ADIRONDACK
Cross-Country Skiing

ADIRONDACK
Cross-Country Skiing

A
GUIDE
TO
SEVENTY
TRAILS

DENNIS CONROY

with Shirley Matzke

Photographs by the author

Backcountry Publications
Woodstock, Vermont

Library of Congress Cataloging-in-Publication Data
Conroy, Dennis.
Adirondack cross-country skiing : a guide to 70 trails / Dennis Conroy with Shirley Matske. —1st ed.
p. cm.
Includes bibliographical references (p.) and index.
ISBN 0-88150-249-9
1. Cross-country skiing—New York (State)—Adirondack Mountains—Guidebooks. 2. Trails—New York (State)—Adirondack Mountains—Guidebooks. 3. Adirondack Mountains (NY)—Guidebooks.
I. Matske, Shirley. II. Title.
GV854.5.N45C66 1992
796.93'2'09747—dc20 92–31476
CIP

Cover and text design by Virginia L. Scott
Maps by Mike Henkle © 1992 by The Countryman Press, Inc.
Cover and interior photographs by Dennis Conroy

Published by Backcountry Publications
A division of The Countryman Press, Inc.
Woodstock, Vermont 05091

Printed in the United States of America on recycled paper

10 9 8 7 6 5 4 3 2

Publisher's Note:

Each trip described in this book has been skied by the author or (in three cases) close friends. Cautions have been included where appropriate. Cross-country skiing is an inherently dangerous sport, however, particularly in the backcountry or with icy conditions. The author and Backcountry Publications, Inc. shall have neither liability nor responsibility to any person or entity with respect to any loss or damage caused or alleged to be caused directly or indirectly by the information contained in this guide. Every effort has been made to give complete and accurate information. Unless otherwise noted in the text, all land crossed in gaining access to the 70 ski trails is either public property or has an easement. If you come across any new signs advising that a property is private or that no trespassing is allowed, please respect them.

With time, trails may be rerouted and signs and landmarks altered. If you find that such changes have occurred on the routes described in this book, please let the author and publisher know so that corrections may be made in future editions. Other comments and suggestions are also welcome. Address all correspondence to:

Editor, Ski Tours
Backcountry Publications
PO Box 175
Woodstock, VT 05091

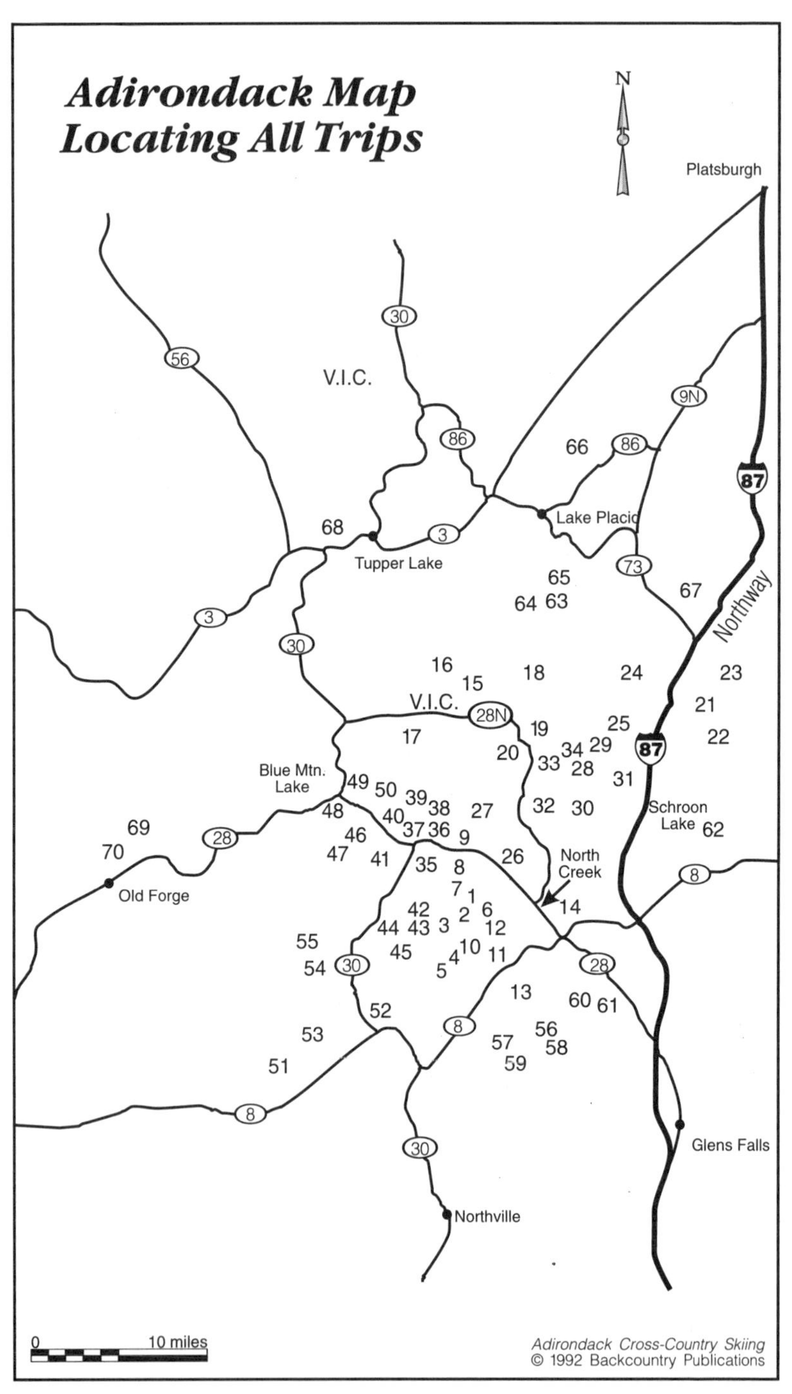
Adirondack Map
Locating All Trips
N
Platsburgh
V.I.C.
Lake Placid
Tupper Lake
V.I.C.
Blue Mtn. Lake
Old Forge
North Creek
Schroon Lake
Northway
Glens Falls
Northville
0
10 miles
Adirondack Cross-Country Skiing
© 1992 Backcountry Publications

Table of Contents

■

Preface

■

Cross-country skiing is one of the main reasons I moved to the Adirondacks, one of the prime cross-country skiing areas in the East. Since then I have been able to put on skis at my door and glide out to the meadow and onto old woods roads four months of the year.

This book grew out of my ski-touring experiences. Seventy ski trips are described, and many other routes are mentioned. I also comment on Adirondack history, lore, and special attractions and discuss skiing safely and healthily, equipment, waxing, dressing properly, finding your way, and give some thoughts on skiing with snowmobiles.

The trails described in this book are grouped by geographic area. Trips can be located by number on an overall map of the Adirondacks at the front of the book. The degree of difficulty ranges from beginner to advanced, and there is a complete list in the back. At the beginning of each trip description you will find the distance in round-trip miles or, in the case of a roundabout where you leave a shuttle car at the other end, the one-way mileage; the average skiing time (not including a lunch stop); the degree of difficulty; the U.S. Geological Survey (USGS) topographic map on which the trip is located; and the page number on which a sketch map of the trip is found.

I have given the average skiing time for each trip. I have not skied every trail under different snow conditions or with the same people, however, and there is a big difference in skiing time when gliding over new, dry snow on a cold midwinter day and mushing along on old, wet snow in the spring.

One of the pleasant treats of cross-country skiing is the opportunity for a close look at nature in winter. Stark, leafless trees glowing in a low winter's sun take on a special aura and pose a greater challenge of identification than in the summertime. Fungus, ferns, and nonflowering plants provide the color highlight of nature in the snow. Some trails are especially rich in plant and animal life, and these are mentioned.

Throughout the book the abbreviation DEC is used; it stands for the New York State Department of Environmental Conservation. The DEC manages most of the public land in the Adirondacks, with a DEC forest ranger in each area. Whether it is information on trails or winter conditions, you will find that the forest rangers are knowledgeable and helpful. Their telephone numbers are found in local telephone books under New York State.

Cross-country skiing is a safe sport, but you cannot expect to do anything physical without an occasional bruise or sprain. Every injury that I remember seeing occurred because the skier was going too fast and skiing beyond his or her ability.

One of the greatest pleasures in life is to put on a pair of perfectly waxed "skinny skis" and head into the woods on a crisp, sunny day. There is nothing better to ease the mind and help you feel right with the world. Cross-country skiing can make North Country winters your favorite season in the Adirondacks.

Many years ago John R. Fisher, husband of the Vermont author Dorothy Canfield Fisher, taught me the telemark on the slopes of Red Mountain. My mother, Etta Seymour Conroy, and the Fishers also gave me a love of the outdoors, an awareness of nature, and an appreciation for quiet, self-propelled sports.

Shirley Matzke of North Creek suggested the book and has been a companion on over half of the trips. We shared the excitement of discovery and the thrill of achievement that comes from finding new places. While the writing is mine, she played a key role in planning and in reviewing its content. In addition she and her daughter, Karla, demonstrated their artistic talents by drawing the draft sketch maps of each trip.

Evelyn Greene skied most of the long, arduous trails with me. Evelyn read a lot of the book in draft and I have benefited greatly from her cross-country skiing experience. She is an advocate of appropriate clothing and layering, and the sections on how to avoid overheating have been strengthened immensely by her views.

Others who were particularly helpful in finding new destinations or skiing with me are Gary Randorf, Richard and Anne Morse, and Erwin Miller. Many others, too numerous to mention, read sections of the book and made suggestions.

The photographs in the book are mine, and their quality is due to the skill and patience of Alan Cederstrom who developed and printed most of them. His studio, North Country Photo, is in Queensbury, NY.

Barbara McMartin introduced me to guidebook writing when I joined with her in writing and updating portions of her excellent *Discover the Adirondacks* series. Some of the pictures were developed and printed by Alec Reid, her husband, when I worked on those books.

I am particularly indebted to Olive Houghton who applied her editing skills to many sections of the book and improved them immensely. I also wish to thank Cannon Labrie for his meticulous yet sensitive copyedit and his helpful suggestions.

If I have not been clear in any of the trail descriptions, or if the trail descriptions have changed, it would be helpful to hear from you.

Dennis Conroy
North River, NY

■
Falls on Boquet River

Cross-Country Skiing Tips

■

Using the Guide and Skiing Safely

As you clamp your boots down and glide along the trails on your "skinny skis" you will see some of the oldest and most scenic mountains in the United States. Created during tremendous upthrusts millions of years ago, the Adirondacks have eroded to relatively low peaks with wide valleys. Glaciers left many distinct landforms such as kettles, kames, and eskers, and dammed deep valleys, forming lakes with steep sides. Anorthosite rock was exposed providing outcrops for sweeping views of snow-covered valleys. An excellent account of this evolution is found in Lincoln Barnett's readable *The Ancient Adirondacks,* as well as other books.

In the last century these mountain slopes were also scarred by men who harvested the bountiful timber resources. Sawed logs for lumber, hemlock bark for tanneries, and pulp for paper mills were removed, leaving behind inflammable slash. Clear-cutting—and the destructive fires that followed—brought strong reactions. The Forest Preserve was created, and Article XIV of the New York State Constitution halted the cutting of timber on most public land in the Adirondacks.

A little more than 45 percent of the six-million-acre Adirondack Park is public land with several forms of land use. Access to these beautiful "forever-wild" forests in the park is surprisingly convenient, and it takes only a brief time to get out of sight of civilization. The wilderness areas are the most remote, with few remaining signs of man; you may travel there only on foot. Another category is Wild Forest; in places it is almost as remote and untouched as the Wilderness areas, but snowmobiles and vehicles are permitted in some places. Most trails in this book are located on these two kinds of public land, although some trails start on easements across private property. The commercial areas mentioned are mostly private.

A sketch map for each trail is provided, usually at the beginning of the trip description. The sketch shows key roads to nearby towns, where to park (designated by the letter P), ponds, brooks, major mountain peaks (designated by a mountain symbol), mountain ranges (without a symbol), direction of true north, scale of the map, and the route of the trail. Topographic maps that show additional man-made and natural features are not reproduced in the book because they are hard to read and to use in that form.

Most of the trails in this book follow old roads that are cleared and marked; it is difficult to get lost on them. A few trails, as noted in their write-up, are not marked and are very hard to follow. A topographic map and compass, or a guide who knows the way, are essential for such routes. An altimeter, which measures altitude, is also helpful to locate your position on a contour line of the map. Even on the well-marked trails it is rewarding to carry a topographic map of the area as it will identify mountains, streams, bogs, and other natural features and heighten the enjoyment of the trip. The relevant topographic map is listed for each trip.

There is a wealth of nature to observe and study as you ski these trails. The forest varies with altitude and type of soil: spruce and balsam fir surround ponds; mixed woods grow on the sandy glacial soils; hardwood stands are found on the lower slopes; and boreal forests exist from 2,500 feet to the timberline. Animals and birds favor specific forest communities and leave telltale signs on fresh snow. Green mosses and various-hued liverworts thrive at the base of trees or on the upper bark; polypody ferns crown rocks with winter greenery; gray fungi protrude from dead trees; insect cases and galls entwine twigs and branches.

One of the best books to help you appreciate this snowy world is *A Guide to Nature in Winter* by Donald Stokes. The Peterson guidebooks on ferns and animal tracks are also recommended. The chapter on precipitation in the Peterson guide, *Atmosphere,* will help you understand the various forms of snow.

These 70 ski trips through magnificent valleys and rolling hills provide a variety of experiences. Some routes will satisfy the beginner; others, the most expert; most fit somewhere in between. All are fun and memorable. The routes can be as fast, and as strenuous, as you want to make them. The sport is great exercise; you will burn about 540 calories an hour in average, recreational skiing. Perhaps the greatest benefit, however, is that skiing relieves tensions and relaxes the mind. Most trails take you into pristine places, quiet glades with only the whisper of wind. Breathing clean air in relative peace and quiet is great for the human psyche.

Accidents can be avoided by skiing under control and using trails that match your ability. But any sport that involves fragile bodies moving around trees and rocks—sometimes rapidly and off balance—in an isolated area, requires precautions. On many trails you will meet few people, especially during midweek, so you should try to ski with someone else. If that is not possible, always let someone know where you are going; if you haven't shown up by dark, they can call the local forest ranger. If there is a trail register, sign in and out; this record tells others where to look and also helps to justify trail maintenance.

The weather in the backcountry changes fast! TV and radio reports seldom forecast mountain storms accurately. You can start out at 10:00 in the morning in pleasant sunshine and be in a blinding snowstorm, with the temperature below zero, at 1:00 in the afternoon. Poor visibility and cold muscles can cause a bad fall—so turn back if the weather threatens.

Skiing on ice can be dangerous because the ice over unknown springholes, inlets, and outlets may be thin. When you cross streams on snow bridges or ski on unsure ice, release the bail on your bindings so your skis will come off if you break through. It is a lot easier to kick and pull yourself out if you don't have skis on!

Anyone skiing more than an hour should carry a day pack or a large fanny pack with food, liquid, and first-aid basics. If you are going out for three hours or more, one person should carry a touring pack with essentials for survival. This sounds ominous, and you will seldom use all the gear, but it can save fingers and toes and even a life. The survival pack should have:

- Space blanket
- Wooden matches in two waterproof containers
- First-aid kit
- Ace bandage (large and wide)
- Flashlight and candles
- Wool sweater or down jacket
- Dry socks and mittens
- Heat packets (Grabbers)
- Granola bars, chocolate, and trail food
- Thermos of warm (preferably sweet) liquid
- Water
- Knife (heavy duty)
- Pozidriv screwdriver and pliers
- Duct tape and wire
- Plastic ski tip

If you do a lot of backcountry skiing, stock a pack with these items and habitually take it along. You will want lunch, water, ski wax, and probably a camera anyway—so a few extra pounds are manageable.

For more information about winter traveling see Craig Woods and Gordon Hardy's *Cross Country Skier's Trailside Guide,* an inexpensive booklet. Another book, *Winterwise,* by John M. Dunn, is a general backpacker's guide, with only short sections on skiing and snowshoeing, but it should be read by anyone who ventures into the backcountry.

The trails in this book have four difficulty ratings: beginner, competent beginner, intermediate, and advanced. An appendix lists each trail by the level of difficulty. The ratings depend on the depth and type of snow and weather conditions. With less snow the trails will be more difficult because of semiexposed rocks, brush, and blowdowns. Deep, fluffy, new-fallen snow slows the skis and makes the trail easier and safer than crust or icy patches. Longer trips are more difficult because you tire and fall more easily.

Use judgment and be cautious on steep hills. A snowplow is the best and easiest way to slow down and stop. If the woods are open, you can make long, wide traverses down the slope. It is better to sidestep down a drop than to lose control and hit a tree. One braking technique is to hold your ski poles together in both hands, brace them almost vertically against your lower leg, and drag the tips in the snow. If you still gain too much speed, you can simply sit down. The key safety rule is to keep your speed under control!

Are a map, compass, and altimeter really necessary? Not for the short easy trips, but you should not travel on any isolated trails without at least a reliable compass, a topographic map of the area, and the knowledge to use both of them. An altimeter is useful but not as essential.

Summing up, remember these points:

- Ski trails that fit your ability and competence.
- Don't ski alone, and if you do, tell someone where you are going.
- Check the weather forecast and know when it gets dark.
- Carry a survival pack and check your gear.
- Know your location.
- When in doubt, don't take chances.

There are unbounded pleasures and satisfactions waiting out there and, with a little preparation and common sense, cross-country skiing can become the quintessential experience of your life.

Keeping Warm and Healthy

The only dress code in cross-country skiing is to wear several layers and avoid cotton. Clothing provides the insulation needed to counter the temperature and windchill. The rub comes because, when you exercise, you give off heat and you must get rid of it. The trick is to sandwich the right amount of warm air between layers of clothing, but allow your perspiration to vent and evaporate.

Cross-country skiing uses all the muscles, and there is no way to ski without perspiring, sometimes heavily. The clothing you wear should wick out this moisture, stay reasonably dry, and be warm even when damp. Polypropylene and wool do this best. Silk is also good for underwear. Cotton is not a good material for cross-country skiing because it absorbs and holds moisture and is cold when damp. No matter how well your clothing insulates, trapped perspiration will make you feel uncomfortable and cold.

Polypropylene is inexpensive and comfortable next to the skin; a lightweight top with a zippered or buttoned front is best since you can adjust the ventilation around your neck. Tops should be long enough for the tail to stay in and prevent a midsection gap.

Over the polypro underwear top put on a long-tailed, light wool shirt that opens at the throat. Next add a full-cut, light wool sweater and, finally, a nylon windbreaker, preferably with a full zipper. Wear or carry a neck-up or a light scarf and carry a silk face mask or balaclava in your pack. This clothing, or a variation of it, is usually enough on the upper trunk for a 10- to 20-degree day. Some may need another light sweater or an outer windproof jacket.

On your lower body, for average temperatures, wear lightweight wool pants with long legs that tuck into wool socks. If it is below zero and windy, add polypro underwear bottoms or substitute heavier wool pants. For extended backcountry, or overnight, wilderness skiing, it is a good idea to carry windproof, water-repellent overpants in your touring pack.

Most skiers wear polypro socks or lightweight wool socks next to their feet. Over the light socks wear one pair of wool socks. Your feet should not be perspiring before you start to ski, or they will be cold during the entire trip. A good idea is to carry an extra pair of socks, and change them if your feet become cold and damp.

Gaiters serve the practical purpose of preventing snow from getting in your boots and keep your feet drier and warmer. Short ankle gaiters are adequate for most trails; knee-length ones are best in deep snow. For long wilderness trips you can buy gaiters attached to a rubber or synthetic overboot that completely covers the boot and part of the sole.

Soft, leather mittens with wool liners are best on your hands. They are usually enough to keep your hands warm, and you can carry extra liners. If you tend toward cold hands, even with good dry mittens, you can purchase heat packs (Grabbers) that, after opening, provide warmth for six to eight hours. Unless the temperature is above freezing, cross-country ski gloves—even those with Thinsulate—are cold.

A knit cap is essential. It is wise to own two; one of lightweight polypropylene and one of heavy knitted wool. On sunny, cold days an earband lets the top of your head vent heat but keeps your ears warm.

Most people make the mistake of starting out dressed too warmly. They become overheated, trap perspiration before they remove a layer of clothing, and then get chilled when their damp undergarments are exposed. The first rule is zip open or take off clothing *before* you start to perspire. Wrap the garments you remove around your waist or tie them to your pack. During a brief stop you only need to button or zip up and put on your hat. During a windy lunch stop put everything back on to avoid a chill.

All this may seem like a lot of fuss, but it is the only way to keep your body temperature regulated and to stay comfortable. For more information, Michael Brady's *Cross-Country Ski Gear* has an excellent chapter on clothing, windchill, and calories.

There are three things to avoid when you are on the trail: hypothermia, frostbite, and giardiasis.

Hypothermia

This health problem comes from a lowered body temperature. When a person is exposed to cold weather the body will keep the torso warm. The body does this by making the blood vessels of the skin smaller in diameter; this routes the blood to the central vital organs. When you become cold, the body will shiver to produce heat. But if heat loss is greater than heat production, your body temperature will begin to fall. The body can function with a certain amount of reduced temperature, but beyond a certain point mental and physical functions decrease rapidly. Because less blood reaches the brain you may not realize that you are losing the ability to think and move effectively.

One of the first symptoms of hypothermia is **uncontrolled shivering.** This involuntary muscle action should never be ignored; it is proof that your body is losing more heat than it can generate.

Another indicator is **slow, slurred speech,** possibly with confusion and disorientation. You will probably not notice this in yourself, so members of the group should be told to look for these symptoms in one another.

A third symptom is **impaired motor functions.** If you fall twice, without reason, you probably have hypothermia. If you lose a piece of clothing such as a hat or glove, you undoubtedly have it. Other concerns are stumbling, abnormally slow skiing or walking, fumbling hands, and the inability to walk without help. The skin will become pale because of decreased blood supply. Respiration will become shallow and the pulse very weak. Hypothermia at this stage is potentially fatal and immediate action is required.

The last phase is **overwhelming drowsiness.** Lassitude and the irresistible urge to sleep mean that hypothermia is in the terminal stage.

The best way to handle hypothermia is to prevent it. Wind and moisture are usually responsible for lowering body temperature. Dressing properly to avoid overheating and wet clothing is very important in prevention. Nevertheless, wet snow or rain, high winds, or a dunking in a stream cannot always be avoided; even with the best planning, hypothermia will occur in a group of skiers at some time or other, more frequently than you think.

If you notice one or more of the above symptoms in a member of your group, do something about it immediately. Hypothermia is a medical emergency, and, at the latter three stages, the person should be taken to an emergency room as fast as possible. Full treatment is a complex task of rewarming and monitoring the cardiovascular condition, requiring professional help.

In the meantime, on the trail, you can take the following actions. First, stop and get the person out of the wind; get behind a conifer or rock, or set up a space blanket as a windbreak. Second, get any wet clothes off the person as quickly as possible and replace them with dry ones. If there is no extra clothing, take dry clothes off yourself or someone else. Wrap the person in a space blanket or a sleeping bag if one is available. Third, feed the skier warm, sweet drinks and high-energy foods such as a candy bar. If the skier is unable to swallow naturally, do not attempt to give drinks. Do not give any form of alcohol to persons with hypothermia; alcohol dilates the blood vessels, is a depressant, and lowers body temperature. Fourth, if the skier is semiconscious try to keep the person awake; take off all clothes, and put the person in a sleeping bag with someone else, also stripped. The transfer of body heat from another person is considerable and may make the difference in survival at this stage.

Remember, beyond the simple shivering that is controlled by adding dry garments and exercise, any symptom of hypothermia should be treated as an emergency. Evacuation is necessary. If the person cannot walk or ski, make a sled with lashed skis and tow the person out. There is no room for complacency if you notice any of the symptoms.

An excellent pamphlet on hypothermia is published by the Adirondack Mountain Club, Inc., RR 3, Box 3055, Lake George, NY 12845; telephone: 518-668-4447.

Frostbite

In frostbite the small arteries in the extremities contract when exposed to extreme chill. The flow of blood slows, then ceases. Ice forms between cells, drains cellular fluids, and damages or kills the cells. The amount of cell damage depends on how cold it is and how long the skin is exposed.

The first sign of frostbite may be when the cheeks turn grayish white. This is actually frostnip and causes no great damage if the area is warmed gradually. A more severe frostbite feels waxy and frozen on the surface but soft beneath. Once rewarmed this skin will turn purple, feel numb, and begin to burn. You can diagnose the most severe frostbite because not only is the skin frozen, but the area *beneath* it is hard. In a severe case the surface tissue will eventually blacken and die; the tips of fingers and toes may slough off; surgery may be required.

Do *not* rub frozen parts with snow or ice. In cases of frostnip or mild frostbite, warm by gentle pressure from warm skin. Cover cheeks with warm hands; tuck numb fingers under the armpits; put numb toes against a friend's bare stomach. Never apply extreme heat, and avoid warming in front of a campfire that may burn numb flesh. In severe cases of frostbite evacuate the person immediately *without* trying to rewarm the flesh. Refreezing, or walking on thawed feet, can increase earlier damage. As in hypothermia, the first signs can be treated in the field but any later stages require skilled medical attention.

Giardiasis

Human pollution in the Adirondacks has introduced *Giardia lamblia*, an intestinal parasite responsible for the disease giardiasis—commonly called beaver fever. You get giardiasis by drinking untreated, contaminated water. The symptoms, which often take two or three weeks to develop, are fatigue, diarrhea, weight loss, abdominal pain, nausea, and gas. You won't ever forget it if you have it. Treatment is available for giardiasis once it is diagnosed, but it is far better to avoid it.

You can protect yourself by carrying full water bottles, considering all streams and lakes contaminated, and boiling or filtering your water when winter camping. Boiling water for seven to ten minutes will kill *Giardia* cysts. Filters, such as First Need, have a 0.4 micron barrier that is small enough to filter out *Giardia* cysts, parasitic tapeworms, and most other bacteria. The First Need filter weighs 12 ounces and treats a pint of water per minute. Iodine is also effective in killing the cysts. (Add four drops of 2 percent tincture of iodine per quart of clear water, shake well, and let stand for 30 minutes. When treating very cold water, double the dosage of iodine.)

The cysts are spread by beaver and other animals, but they originate with humans. *Giardia* cysts are passed in human feces, and some people may be carriers without having the symptoms. Camp at lean-tos, if possible, and use the latrines. If no latrines are available, dig a hole as deeply as you can, *at least* 150 feet from water. Giardiasis can also be passed along by hand-to-mouth transfer of cysts, so personal hygiene in camp is important. A pamphlet on *Giardia* is available from the Adirondack Mountain Club.

■

Brook in Hoffman Notch Wilderness Area

Choosing Equipment

Skis

Your first decision is the type of skis to buy; most of the other equipment should match them. Twenty years ago wooden, waxable touring skis were the only cross-country skis available; many people still use them. Now high-tech skis, made from a variety of synthetic materials, have been developed, and prices have kept pace.

There are five types of skis, designed for different kinds of skiing: light touring, heavy touring or backcountry, telemark, racing, and skating. The most popular skis are made for light touring. They are skinny skis, about 50 millimeters wide at the waist; the sides are almost straight and they have little camber (arch in the middle). They are appropriate for prepared track skiing, groomed trails, or for making your way over a meadow or golf course. You can use them on nongroomed trails and in deep snow, but they will sink deeply and will not turn well. They are the least expensive, and, for light skiing, will give a lot of pleasure.

Rapidly gaining in popularity are off-track, heavy-touring, or backcountry skis. They are sidecut—wider in the front and rear than at the waist. (The more expensive ones have steel edges, at least along the middle section of the ski.) The increased width helps the skis ride over deep snow; the sidecut makes them turn more easily. They have a lot of camber to get maximum unweighting when turning, but they are not so stiff that they do not contact the snow when you kick off. With these skis it is easier to snowplow down a long hill; you can even do a telemark turn. The skis are rugged enough to survive off-trail bumps and dips but are still relatively light.

Telemark skis are for heavy-duty mountaineering. They are about 60 millimeters wide at the waist to help support a heavy pack on your back. They have a wider and softer "shovel" (the front upturned part) in order to ride up in deep snow and turn under rugged conditions. Racing skis are a different breed; they are very light and narrow and are used for speed—usually in competition. Skating skis are also light but have blunt tips and no groove; they require a wide, packed trail and a lot of stamina to use them.

Most ski shops carry several makes of the popular ski types and will let you try them out. The construction and design of quality skis have characteristics that affect performance, so don't buy the cheapest pair. Try out various skis and buy the ones that perform best for you, even if they cost more. You will enjoy them for many years.

After you decide on the type of ski, you must decide on a waxable or waxless base. Waxable skis are faster and quieter. For temperatures of 30 degrees and less, with fresh snow and the correct wax, they will climb, kick-off, and glide better than waxless skis. The section on waxing should help convince you that it is not difficult to wax correctly under most winter conditions. In late winter, with the temperature around freezing, the snow is in transition between dry and wet, so waxing is difficult. You might buy a less expensive or secondhand pair of waxless skis for such wet snow conditions. Some people, however, accept somewhat less performance in exchange for convenience and own only waxless skis. Try both kinds on the trail before you make a choice.

Proper ski length depends upon height, weight, and ability. Some people prefer shorter skis that turn more easily and are lighter; others like the speed and glide of longer lengths. The length is measured in centimeters from the floor to the wrist with the arm extended above the head; if you are heavier than average, add five centimeters to the total.

Catalogue stores, such as L. L. Bean, and some ski shops sell skis, bindings, poles, and boots as a package at considerable savings.

Bindings

The Nordic Norm is a standard, three-pin, 75-millimeter toe binding. It has been the most popular, but other toe binding systems that fit special boots are made by different companies, such as Salomon, Rottefella, Adidas, and Tyrolia, and are gaining popularity. The special bindings perform well and are durable but are not interchangeable with each other or the Nordic Norm.

Bindings are made for different levels of skiing and types of skis: lightweight for light touring, heavy duty for rugged backcountry use, and so forth. The two most frequent Nordic Norms found in ski shops are made by Rottefella and Normark. At least three companies, Rottefella, Chouinard, and Ramer, make a cable binding that adds lateral stability and prevents toepiece wear under extreme skiing conditions, such as ski mountaineering in heavy snow. The rule in selecting bindings is to buy a well-made, strong pair that match the ski. Have the bindings mounted by the store.

Poles

Fiberglass poles for light touring have small baskets for groomed, track skiing. Heavy-duty poles have wide baskets for deeper snow conditions; they cost two to three times as much as the lighter poles. You can also buy ski poles that adjust for height and lightweight poles for racing. Correct pole length is measured from the floor to the palm of the hand, with the arm held out at chest level.

Boots

Your choice will depend on the type of skiing you plan to do and the skis you buy. Below-the-ankle light touring boots are for short trips with groomed tracks. They are sometimes made of flexible nylon, instead of leather, and are very light. If you ski off-track or want the stability needed with a wider ski, then buy over-the-ankle touring boots; many are water-repellant with thermal insulation. For rugged backcountry use you can get an even heavier boot with a thicker sole for lateral stability and more support. Finally, very heavy telemark boots provide even greater control. Boots should provide sturdy ankle support but have room for toe movement when wearing one very lightweight and one heavy wool sock. Feet take a lot of strain and abuse when skiing and comfortable boots are essential. It is wise to try boots on because fit varies with manufacturers.

Packs

Fanny packs strap around the waist with a wide belt and can hold a small camera, several sandwiches, candy, wax, a space blanket, and other small items. The main drawback is that they are not large enough to carry a thermos or extra clothing. One unique fanny pack design has a net attachment that slips over your shoulders to hold clothing removed as you get warm.

A day pack is larger and will carry the basic items needed for an all-day backcountry trip. It should fit well, which requires adjustable shoulder straps and an adjustable belt to prevent sway. Packs should be waterproof and light. Internal dividers are helpful to separate food and thermos from camera and other gear. Put a small closed-cell pad on the inside next to your back; you can use it to sit on during lunch stops.

A touring pack is necessary for overnight trips and for someone leading a group on a wilderness trip. It should be large enough for a sleeping bag, extra food and clothing, and emergency survival gear. Load the pack with the weight distributed along your back, not high up as in hiking, because you bend over and sway more when skiing.

Climbing Skins

Climbing skins attach to the bottom of cross-country skis and allow you to climb very steep hills. They are used only on long climbs because you take them off before skiing downhill, and they are a nuisance to attach. In the old days climbing skins were made from real sealskins. The skins were attached to the ski with the fur facing down and pointing backward. You could glide forward but, when pushed in the wrong direction, the fur stuck into the snow and held you back. Now the skins are made of heavy plastic with very fine protrusions running in one direction.

One type of skin is stretchable. It loops over the tip of the ski and is stretched until a metal bracket catches on the rear end; several buckles go around the center of the ski to hold the skin in place. Another skin has an adhesive base that is pressed onto the bottom of the ski. It is easier to apply but the ski should be dry and the skin may not adhere well after repeated use.

Only two or three trips in this book require skins, so you need to purchase them only if you plan a lot of serious climbing.

Snowshoes

Snowshoes are useful for winter recreation. Some of the trips in this book require snowshoes because the tracks are narrow and steep or have too many fallen trees to use skis. Other trips, such as Trip 9 to Whortleberry Pond and Trip 36 up McGinn Mountain, start out easy but you can't ski all the way.

There has been a major evolution in snowshoe design in the past few years. The Yukon snowshoe and Maine-type snowshoe (with a large frame with a tail) were awkward to use but provided extensive flotation on snow for carrying large loads. Today a new breed of snowshoe has been developed for recreation. It is a smaller bearpaw design—made in sizes from 8 inches by 25 inches to 10 inches by 36 inches, depending on your weight. These shorter, narrower snowshoes have a turned-up tip, neoprene or urethane lacing, and an improved binding.

It is a good idea to rent or borrow several different types of snowshoes and try them out before you purchase them. For use in conjunction with skiing, the binding should fit your cross-country ski boots so you can switch from one to the other. One snowshoe that you see on the trail is a Sherpa with an aluminum frame. The Sherpa has a hinged toe with a serrated crampon-type device for traction and comes in four sizes. An Adirondack craftsman, author, and photographer named Carl Heilman makes a lightweight wood frame snowshoe out of split ash with urethane lacing. He has developed a binding that provides traction but is easy to walk in—you can even race with them. His wood frame snowshoes are made in three sizes: Catpaws (8 by 26-inch), Trailpaws (9 by 31-inch), and the larger Green Mountain Bearpaws for heavier persons. Write: Heilman's Snowshoes, Box 213A, Brant Lake, NY 12815 for information.

The advantage of lightweight snowshoes is that they can be tied to your pack and carried with you on the trail. When you reach a section that can't be skied it is easy to switch to snowshoes. Your skis can be left at the foot of the mountain for a short time (such as the McGinn trip) or, if you do a lot of this type of skiing, buy a pack with slots that hold your skis in an upright position on your back. The ski poles are as useful for snowshoeing as for skiing.

Cross-country skiing books have chapters on each of these equipment items; *Cross-Country Ski Gear* by Michael Brady is one such source.

Waxing

Waxing need not be difficult, at least under most conditions. The easiest and best way to wax is to use only a few waxes, and learn to wax only for the conditions where you ski.

Wax is put on skis to accomplish three things: the first is to grip the snow so you can kick off to move forward and not slide back, the second is to allow the skis to glide over the snow once they are set in motion, the third is to prevent snow from sticking to the bottom of the skis. To understand how the wax/snow bond works we must examine the makeup of snow crystals.

Five of the ten categories of snow listed by Vincent Schaefer in *Atmosphere* fall in symmetrical crystalline forms. The most beautiful is the perfect hexagon with tiny barbs protruding from the crystal. The other four are crystals that are shaped like columns and needles, also with rough protrusions. In general, the colder and fresher the snow, the sharper the protrusion. Wax keeps you from sliding back because the barbs or protrusions of these snow crystals actually stick very minutely into the wax on the base of the ski. The secret is to match the wax to the snow. With warmer snow and older snow, the barbs are blunter, so you use "hard" stick wax if it's cold and "softer" wax for warmer or reconstituted snow. When the other categories of snow—sleet, hail, and graupel—are falling, stick waxes don't work well.

Waxes in sticks are color-keyed by degree of hardness to match the temperature and the age of the snow. The hardest wax is arctic; then, in decreasing order of hardness, the colors are special green, green, blue, violet or purple, red, and yellow. Companies vary the colors somewhat and add "special" colors, but the principle is the same; there are color/temperature charts to help you choose the right wax.

Skill in waxing comes from being able to gauge the snow. Powdery and grainy snow that falls when the temperature is under 30 degrees is easiest to identify. When in doubt apply a hard wax, usually special green, to the entire base and smooth it evenly over the surface with a cork. Place the ski lightly on the snow and then look at the base; if the snow is sticking to the wax it should be right. Now put the ski on and try it; if you slip back when you try to move forward, add a thin layer of green or blue (depending on the temperature) a distance of two feet along the center bottom of the ski. The center section is where your weight falls that gives you the kick.

If the barbs of the snow crystals stick into the wax, how does the ski slide? The answer lies in friction and melting. When the ski is moved forward, friction and pressure occurs between the snow and the wax. This action generates a small amount of heat that forms a thin water film, and your ski rolls on the small drops of moisture, as if they were ball bearings. If you apply too soft a wax for the snow temperature, you will climb hills but not be able to glide. This is because the sharp snow crystals will have penetrated the wax deeply, and won't pull out and release the ski. (Some people use blue or purple wax all of the time because they want to climb without slipping back, and prefer to move downhill more slowly.)

The difficult phase of waxing comes when the snow is at 32 degrees or warmer, or when the snow is old, crusty, and icy. This is where you put on klister, which comes in tubes of blue, violet, red, or silver. It oozes out of the tube like cold molasses, is very sticky and gooey when warm, but hardens when cold. In a warm room apply a ribbon for about two feet under the center of the ski; then spread it evenly with a plastic tool. Set the skis outside to cool before you handle them or the klister will stick to everything.

You can apply softer wax over harder wax but not the other way around. Usually the day warms up as you ski, so this quirk is no problem. Carry a small scraper in your pack and, if the day gets colder, scrape the ski bottoms clean before going to a harder wax. At

▪
Trail to Puffer Pond

home you can use a special solution (lighter fluid will work) to dissolve the remaining wax after you scrape. This is easy with stick wax, but klister is more difficult and messy to remove. Many people who use waxable skis never use klister for this reason. Instead they buy a pair of waxless skis to use in wet snow and spring conditions.

If you use only stick waxes below freezing, waxing is a simple process that becomes second nature. Key points to remember are:

- Clean and dry the base before applying wax.
- Apply softer wax over hard.
- Apply and cork wax from tip to tail.
- Smooth and even out wax with a cork.
- Spread wax on thinly in layers.
- Adjust performance by waxing thicker, then longer, before changing colors.

Carry the wax of the day and at least one colder and two warmer waxes; a scraper to remove hard wax (or ice); a cork for smoothing wax; and a small towel to dry and clean the ski base before putting on wax. For overnight trips or changeable conditions, take more wax and some wax remover in an unbreakable container.

Ski-touring centers post the wax-of-the-day on bulletin boards. An inexpensive booklet by Wendy Williams, *Cross-Country Ski Waxing and Maintenance,* provides valuable additional information on the maintenance of skis.

Using Map and Compass

Two different map series are published by the U.S. Geological Survey for the Adirondack region. Where a name and 15' follows USGS in the trip descriptions, the map quadrangle is the 15 minute series published in 1953 or 1954 (or before). This series has a scale of 1:62,500. The contour intervals are every 20 feet, and 1 inch on the map represents 1 mile. The northern portion of the Adirondacks (and recently some of the southern) is covered by newer metric maps. The metric 7.5' x 15' series is a much larger scale (1:25,000) with contour intervals every 6 or 10 meters (1 meter equals 3.2808 feet). One centimeter on the metric map represents 250 meters on the ground (2½ inches equals

1 mile). In the field you can roughly convert meters to feet by multiplying the figure in meters by three; conversely, change feet to meters by dividing by three.

A map becomes really useful in finding your way when you use it with a compass. Excellent compasses are made by Silva and Suunto. The liquid-filled Silva Polaris 7 has jewel bearings and a transparent housing for easy map use. It will serve you well for the needs of this book. Foresters and geologists use the more professional Silva Ranger 15CL, which has many additional features, including an adjustable declination.

A basic understanding of map and compass is adequate for off trail, backcountry skiing. Generally you will want to perform only three functions.

First, you know where you are and want to identify mountain peaks, valleys, or other natural features. To do this you need to orient the map using the declination scale. The vertical lines on the map indicate the true north-south direction. The declination scale is at the bottom left of the 15' series. One line points true north; the other, marked MN, points to the left of true north. The wedge-shaped space between these two lines is the declination between true north and magnetic north for that specific map area. In this part of the world it ranges from 13 to 15 degrees, depending on your location. Place your compass with the center of the dial over the point of the wedge and turn the map until the north (red) point of the compass needle is aligned over the MN line on the map. Your map is now aligned in a true north-south direction. You can now look at the terrain around you and identify its features. Using the scale along the edge of the compass, you can tell about how far away an object is.

If you want to know height, the brown lines on the map indicate altitude above sea level. Each contour line is 20 feet (6 or 10 meters on metric maps), and there are heavier brown lines every 100 feet (50 meters on metric maps). The heavier lines have altitude numbers. The closer the brown contour lines are together, the steeper the slope.

In the second use of a compass and map, you want to walk in a specific direction by taking a "bearing." In this case you can use only magnetic north, which is the way all bearings are given in this book.

Assume the bearing given on a trail is 80 degrees magnetic. Turn the compass dial until the number 80 is aligned with the line of the "direction of travel" arrow on the compass. Hold the compass level in your hand at waist height, with the direction of travel arrow pointing straight ahead of you. Turn yourself and the compass around until the north (red) end of the magnetic needle points to the letter N on the dial. The direction of travel arrow now points to 80 degrees magnetic. To walk this bearing, choose a distant landmark and walk to it without looking at the compass. When you get there, repeat the procedure until you reach your destination.

Third, you may want to go from where you are to another location. Orient the map to true north by adjusting for magnetic declination as in the first instance. Place the compass on the map with the edge along the desired line of travel (from where you are to where you want to go). With the compass still on the map, turn the compass dial until the compass meridian lines in the clear bottom of the round dial are parallel with the meridian lines of the map (north on the *dial*, not the needle, now points to north on the map). Now remove the compass from the map, and, without changing any setting, rotate the compass horizontally until the red end of the needle points to N. Now get the compass reading of the direction of travel arrow and walk in that direction.

Compasses come with additional instructions. For further information, see Kjellstrom's *Be Expert with Map and Compass.*

Metric maps sell for about $2.50 each, and the 15 minute series sell for about $2 (in 1991). They are available in outdoor stores and some other stores, or you can order them from the U.S. Geological Survey, Reston, VA 22092. A pamphlet showing topographic maps produced by the USGS is available upon request.

Map reading will bring a lot of pleasure to your cross-country trips. There is a chance, as well, that at least once each winter you will be on a trail where you are not sure which way to go. If you have a map and compass you can save a lot of time and discomfort by going the correct way.

Sharing Snowmobile Trails

Cross-country skiers, like canoeists and bicyclists, are dedicated to the self-propelled and quiet mode. Some are purists who will not use any trail or lake where they might be disturbed by the "racketeers" and smelly exhaust. It is commendable to try to live by such principles but difficult. Your favorite lake may have a few fishing boats with small motors that you tolerate. You compromise in that case, but you refuse to accept paddling among high-powered speedboats pulling water skiers.

There is a similar situation with cross-country skiers in some areas of the Adirondacks. Snowmobiles are not permitted in Wilderness areas but are allowed on designated, marked trails in Primitive and Wild Forest areas. Some routes are wide, groomed speedways for heavy double-tracked machines; skiers should stay clear of them. On the other hand, some snowmobile trails are narrow, winding, and scenic. These trails are used predominately by local residents, and the newer small snowmobiles are fairly quiet. True, the smell of exhaust lingers after the machines pass, but sometimes, especially on weekdays, you have the trails to yourself.

If certain precautions are followed, there are trails in this book that can be safely shared with snowmobiles. Try them after a heavy, deep snow, because snowmobilers will pack them. You can also seek out snowmobile trails in the spring because the packed snow stays longer and the bridges will help get you across streams after they begin to flow. (In the spring it is better to use waxless skis because the petroleum residue from the exhaust, which remains on the packed trail, sticks to the wax and clogs the bottom of the skis.)

There are several, perhaps obvious, rules that should be followed when you ski on snowmobile trails. First, listen for the snowmobiles, and warn others in the group who may not hear them, especially on a cold, ear-covered day. Second, stop and step to the edge or off the trail and let snowmobilers pass. Third, be especially cautious skiing down winding trails, or through groves of conifers, where you can't see ahead. Help each other to look and listen.

■

Trail from Old Farm Clearing: Trip 3

North River Area
Treks in the Wilderness

■

This scenic portion of the Adirondacks, where the Hudson River tumbles through a gorge as it leaves the high peaks, offers some of the best, and most varied, cross-country skiing. The public trails are primarily in the 108,503-acre Siamese Ponds Wilderness Area that extends from Thirteenth Lake and Kings Flow in the north to the wilderness' southern flank along NY 8. The gem of the area is beautiful Thirteenth Lake, which lies in a deep fault. The narrow, 2-mile-long lake is 3.6 miles southwest of NY 28 at an altitude of 1,674 feet. A steep scarp on the northwest side of the lake is penetrated by a valley that leads to Peaked Mountain Pond. Most of the public ski-touring trails begin on the southeast side of the lake on the wide, unplowed road to Old Farm Clearing. From the clearing—now a grove of Norway spruce—trails radiate into the wilderness. There are no provisioned huts in this backcountry, but there are lean-tos to stay in overnight if you carry food and a warm sleeping bag. All of the trips are short enough for day trips, however, so you don't have to camp out to enjoy these memorable, and sometimes strenuous, outings.

Nine public trails offer a rich variety of pleasures. Beginners can start out on scenic Thirteenth Lake or take the easy and popular track into Old Farm Clearing. More experienced, and stronger, backcountry skiers will find the all-day wilderness treks a real challenge, particularly when the temperature drops below zero, as it often does. The skiing is between the 1,650-foot rolling foothills and the 3,130-foot top of Pete Gay Mountain. Snowfall at these altitudes is excellent, so there is usually skiing from mid-December until early April, barring an unseasonable thaw.

Beginners will enjoy Trip 1 on Thirteenth Lake. From Old Farm Clearing Trip 2 takes you east to Botheration Brook. Intermediate skiers should try Trip 3 west to Puffer Pond, and go south from the clearing on Trips 4 and 5 to NY 8 and the Siamese Ponds. Another intermediate trail begins at Halfway Brook as Trip 6, and Trip 7 is a snowshoe challenge to Peaked Mountain Pond. Nearby, reached from NY 28, are Trips 8 and 9 to Prier, Ross, and Whortleberry ponds.

Two topographic maps issued in 1990, the USGS Thirteenth Lake and Bakers Mills 7.5 x 15 minute metric, cover the area, but the single Thirteenth Lake 15 minute quadrangle issued in 1954 can still be purchased and shows the full area in less detail.

There are two commercial cross-country skiing centers, described below. The centers are linked by a four-mile trail that passes through portions of the wilderness. The genesis of both of these ski-touring centers is, strangely enough, mining. The jointed rocks of these peaks are unusually rich in garnet. The old Hooper Mine site is one mile east of the northern end of Thirteenth Lake; you can ski to it from the public road. From the rim of the mine there is a fine view of the lake and the surrounding mountains. See Barbara McMartin's *Discover the South Central Adirondacks* for an interesting history of the mining operations.

Highwinds Ski Touring Center

The first Barton Mine, on the north side of Gore Mountain, is now the site of the Highwinds Ski Touring Center. Carved high beside the deep crevice of the open-pit garnet mine, Highwinds offers diverse and challenging trails for the beginner or the most expert skier.

Competent beginners can take the Sunset Trail down to Flat Bush, then to the Vly Trail where you can enter the wilderness area and come out on Thirteenth Lake Road. Intermediate skiers can climb the wide, groomed trail to the summit of Pete Gay Mountain for a panoramic view. Descending you can practice telemarks, and enjoy the winding Sheepskin Brook Trail. Some sections are perfect for skating, the newest cross-country way of discovering that you are not in as good condition as you used to be. Expert skiers can traverse the Panorama Trail, climb the Garnet Trail, or take the steep track to Upper Dam for a challenging run back in deep powder.

You reach Highwinds on a sanded road by turning off NY 28 at the Barton Mines Road, 4.5 miles northwest of North Creek. Drive for 5.0 miles. Highwinds Ski Touring Center is currently open only to guests at the inn or by special arrangement with other touring centers. So call telephone number 518-251-3760 before driving to it.

Garnet Hill Cross-Country Ski Center

The 50-kilometer trail network at Garnet Hill has something for every skier—flat areas for beginners, forested loops and runs for intermediates, and steep downhills for the experts. Located at 2,000 feet, the area receives a lot of snow, and because many of the groomed trails are north-facing, they hold the snow longer in the spring.

A main trail, Trapper, winds through the woods for a gradual descent to Harvey's Tailings. From here you can continue on Trapper, or on Cougar Run to the Sugar House Warming Hut, then to Rogers Road. Side routes branch off from the main trail. Other routes from the ski center take you toward Thirteenth Lake.

A convenient shuttle bus service picks up skiers from the lower ends of the trail system and brings them back to the ski shop. The bus also takes skiers to neighboring Highwinds from whence they can ski the wilderness route back to Garnet Hill. The well-equipped ski shop gives lessons and has rentals and sales. For information and rates contact: Garnet Hill Cross-Country Ski Center, 13th Lake Road, North River, NY 12856; telephone: 518-251-2444. For ski conditions call 518-251-2150.

Adirondack Hut to Hut Tours

A delightful and entertaining skier, Walter Blank, arranges exceptional experiences in the Siamese Ponds Wilderness Area. Hut-to-hut, or lodge-to-lodge, treks are known in Vermont and New Hampshire but are not common in New York. These trips, which can be customized to last a weekend or up to five days, are well organized and have excellent guides. The trips can take you into some of the most remote parts of the wilderness and they are strenuous, but they make for a grand time.

A group might start at the Gore Mountain Ski Center where, with special arrangements, they take a lift that leads to a trail down to Highwinds, up Pete Gay Mountain, and across to Thirteenth Lake. On the second day, the tour goes west to Kings Flow for supper and a video show in heated cabins. The third day the group (up to thirteen with two guides) might ski past Round Pond along old Kunjamuk Road and stay in a wilderness cabin. (Personal gear is brought around by van and snowmobile.) The fourth day is on to another cabin or back to Kings Flow. Trips vary depending on snow conditions and availability of accommodations.

Information on tours and the rates can be obtained by writing: Adirondack Hut to Hut Tours, RD #1 Box 85, Ghent, NY 12075; or telephone: 518-828-7007.

1. Thirteenth Lake

■

4.0 miles round-trip
Skiing time: 2 hours
Beginner
USGS Thirteenth Lake 15' or 7.5 x 15' metric
Map—page 45

You reach the lake from a spur off Thirteenth Lake Road. Turn off NY 28 in North River onto Thirteenth Lake Road, going west, away from the Hudson River. Drive uphill for 3.1 miles to a fork and a sign

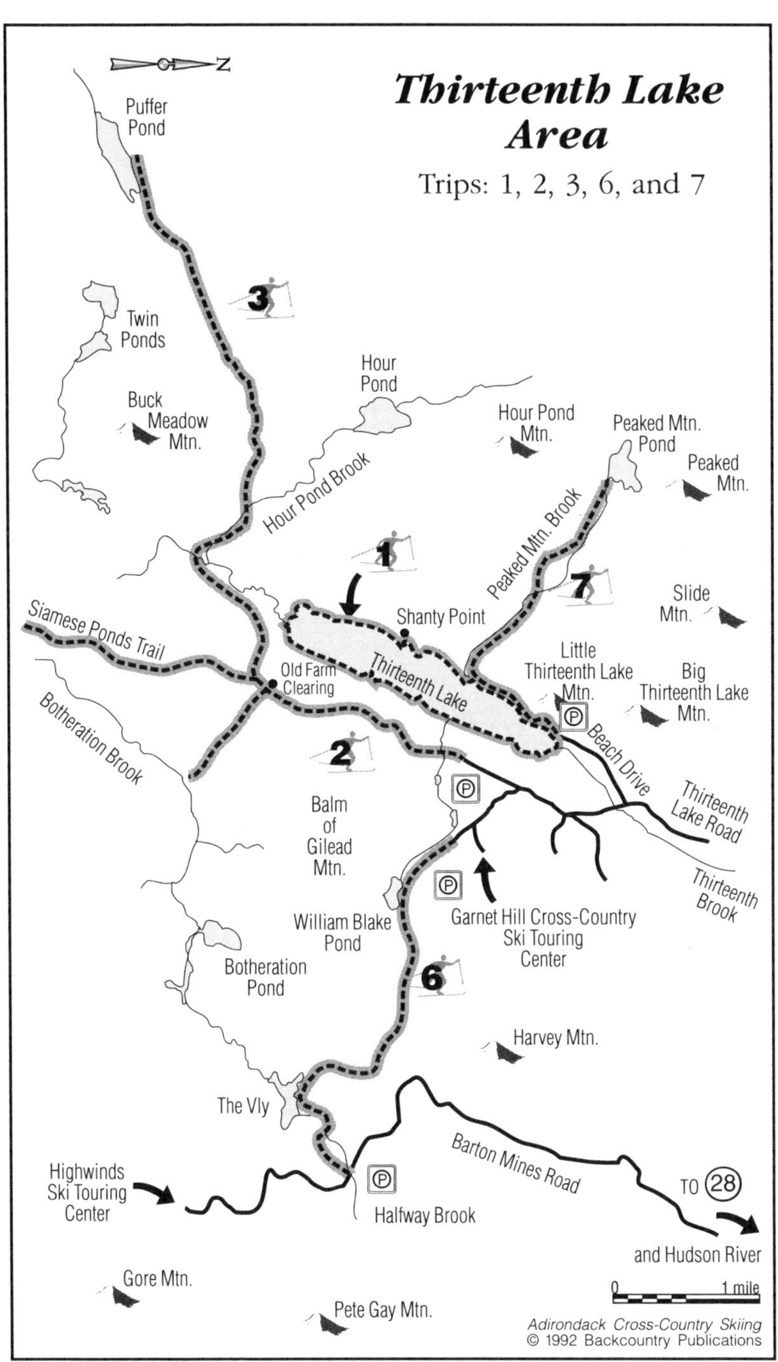

Thirteenth Lake Area
Trips: 1, 2, 3, 6, and 7
Z
Puffer Pond
3
Twin Ponds
Buck Meadow Mtn.
Hour Pond
Hour Pond Brook
Hour Pond Mtn.
Peaked Mtn. Pond
Peaked Mtn.
Peaked Mtn. Brook
1
7
Slide Mtn.
Shanty Point
Siamese Ponds Trail
Old Farm Clearing
Thirteenth Lake
Little Thirteenth Lake Mtn.
Big Thirteenth Lake Mtn.
Botheration Brook
2
Beach Drive
Thirteenth Lake Road
Balm of Gilead Mtn.
Thirteenth Brook
William Blake Pond
Garnet Hill Cross-Country Ski Touring Center
Botheration Pond
6
Harvey Mtn.
The Vly
Barton Mines Road
Highwinds Ski Touring Center
TO 28
Halfway Brook
and Hudson River
Gore Mtn.
0 1 mile
Pete Gay Mtn.
Adirondack Cross-Country Skiing
© 1992 Backcountry Publications

pointing to Thirteenth Lake and the Siamese Ponds trailhead; go right on Beach Drive for 0.5 mile to the parking lot. Ski south along a path 200 yards to the lake. It is wise to telephone the forest ranger or the Garnet Hill Ski Touring Center to determine if the ice is thick enough to ski on. You can also look for tracks of other skiers. Do not ski to the left as you go out on the lake because it is the outlet, and the ice is thin.

The best way to enjoy the lake is to ski along the right (west) shoreline and continue around it counterclockwise. The winter woods and shrubs are a beautiful mix of birch, poplar, pine, and spruce. As you ski along the shore, the first landmark is a point with two handsome white pines. Later, multicolored ice-falls glisten on rocky, lichen-covered cliffs. In 0.75 mile, after passing a rocky promontory, you cross a small cove. Peaked Mountain Brook flows gently into the lake from the birch-covered shore. Because of the moving water, the ice can be thin here, so release your toe bails and keep 50 feet out from the shore as you round the point. About two-thirds of the way down the lakeshore, you pass Shanty Point. Enjoy the beauty, solitude, and peace all the way to the far end, 2 miles from the start.

Hour Pond Brook enters through terraced beaver ponds at the shallow southern end of the lake. There are active beaver lodges and sometimes signs of otter. Looking north, you can admire distant high peaks shining in the notch to the right of Ruby Mountain. Ski around the lake to pine-studded Elizabeth Point, a good place for lunch in the afternoon sun. A trail leads from here up to the Old Farm Clearing Trail described below, but it is steep and narrow for beginners.

If the ice in the center of the pond is safe, you will see the tracks of skiers, and in that case you can continue along the eastern side. You will come to a clearing where canoes are stored, and from there you can cross the ice back to your car to complete the loop.

2. Old Farm Clearing and Botheration Brook

▪

4.0 miles round-trip
Skiing time: 1 hour and 40 minutes
Competent Beginner
USGS Thirteenth Lake 15' or 7.5' x 15' metric
Map—page 45

Thousands of people have learned to kick and glide into Old Farm Clearing. It is one of the all-time favorite places to get out for a short, pleasant jaunt. Beginners can handle it because it is almost level, but experienced skiers also enjoy the beauty and solitude of the old road.

The trail to Old Farm Clearing runs parallel to the eastern lakeshore. You reach the parking area for this trailhead by turning left at the fork on Thirteenth Lake Road (3.1 miles from NY 28). Continue up the road and bear right at an intersection (3.55 miles) to another fork at 3.8 miles. Go straight on the level following the Old Farm Clearing trailhead sign. Park at the end of the road in an open plowed area 4.35 miles from NY 28. This access is a public trail into the Siamese Ponds Wilderness Area.

The old road is gentle and wide. There are usually tracks on each side if you like to ski in them; otherwise, ski down the center. In a few minutes you enter the Siamese Ponds Wilderness Area, marked by yellow blazes. Five hundred feet along there is a summer parking area and a barrier to vehicles. Sign in at the register. A sign reads: Hour Pond 4.1 miles, Puffer Pond 5.3 miles, Siamese Ponds 9.2 miles, NY 8 10.2 miles.

Ten minutes from the barrier a sign high on a tree to the right marks the way down to Elizabeth Point on the lake. This steep side trail is not for beginners. Continuing along the old road, you reach a dense grove of Norway spruce, planted by the Civilian Conservation Corps over 50 years ago. Prior to reforestation this was a very large clearing, and the site of a popular summer lodge. (It burned in the 1920s and the owners rebuilt the lodge closer to Thirteenth Lake in the clearing where you parked. The new hotel also burned.)

It takes 25 to 30 minutes from the parking area to glide into the small clearing. Five large maples grow in front of the former homestead; if you look carefully, you can see the cellar holes to the right. A lumberman named Van Dusen opened up this area about 1877; later, it became a working farm. In the early 1900s, guides took fishermen and hunters from here into the woods and ponds where game and trout were plentiful. These trails still exist, for the most part, and are used by sportsmen and hikers as well as cross-country skiers. A sign here gives distances to the Sacandaga Lean-to 5.5 miles, John Pond 8.8 miles, and Rainbow Lake 10.8 miles.

Beginners have an easy run back to the car from Old Farm Clearing. The more adventurous and capable can continue with a choice of three trails. If you go straight ahead through the clearing, the trail branches within 50 yards; the right fork goes to Puffer Pond (Trip 3); the straight route goes through to NY 8 (Trip 4) and the Siamese Ponds (Trip 5). They are the portals that lead you into the northeast corner of this secluded and beautiful wilderness.

The route to Botheration Brook is the easiest but a little harder than the road coming in, and it requires more snow. On a tree at the far left end of the clearing there is a DEC sign which states: Unmarked Trail to East Branch of Sacandaga 1.0 mile. The DEC and the topographic map call this northern part of the stream the Sacandaga River. Local residents call it Botheration Brook; they claim that the East Branch of the Sacandaga River does not begin until Second Pond Brook joins Botheration Brook several miles downstream.

At the sign a path climbs gently left (east) through the dense Norway spruce. This trail is sometimes icy and fast because the thick spruce branches catch the snow and prevent it from reaching the ground.

In 10 minutes you leave the thick grove, and the path levels off as it passes through beautiful hardwoods. Soon you drop down a narrow spot in the trail and arc around a small hill, generally heading southeast. There is a nice ambience to the long glides and short climbs. Rabbit, coyote, and other tracks are numerous. You reach the partially frozen brook in 55 to 60 minutes from the car, 20 minutes from the clearing. If the weather has been cold, you can ski across the brook on an ice-and-snow bridge. Look for a blazed but hard-to-follow trail on the other side if you want to explore a little farther.

The return trip takes the same amount of time. You enter the spruce in 20 minutes, and after a fast 5-minute run, you are back at the clearing. Turn right for the 1.25-mile glide, slightly downhill, to your car. The entire trip can be skied in 1½ hours if you push it, and it's very pleasant.

3. Old Farm Clearing to Puffer Pond

▪

11.0 miles round-trip
Skiing time: 4 hours and 20 minutes
Intermediate
USGS Thirteenth Lake 15' or 7.5' x 15' metric
Map—page 45

Strong skiers will enjoy this outing into the wilderness area because the trip back is fast and demanding. The trail gains altitude most of the way to Puffer Pond, but there is beauty and variety, so the climb goes fast.

You can ski through to Kings Flow and make this a one-way trip. It is shorter, and somewhat easier, than a round-trip, but you must first drive a shuttle car around to Kings Flow (see Trip 43). A longer one-way trip (12.0 miles) is possible if you go to John Pond from Puffer Pond and then out to the trailhead near Wilderness Lodge (Trip 42), but you must traverse a long flat area in the valley below Bullhead Mountain leading to John Pond.

For the round-trip, leave your car at the trailhead for Old Farm Clearing (Trip 2), sign the register, and stride out fast to the clearing. Continue straight for 50 yards to a DEC signpost. Go right (Puffer

■
Puffer Pond: Trip 3

Pond 4.3 miles, John Pond 8.8 miles, and Rainbow Lake 10.8 miles) through the Norway spruce for a few minutes; then downhill on a steep, narrow path. Steel edges help to hold a snowplow on this short difficult stretch. At the bottom, the path veers left (southwest) for a pleasant stride-and-glide to a tributary of Hour Pond Brook. The log bridge has collapsed but, with care, a crossing is possible just upstream on a snow bridge. Across the narrow valley you face a very steep hill and a steady 15-minute climb. As you rest, enjoy the beautiful glen of Hour Pond Brook where it falls precipitously into snow-covered pools; only a murmur of water is heard through the dense snow blanket. Snow-crowned rocks, with a fringe of green moss and polypody ferns, lie where they tumbled among the moisture-loving hemlocks. Thirty feet above the stream the trail passes through yellow birch, beech, and maple. Abruptly, trail and brook converge and cross; now your route is a narrower path parallel to the brook on your left. Study this section of the eroded path carefully because you will ski it on the way back. Upstream from the crossing a large rock in the bed of the brook has a 30-foot hemlock growing out of it, seemingly thriving without soil. At the base of the rock you should see otter tracks where this sleek animal emerged from the ice after fishing the pool.

One hour and ten minutes from the car, a trail to the right goes off to Hour Pond, marked by a sign. The Puffer Pond route goes left here, crosses the brook, and swings farther left in a west-southwesterly direction. The trail is easy to follow as it is marked by blue disks. Continuing to climb, you see an open area through the deciduous forest. A steep hill descends to this large beaver meadow containing many dead trees. You swing around an arm of this stark expanse, foreign to humans but

▪

Lunch at Puffer Pond lean-to: Trip 3

familiar to wildlife, and begin to climb again. Large hemlocks thrive in the wetland; the understory is a tangle of hobblebush. If you must detour around a blowdown, this low, arching shrub catches your bindings and ski pole baskets; you wish the deer were more fond of this *Viburnum*, but they only browse the tips. Long, delightful glides are followed by short climbs as you follow the contour below the slope of Bullhead Mountain, which soars on your right.

You are almost to the pond when you reach a very pretty rock-strewn slope. The various-sized rocks appear to be fractures from the upper cliffs. After you see a large rock on the right, the trail drops sharply into a tricky section. Following the drop it is an easy run, with maybe a few blowdowns, to the lean-to at the eastern end of Puffer Pond. You reach it in 2 hours and 20 minutes. The lean-to is close to the water, so it is scheduled for removal when it deteriorates. It is still in good condition, however, and a favorite place for lunch. There is another lean-to halfway down the pond on a knoll. If you are skiing through to Kings Flow, see Trip 43 for how to proceed from this second lean-to.

On your return, you climb back to the stretch with the large rocks in about five minutes; then you level off with the sun on your back. In 30 minutes you are back at the flow; there are usually otter slides along the brook. Forty minutes after starting back be careful on a very abrupt hill, which is often icy and may have a log across the trail. At the bottom of the hill you are at the beaver meadow with the dead trees. A short climb, and then there is a great run down to Hour Pond Brook. After crossing it, try to ride above, rather than in, the eroded trail as you ski down to the lower brook crossing. The next downhill is very steep and takes a strong snowplow or a sidestep to navigate it safely. After this hill you ski a flat area, a brook crossing, a nice level stretch, and then climb to the spruce forest.

You are back at Old Farm Clearing 1 hour and 40 minutes after leaving the Puffer Pond lean-to; 20 minutes more and you are at your car. The round-trip is 4 hours and 20 minutes, not counting lunch. It is a sporty trip and popular with intermediate skiers.

4. Siamese Ponds Wilderness Trails

▪

9 miles one way
Skiing time: 4 hours or more
Intermediate
USGS Thirteenth Lake & Bakers Mills 7.5' x 15' metric
Map—page 54

This is one of the longest trips described in this book, and aside from one steep ridge and the possibility of becoming tired (particularly if you are breaking trail), it is a delightful and pleasant trek. It cuts through the eastern portion of the Siamese Ponds Wilderness Area. The beginning and end of the trip are both at an 1,800-foot elevation, but in between is a 200-foot climb followed by a 400-foot drop to the Sacandaga River. Much of the route follows this uninhabited river valley which, despite its current isolation, has a rich history. In the late 1800s settlers moved into this narrow band of flatland along the East Branch of the Sacandaga River from the south, climbing the shoulder of Eleventh Mountain (the route you follow). Burnt Shanty Clearing, Curtis Clearing, and, at the northern end of the route near Thirteenth Lake, Old Farm Clearing, mark the openings these pioneers cleared in the forest to get reasonably level land and good soil. The crude wagon road was gradually improved, and at one time a stagecoach came this way en route to Indian Lake past Puffer Pond. During the 1800s the road was used to haul hemlock bark and pulp. Now the trail is kept open by forest rangers and by hunters and fishermen whose gear is brought into the backcountry by wagon.

This well-marked tote road makes a memorable all-day cross-country excursion. It is not often skied, however, and storms can come up suddenly or accidents can happen, so you should follow the precautions on first aid and wilderness skiing in the opening chapter. The trip can be skied from north to south, but traveling in that direction requires a 400-foot climb over the shoulder of Eleventh Mountain and a fairly steep run down to NY 8 at the end of the trip.

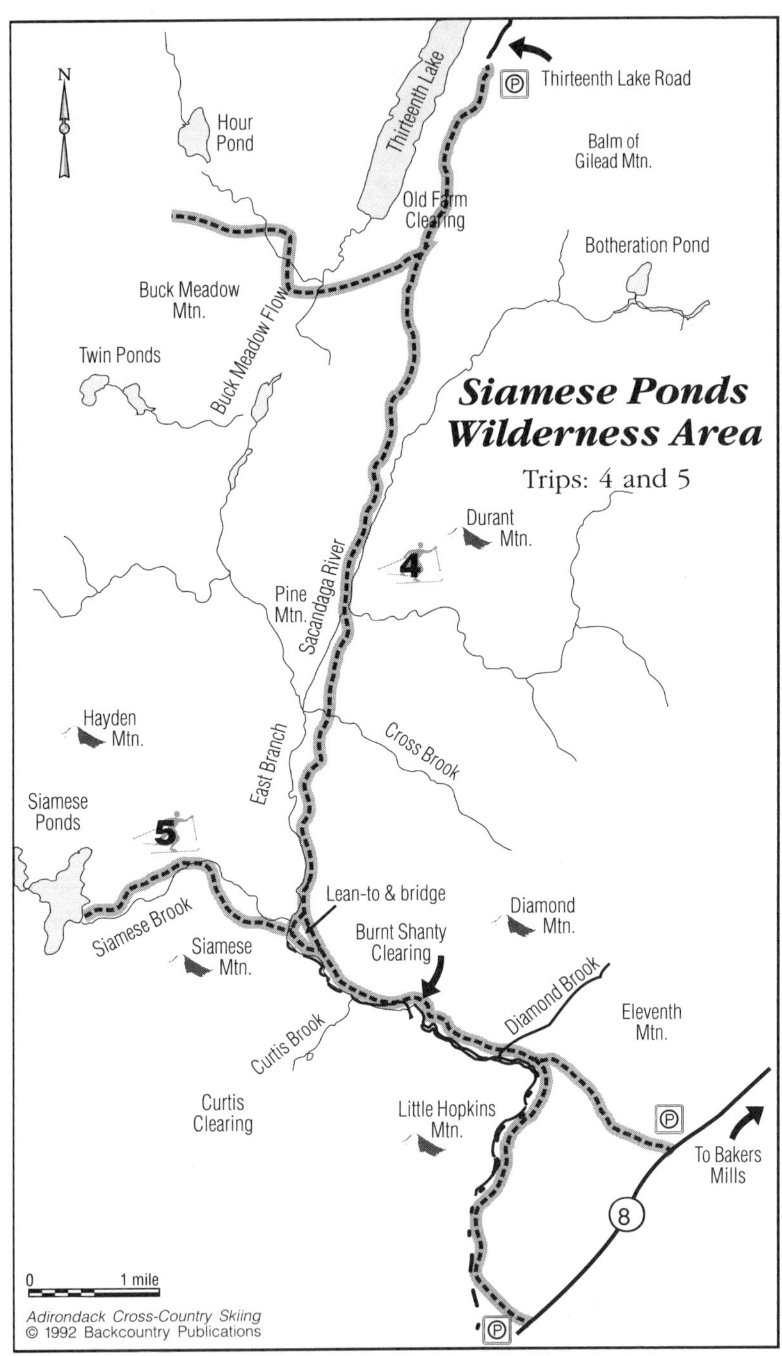
Thirteenth Lake Road
Thirteenth Lake
Hour Pond
Balm of Gilead Mtn.
Old Farm Clearing
Botheration Pond
Buck Meadow Mtn.
Buck Meadow Flow
Twin Ponds
Siamese Ponds Wilderness Area
Trips: 4 and 5
Durant Mtn.
4
Sacandaga River
Pine Mtn.
Hayden Mtn.
Cross Brook
East Branch
Siamese Ponds
5
Lean-to & bridge
Siamese Brook
Diamond Mtn.
Burnt Shanty Clearing
Siamese Mtn.
Diamond Brook
Eleventh Mtn.
Curtis Brook
Curtis Clearing
Little Hopkins Mtn.
To Bakers Mills
8
0 1 mile
Adirondack Cross-Country Skiing
© 1992 Backcountry Publications

It is better to ski from south to north and this description guides you that way.

Leave a car at the parking lot at the end of the spur road going toward Old Farm Clearing, as in Trip 2. Drive back down Thirteenth Lake Road to NY 28; turn right (south) and go 10 miles to Wevertown; turn right at the blinker and drive through Bakers Mills. Continue southwest on NY 8 almost 4 miles from the Edwards Hill Road intersection in Bakers Mills to a large historical marker and a plowed parking lot on the right (north) side of the road. A trail sign at the head of the parking lot (you have to climb the snowbank to read it) says: Trail to Siamese Ponds 5.8 miles, Sacandaga Lean-to 3.5 miles, 13th Lake 9.0 miles. No Snowmobiles.

You start with a climb up the old, eroded wagon road. It is not steep enough to require skins, if the snow is fresh and you have waxed correctly, but they help if you have them. As you climb, look back often to enjoy the open hardwood forest and glimpses of Kettle Mountain and Mount Blue through the trees. Blue trail markers and yellow cross-country skiing disks mark the route, but the trail is obvious. It crosses a low shoulder of Eleventh Mountain, marked by steep cliffs rising toward the hidden summit on your right.

After 10 minutes of stiff climbing you have conquered the steepest part; in another 10 minutes you are at a height of land 200 feet higher than your car. (As you climb, you should remove outer layers of clothing to keep from getting too warm.) Now the fun begins with a 400-foot run down to the East Branch valley. The trail is wide and can be handled by good intermediate skiers, but keep your speed under control, as the descent is continuous. In 10 minutes you level out, exhilarated, at a spot where the trail crosses a small brook. What a great schuss! Look right, up the brook valley through the alders, for a beautiful view of the cliffs on Eleventh Mountain. Get out your camera and keep it handy for the next 2 or 3 miles!

From here, for about 5 miles, you ski along the river valley. At first the trail winds through a picturesque stand of red spruce and balsam fir, a sharp change from the hardwoods on the hill. In 5 minutes you reach the frozen flow of the Sacandaga River on your left. The wide trail continues along the east side of the river. A new log bridge marks the crossing of Diamond Brook. Forty-five minutes after leaving your car, you will reach a spot where beaver have made a deep pond; the water may be frozen, but be cautious and ski across the top of the beaver dam—you are a long way from dry clothes. The view to the right is Diamond Mountain, a blend of cliffs, snow, and evergreens in a magnificent setting. Continuing on, you reach Burnt Shanty Clearing. It is recognized by berry bushes and shrubs, but in the winter you may miss this farm site, occupied not too many years ago.

In 1½ hours from the start there is a marked fork. A sign shows that the Siamese Ponds are 2.8 miles to the left, and that Thirteenth Lake is 5.5 miles if you go straight. You have skied 3.5 miles to this point. Go straight and in 10 minutes you reach another sign; it marks the fork to Siamese Ponds if you are skiing in from the north. At this point the river wanders through a broad marshy area, so the trail moves away from it. An array of red and brown reeds poke out of snow hummocks in the marsh for a show of winter color. Stately red spruce flank the trail. Many dead, limbless elms stand like huge sentinels. In 2½ hours, counting a brief stop for some hot soup and a sandwich, you reach a log bridge over Cross Brook. For years hunters have come into this area in early winter to camp and search for deer and bear.

The trail is clear and almost level; you can lapse into a smooth pole-and-glide rhythm. Open hardwoods create shadows on the snow as you slide easily by. Just under three hours from your car you reach the Sacandaga River crossing. It is shallow here and safe to cross anywhere. If there is running water, which is unlikely unless there has been a thaw, find a rocky outcrop with snow that will support your skis. After you cross the river, the trail bears right uphill, angling away from the valley. Looking downhill you can see Second Pond Brook coming in from the east. It marks the beginning of the Sacandaga River; above here the stream is called Botheration Brook.

You climb gradually but steadily for the next 25 minutes. Hemlocks border the trail, a reminder of history. In the mid-1800s hemlock bark was taken out to the tanning factories located on streams at Wevertown, Griffin, and other waterfall locations. In the spring and summer when the bark would peel, lumbermen cut the hemlock, and "spudders" stripped it. Teamsters hauled the bark out on huge sleds in the winter. The mammoth, skinned tree trunks were left to rot in the forest. The trees are rich humus now, but you can still see the stumps of some of the largest trees. (A comprehensive study of the industry is found in Barbara McMartin's *Hides, Hemlock and Adirondack History.*) By 1890 hemlock was used for building; pulp mills, which previously preferred white pine and spruce, also began to accept it. The logs were floated down the river, with bark stripped off to make them float better, and dams were built upstream to increase the flow of water. It was a busy place in contrast to the peace and quiet of the forest today.

Twenty-five minutes after crossing the river, you pass a large split rock on the right. It is a glacial erratic, carried there by an ice flow tens of thousands of years ago. Freezing and thawing have split it, and the crevice sprouts evergreen spinulose wood ferns. You are halfway from the river to Thirteenth Lake. Through the trees to the east you can see Gore Mountain, marked by several towers. Below the summit, if you peer carefully through the trees, you will notice the open area created by the garnet mine, now the site of the Highwinds Ski Touring Center.

The trail drops steadily from the height of land. There are no steep hills, and the route should be clear, so you can speed up for maximum glide. You will recognize the clearing by an opening with old maple trees in the middle of a large grove of Norway spruce. Your car is 20 to 30 minutes straight ahead on a heavily skied, mostly level, route. The through trip should take about four hours, but it can easily take longer if you are with a large group or if you stop frequently. Pick a good day with new-fallen snow and enjoy it.

5. Spur to Siamese Ponds

■

13.4 miles round-trip
Skiing time: 6 hours
Intermediate
USGS Thirteenth Lake & Bakers Mills 7.5' x 15' metric
Map—page 54

This trip to the two ponds, for which this wilderness area is named, is long and arduous. There are some steep downhills to the Sacandaga River valley from NY 8 (see Trip 4). From the river it is a 5-mile round-trip to the ponds, and then you have the climb over the shoulder of Eleventh Mountain on the way out. Alternatively, you can leave a second car farther south on NY 8 and ski out down the Sacandaga River. This river route obviously requires safe ice and a good snow cover. You should ski it with a group, including someone who has done it before.

The trip begins on the NY 8 trailhead as described in Trip 4, or you can start at Old Farm Clearing (Trip 2) and ski in from north to south. If you want to ski out along the East Branch of the Sacandaga, drive a shuttle car 1.9 miles southwest from the trailhead parking lot along NY 8. Look for a narrow, woods road on the right that angles back to the river. Scout it to the stream; leave a temporary colored marker on a prominent bush, so you will know where your car is (the shore all looks the same as you ski along it).

Ski in over the shoulder of Eleventh Mountain (as in trip 4) until you reach the river; this is the spot where you start down it on the way out. Go north to the fork, which you will reach in less than 1½ hours; then follow the sign left to the Siamese Ponds (2.8 miles). Fifteen minutes from the fork, you reach a lean-to beside the river, and surprisingly, a metal bridge that spans the wide stream. The bridge surface may not hold snow but you can walk across it, or ski across the river 100 feet downstream where the banks are low.

The river here is at an altitude of 1,640 feet; the twin ponds you are headed for are at 2,118 feet, so there is a climb ahead. The first 0.75 mile is fairly level as you follow the path west. As you climb, the way bears more to the north, following the contour around the base of Siamese Mountain on your left. Before long it climbs over the shoulder of the mountain and rises steadily. It should be a cleared trail if local teamster Earl Allen and his horses have taken camping gear into the area for hunters and fishermen; sometimes, however, early wet snow followed by winds blow down many trees. The trail is narrow in places with sharp turns. Skiers should be cautious on the return.

It is hard to say how long it takes to ski from the lean-to to the first pond; it depends on blowdowns and how frequently you rest. In about 1½ hours, on the average, you will cross the outlet of the first pond and can explore its long shoreline. If you started early enough, there may be time to ski up to the smaller pond that lies to the northwest. The area is heavily used in summer so there are various paths to follow on the shore.

With no blowdowns you can ski back to the Sacandaga River bridge in about 1 hour. It takes over 1 hour from the bridge to the place you start downstream, near the foot of Eleventh Mountain. The trip downriver to your shuttle car takes another hour. The climb over Eleventh Mountain to the point where you started is shorter and safer but more tiring.

At least three persons should be together skiing down the Sacandaga. One person should lead and cautiously test the snow-covered ice along the edge and the ice-and-snow arches where you switch sides, as you must do frequently. If someone breaks through, the water is not deep in most spots, but you may be standing in a hole with snow at the level of your waist, and you may not be able to reach your skis; leave the bail of your bindings loose so you can easily kick them off. The last person should have a rope to pull someone out. It will be slow going and perhaps a bit unnerving to ski near patches of open water.

As in many trips into the winter wilderness, it is advisable to have at least three people and to go with someone who knows the route. An accident, such as a twisted knee, can happen anytime and the third person can summon help while the second person attends the injured skier. Once you are in this secluded wilderness, it is a long way out and the trail is seldom traveled in winter.

■

Fungus along Halfway Brook trail: Trip 6

6. Halfway Brook to Thirteenth Lake Road

▪

2.5 miles one way
Skiing time: 1 hour and 30 minutes
Intermediate
USGS Thirteenth Lake 15' or 7.5' x 15' metric
Map—page 45

It is a mystery where Halfway Brook got its name; it seems halfway from nowhere, about two-thirds of the way up the north side of Gore Mountain. Skiing this trail makes for a varied and challenging trip through part of the Siamese Ponds Wilderness Area, past two interesting ponds and a beaver meadow. The finish is at the end of Thirteenth Lake Road. The trip is on public land, following old tote roads and a trail used by Frank Hooper when he walked from Thirteenth Lake to the Barton Mine on the backside of Gore. Hooper was an outdoorsman, hunter, and fisherman, as well as a competent geologist and manager; he would probably like to have his trail enjoyed on cross-country skis. Part of the trail is hard to follow, so it is wise to carry a compass and map.

Park a shuttle car on Thirteenth Lake Road (actually 4-H Road) in the vicinity of the Garnet Hill Cross-Country Ski Touring Center, 5 miles up Thirteenth Lake Road from NY 28. The trail from Halfway Brook is not part of the maintained system, so it is not necessary to pay a fee (although you will certainly want to ski the ski shop's well-groomed trails another time). Drive the other car back to NY 28, turn right (east) toward North Creek, then right again on Barton Mines Road between the Jasco Minerals Shop and the North River General Store. There is a Highwinds Inn sign at the turn. Go up the paved road for 3.9 miles to where the road dips in a slight valley. Halfway Brook flows under the road through a large culvert at this point; if you look to the right, you will see the narrow, unmarked opening of the trail. You'll have to leave your car off the road as far as possible as there is no plowed parking space.

The first 0.5 mile follows an old woods road with a straight and gradual drop to The Vly. Young evergreens are beginning to crowd the trail. Halfway Brook is on your right, hardly distinguishable except where beavers have created two new dammed areas. (Large balsam trees have toppled over because the soil has been softened by the water in the beaver pond, part of the constantly changing succession that occurs in nature.) The route continues through a new grove of balsam fir; in 10 minutes it crosses the brook, an invisible trickle unless there is a thaw. In about 20 minutes from the start you will see an opening on the left, the frozen surface of The Vly. Detour down to it, and ski out for a fantastic view of Gore Mountain. A fire tower and two radio antennas identify the 3,583-foot summit. In the early morning the trees on the upper slopes are often covered with a heavy coating of hoar frost. The red buildings and treeless, waste-rock piles are the remnants of the former garnet mine, now the Highwinds Ski Touring Center.

A *vly* is a very shallow pond, sometimes created as a result of beaver dams. As years go by, it becomes filled with silt and humus, or sometimes the dam washes out, and you have a "beaver meadow." If it has been cold, you can ski out onto the surface to a large beaver lodge. Beavers come and go, so it may not be occupied; one way to tell is to go up on top and see if there is an ice-glazed opening where the heat from the beavers' bodies and their breath escapes.

Retrace your ski tracks to the shoreline and back to the trail in the woods. The trail goes up 20 feet and then left (west) uphill to the right of several yellow birches. It then bears uphill to the right. Look carefully for blue paint marks on trees since it is hard to find the way through the hobblebush if there are no tracks from previous skiers. About 50 feet up the hill on a tree there is a blue arrow designating a sharp right turn. From here zigzag back and forth up the hill. Be sure to follow the blue blazes. In this section, 30 minutes after leaving the car, not counting a detour on The Vly, you will see a trail on the left; it comes from Highwinds. A sign shows Garnet Hill to the right. The woods are magnificent; they harbor some of the largest yellow birch trees you will find.

You climb westerly, and after about 0.5 mile the trail levels off, swings northwesterly, and parallels a steep, rocky outcropping on the right. As you drop into the drainage to the west, there are some nice glides through a handsome maple forest, punctuated by tight turns over narrow snow bridges. Interesting brown fungi grow on a dead beech; huge ash trees tower overhead; two large rocks make a gateway to the trail. Too soon, because this long stretch through open hardwoods is pleasant, you come to the upper end of a beaver meadow. It is spiked with picturesque dead trees. After crossing it and reentering the woods you reach a steep slope. There is no place at the bottom for a run out, and it is too steep under most conditions to hold a snowplow, so be cautious. Unsure skiers should sidestep the upper part; others may want to try wide turns through the semiopen woods.

You can continue straight ahead through open woods, with William Blake Pond down the slope to the left. A better route is to descend to the shallow pond and ski on its frozen surface. The scene is a typical Adirondack wetland with dead trees standing as bleak sentinels among the tufted hummocks of snow-covered grass. This pond was a source of water for the original Hooper Mine; it is deeper at its western end.

The outlet of the pond is toward Thirteenth Lake; it is about 0.6 mile from there down to your car. This last section of trail is heavily skied and fairly fast, dropping over 100 feet. Look out for other skiers climbing up, as many are novices, and they may have trouble getting out of the track. The wilderness area ends virtually in the yard of a large house. Before reaching it, there is a right turn that detours around the private land and over to Thirteenth Lake Road and your car. It takes about 1 hour and 30 minutes to make the trip, not counting stops. If you have only one car and want to make this a round-trip, it will take 1 hour from the western end of William Blake Pond back to your car.

7. Peaked Mountain Pond

▪

5.5 miles round-trip
Climbing time: 3 hours and 40 minutes
Snowshoeing
USGS Thirteenth Lake 15' or 7.5' x 15' metric
Map—page 45

It is a 422-foot climb from the shore of Thirteenth Lake to Peaked Mountain Pond on a narrow trail. It is possible to make it on skis, but the trip is more enjoyable on snowshoes. There are no trail markers, and the route is not usually traveled in winter; therefore, it is wise, the first time, to go with someone who knows the way. If you use a compass and stay in the valley of Peaked Mountain Brook, however, there is little chance of getting lost.

The trailhead is the parking area at Thirteenth Lake. To reach it follow the directions in Trip 1 (up Thirteenth Lake Road 3.1 miles, right on Beach Drive to the end). Walk to the lake and along the path that runs on the right (west) side of Thirteenth Lake or snowshoe along the shoreline. In 0.75 mile (20 minutes) you will reach Peaked Mountain Brook, which comes in from the right (west) down a valley between two mountains. Turn right before crossing the brook, and look for the path along the north side of the brook. It climbs steeply to 2,100 feet in the first 0.75 mile; snowshoes are preferable to skis in this section.

The trail levels off at a large, frozen beaver meadow. Trunks of trees, drowned years ago by high water created by the beaver dam, rise from the ice and snow. If you look ahead, there is a view of the snow-covered, rocky peak of Peaked Mountain. The trail crosses the brook and follows along the left (south) side of this open area. Here the path is less defined, particularly in winter, but continue with the brook valley on your right. In 10 minutes you come to another beaver meadow and the path crosses to the right (north) side of the brook; from here continue west and cross the brook again. You should reach the pond in 1½ hours from Thirteenth Lake.

The pond is nestled between Hour Pond Mountain, hidden to the south, and Peaked Mountain, nearby to the north. The small bay, at the place where you reach the pond, is shallow, so it is safe to snowshoe on it. The dead trees rising from the ice make a photogenic foreground for a picture of the mountain summit, which rises 670 feet above the pond. Peaked Mountain is too steep to snowshoe, but it can be climbed if the snow is not deep. You get to the path by walking north along the shore to the farthest bay, and then inland; look for red ties or blazes on shrubs and trees. The path starts up a ridge, and continues up a draw. The final ascent is from the southwest side of the peak onto the open rock. If the rocks are icy you should turn back, as there is no alternative route except bushwhacking through the spruce thicket. The top of the mountain has excellent views in every direction. It is interesting to look at the series of beaver-cleared patches of land in the valley. Be very careful and stay back from the steep rock face as you move around the top of the mountain.

8. Prier Pond

■

1.0 mile round-trip
Skiing time: 1 hour or less
Beginner
USGS Newcomb 15' or Dutton Mountain 7.5' x 15' metric
Map—page 67

If you want a short trip to a small secluded pond, try this one. The trailhead starts on a loop road off NY 28. Drive west uphill on NY 28 for 4.4 miles from Thirteenth Lake Road, then left on an unmarked plowed road. Go past the house with a porch on two sides to an apple tree on the left, and park beside the road.

Ski south into an open area beyond the apple tree and down a small hill. Look for old blazes on trees and follow the path, going south. In less than 10 minutes you will see the frozen pond through the open woods to the left. Ski down the gradual hill onto the frozen marshy shore. Davis Mountain rises, cone-shaped, to the east. The right (south) end of the pond is shallow. Bog shrubs such as sweetgale (*Myrica gale*) peek through the snow. Attractive, tall tamaracks line the south shore. As you ski toward the north end of the pond, you will see Casey Mountain ahead, beyond NY 28. The pond is deeper on this end; high ground with white pines mark the outlet. After you complete the circle of the shore, follow your tracks for the gradual climb back to your car.

9. Ross and Whortleberry Ponds

■

7.2 miles round-trip
Snowshoe time: 4 hours

Bell Mountain Brook

■

2.8 miles round-trip
Skiing time: 1 hour and 30 minutes
Competent Beginner
USGS Newcomb 15' or Dutton Mountain 7.5' x 15' metric
Map—page 67

Bell Mountain Brook, where otters roam, can be reached on skis along a fairly clear trail in the Hudson River Gorge Primitive Area. The last section of this trip to Ross and Whortleberry ponds had so many blowdowns (in 1991) that it is only for snowshoes. The land from Whortleberry Pond to the Hudson Gorge is owned by the Finch & Pruyn timber company. At one time negotiations were underway between the owners and the state of New York for the state to buy some or all of this land. Public access would add many new vistas and

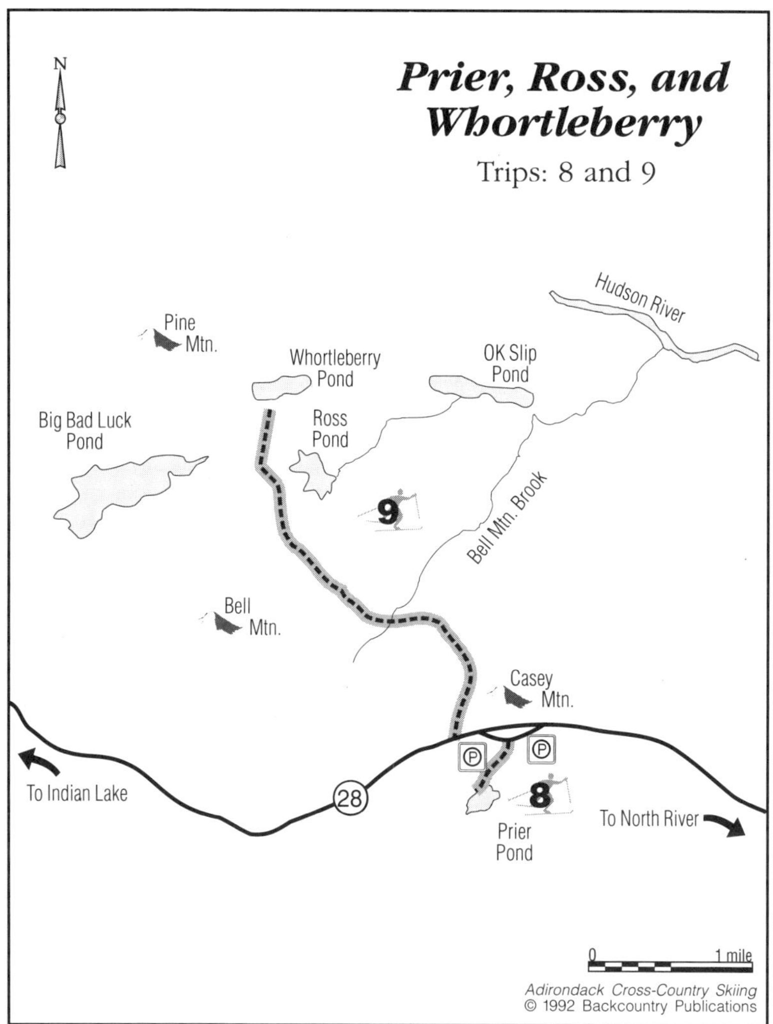

opportunities for new ski routes, including a loop back on a road past OK Slip Pond.

The beginning of this trip is on NY 28 just 5.05 miles northwest of North River (measured from Thirteenth Lake Road). As you reach the crown of the hill at 4.6 miles, the flank of Casey Mountain is on your right. Just beyond, at 4.85 miles, there is a wide, plowed road on the left. Park there, walk across the road, and ski or walk along NY 28 west for 340 yards (4 minutes). Looking down the bank, you see a Forest Preserve sign on a tree and a Posted sign to its left on a pole. Go down to the Forest Preserve sign, and continue past it on a narrow trail that follows yellow boundary blazes. In 100 yards you will come to a wider trail with large rocks. You start skiing here, going due north.

Although the area is near the highway, it harbors many deer, coyote, and fur-bearing animals. (On one trip, the skin and bones of a deer were found beside the trail where it had been killed and devoured by a coyote.) In the beginning, short runs are followed by easy climbs, although you are generally going downhill. The unmarked trail through maple, birch, and a large white pine grove is generally wide and clear. After skiing about ½ hour, however, you reach a section with blowdowns. Here you move north, or a little northeast, with the marshy area of Bell Mountain Brook on your left, and the cliffs of Bell Mountain beyond. Look for dead spruce; if there is a lot of bark on the ground under them you can be sure that a three-toed woodpecker has been at work.

After 40 minutes (about 1.4 miles), the trail swings northwest and crosses Bell Mountain Brook on the broken remains of a plank bridge.

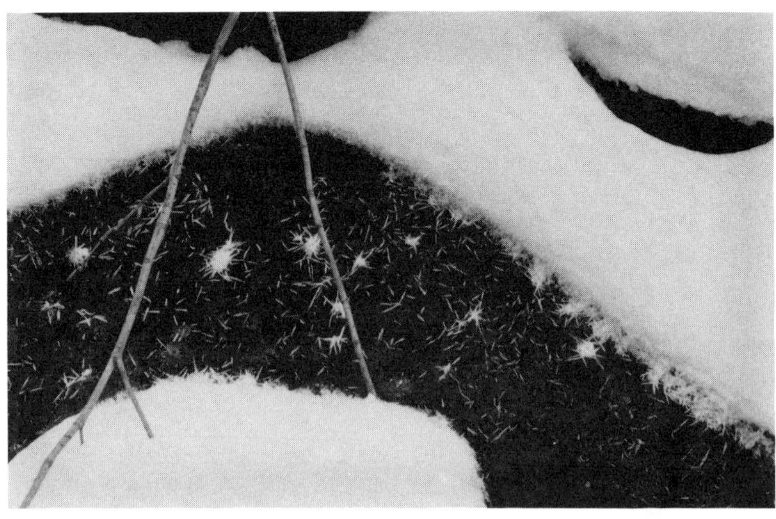

■
Ice crystals on black ice

Along the brook, or just beyond it, you will usually see otter tracks: undulating troughs in the snow with two rear paw prints visible. Occasionally, the track will disappear at a hole in the ice where this fine swimmer has gone into the water in search of a meal.

In the late 1980s you could ski on from here but now the trail is overgrown and covered with blowdowns so you need to switch to snowshoes. The trail climbs steeply for 200 feet, narrow and eroded in spots, over one of the ridges of Bell Mountain. One hour and fifteen minutes (about 2 miles) after leaving the car, you top the 2,000-foot-high saddle and begin a gradual descent to the ponds. About 20 minutes from the saddle (less than 1 mile), you will see Ross Pond through the woods on your right. Bear north from here. (It is essential to carry a compass on this route, as it is not traveled often and you can miss the trail.) After a small rise you reach a camping spot near Whortleberry Pond. It lies at the same altitude as Ross Pond, just under 1,700 feet. It would be nice to ski down the outlet beaver ponds to the dirt road that goes past a summer camp, but this is private land and you cannot do it without permission.

Heading back along the main trail, you top the saddle and descend through open hardwoods to the brook. After this you can put on skis and enjoy the downs and ups on the way out through the attractive and relaxing woods. If you want to see the tracks of an otter, Bell Mountain Brook is a sure place to find them.

■

Paper birch along the trail

North Creek Area

Between Mountain and River

■

The small community of North Creek nestles below the 3,583-foot summit of Gore Mountain beside the Hudson River. In winter, the hills around the village get a lot of snow and the river partially freezes over. North Creek was a larger town in the old days. Loggers cut pine and spruce on the surrounding mountains for lumber and pulp, and woodsmen peeled bark from hemlock for use in nearby tanneries. These lumbering activities created many tote roads and in the early 1930s enterprising local people decided these roads could be used for the growing sport of skiing. Since then, skiing has been an important part of North Creek winter life.

In an account in the February 23, 1989, *North Creek News-Enterprise,* Vincent Schaefer recalled that the first snow train traveled from Schenectady to North Creek on March 14, 1934. Skiers were taken from the station up the road to Barton Mine, where they put on skis. In those days ski boots were leather with flexible soles, much like sturdy, over-the-ankle cross-country boots are today. The early boots fit into a metal toepiece with a strap over the toe that held your forefoot rigidly. A heavy leather and metal strap ran from a pivot on the toepiece around the heel of the boot. This allowed your heel to rise, much like current telemark bindings. In many ways downhill skiing then was similar to telemark skiing today.

The Roaring Brook Trail started from Ives Dam; at a left fork it became the Rabbit Pond Trail which ended at the edge of town. The Pete Gay Trail followed Raymond Brook to the road near the Hudson. Schaefer said it was Bill Gluesing who coined the phrase, "Ride up—slide down," which became a popular slogan in the "Crick."

The sport grew and more tote roads were brushed out. You could glide down Halfway Brook Trail, Ridge Trail, Lower Cloud Trail, and others. Little Gore was opened on the outskirts of the village, with ski tows, a toboggan slide, a skating rink, and a small jump. A 1937 Trail Map issued by the Gore Mountain Ski Club (which you could join for $1) had eight ski trails starting on Gore Mountain, most of them 6 to 8 miles downhill.

After World War II, New York State developed a major downhill facility at Gore Mountain. Little Gore eventually closed, and the old trails down the mountain became choked with brush. Now, with the growth of cross-country skiing, some of the old trails have been opened and more are planned. Ride up—slide down is back.

The trips in the North Creek area lead to bogs and ponds beside the river. Competent beginners will enjoy Trip 10 to Bog Meadow. Intermediate-level skiers will be challenged by Trip 11 to Second Pond. Trip 12 to Second Pond from the North is for advanced skiers only. Beginners will enjoy Trip 13 to secluded Nate Davis Pond and Trip 14 along the upper reaches of the Hudson. Two commercial facilities are described below.

Cunningham's Ski Barn

As you drive into North Creek from the southeast, you'll come to a large barn with a light brown roof and a Ski Barn sign. The Cunninghams have been in the skiing business since 1934; this is their headquarters for the Adirondacks. From the Ski Barn, you can enter 25 kilometers of track-set trails with a skating lane, groomed regularly with the latest equipment. The trails cross open fields and wind through mixed hardwoods and dense pine forests as they weave between the Ski Barn and the Hudson River. Some trails climb to views of the high peaks; others reach almost to the murmuring water.

The trails provide a varied and interesting choice of cross-country experiences for the beginner and intermediate skier. Rental equipment and instruction are available.

Tours for groups of experienced cross-country skiers can be arranged down some old Gore Mountain trails and into the Adirondack backcountry. Information including rates is available from: Cunningham's Ski Barn, Route 28, North Creek, NY 12853; telephone: 518-251-3215.

Gore Mountain Cross-Country Trails

Eleven kilometers of groomed cross-country trails start from the Gore Mountain Base Lodge, managed by the Olympic Regional Development Authority (ORDA). These Gore Mountain slopes range from the easiest to the most difficult. Two loops are easy one half-mile glides. Doe Brook and Tannery Loop combine for about four miles of more challenging skiing. The Straight Brook Loop is two miles of the most advanced Nordic skiing at Gore. All trails are about 12 feet wide and are groomed and tracked.

Telemark skiing on downhill slopes is welcome at Gore, and their alpine trails provide ideal conditions; a separate lift pass can be purchased. Further information and rates are available from: Gore Mountain Cross-Country Area, Peaceful Valley Road, North Creek, NY 12853; telephone: 518-251-2411 or 1-800-342-1234.

10. Bog Meadow and the Flow

▪

7.0 miles round-trip
Skiing time: 4 hours and 30 minutes
Competent Beginner
USGS Thirteenth Lake 15' or Bakers Mills 7.5' x 15' metric
Map—page 75

This moderately long tour takes you deep into the Siamese Ponds Wilderness Area on a cleared trail. It can be handled by beginners with the attitude and stamina for an all-day trek. Pick a day with sun and fresh snow. Get several friends and take a lunch and your survival pack because you are far from help if you should twist a knee or an ankle. You may want to pack binoculars and a book on mosses and lichens if there is room.

From the intersection in Wevertown go west on NY 8 to Edwards Hill Road (2.1 miles). Turn right (north) on this rural road and drive up 1.5 miles. There is a green house on the left, then a white trailer; the driveway you ski into is just past the trailer. A sign near the mailbox reads Fogarty. Park as far off the road as you can.

Ski in to the left (west) up a narrow roadway. On the right, within 100 yards, you pass a white summer residence with a porch and an apple tree. Continue straight on the narrow road into the woods where, in a few minutes, you will see a well-preserved cabin over 100 years old. You are at 1,900 feet and starting to climb over a shoulder of Eleventh Mountain. Continuing to loop right, you reach a private boundary sign that excludes motorized vehicles. After a climb up a hill that will start you puffing, you reach the Forest Preserve, 25 minutes into the trip. Ten minutes later, you cross a small brook and cruise along a flat but undulating trail through mixed woods. You will see many large dead spruce in this area and evidence of three-toed woodpeckers who scatter the bark on the snow as they search for insects.

In just under one hour a very pretty grove of balsam fir greets you; with a coating of snow on its dark green, symmetrical branches,

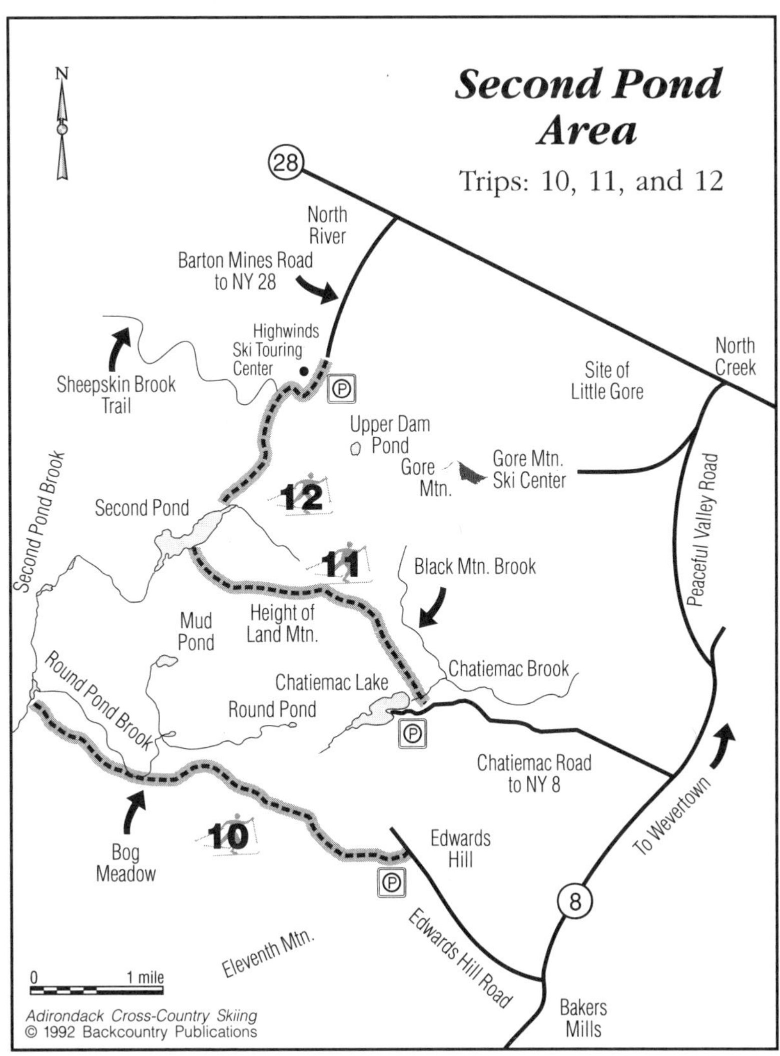

balsam seems made for winter. Gliding on, you enter a stand of white birch at about 2,200 feet. Begin to look for lichen, mosses, and liverworts; bryophytes thrive on the dead wood found in this area. You can spot a round gray-green lichen on birch trees. Another nonflowering plant, *Frullania,* is a liverwort identified by its rusty red, fingerlike growth on tree trunks. Various mosses are common.

If you don't tarry too long, you will reach Bog Meadow in 1½ hours. You can ski out onto this acre-size area surrounded by evergreens. The trail, however, because it is used for hiking, goes around the right side of the wetland. Cross over small Round Pond Brook where it enters the meadow from your right and skirt the bog just inside the woods. After crossing the outlet, continue on a visible trail (although there are no markers to guide you) in a northwesterly direction on a level contour. About 55 minutes from Bog Meadow you will see an open area ahead and below you. As the trail swings around to the left, watch for a place to ski down to the open meadow created by Second Pond Brook. Bordering the opening are some scratchy, impenetrable spruce trees; keep bearing left until you find a place to get through them. Once out in the open, you will see a tall single pine across the frozen flow to the left. That high ground is a sunny place to contemplate the beauty of the woods, sky, and distant hills. There may be ravens doing acrobatics from the high branches, and you are likely to see chickadees and blue jays.

In the late 1800s a wagon road continued beside Second Pond Brook to the Sacandaga River. Hemlock bark was skidded up this road on sleds, out on the trail you have just skied, and on to the tanneries. Now the skid road is overgrown, and a route isn't apparent. It would be a wonderful trip if you could loop around Eleventh Mountain down to the Sacandaga River and NY 8.

Retrace your tracks for the trip back. It is faster than skiing in. It will take about 50 minutes to reach Bog Meadow. Look around on the north side of maple trees for shield lichen (*Parmelia*). Close to the end there is the long downhill slope. You should be back to your car two hours after leaving the flow.

11. Second Pond

▪

5.5 miles round-trip
Skiing time: 4 hours and 10 minutes
Intermediate
USGS Thirteenth Lake 15' or Bakers Mills 7.5' x 15' metric
Map—page 75

The first part of this trail is wide and clear, with only one steep hill to climb and to create a challenging glide on the way back. The last half of the trail is a challenge of a different sort: blowdowns, hobblebush, and finding your way. Until the trail is cleared all the way (you could check with the local forest ranger or go halfway in and see), it takes stamina and patience to go the distance. It is wise to travel with someone who has been there, and compass and map are essential. Once you have arrived at this secluded pond setting, with the low sun streaming across the crust and massive Gore Mountain looming nearby, it will be worth it. At Second Pond there is the feeling of wilderness, which somehow is only slightly diminished by the radio antenna on the mountain.

The unmarked trailhead starts up Chatiemac Road, from NY 8. Go west from Wevertown for 3.5 miles, then right (north) on Chatiemac, a plowed dirt road. Go uphill for 2.3 miles from NY 8. Then look carefully on the right for an opening with a low sign in the middle of an old logging road that says, No Motorized Vehicles. If you miss it you will reach Chatiemac Lake, a private club, so turn around and look more carefully coming back.

The trail heads north from Chatiemac Road. Within 100 yards you reach the outlet of Chatiemac Lake, a small stream that you cross by jogging left over snow-covered rocks and a onetime beaver dam. In 10 minutes you are gliding along an old logging road, following blaze marks, at a heading of 350 degrees magnetic. The open hardwood forest is extensive and attractive; a frozen flow, created by Black Mountain Brook, appears in the valley. In about 50 minutes, you slide into a low, flat area where the trail seems to disappear. It is the first of many such places. Instead of going left up the draw, which appears to be the route, go straight across the flat area onto a hill, which becomes a flattened ridge, or hogback. There may be blue strips of ribbon (flags) tied to trees to guide you and if you look closely, you can see old blazes. Straight and somewhat steep, the trail follows the spine of the hogback. Beyond the valley of Black Mountain Brook is the large southwest shoulder of Gore Mountain with snow-covered ledges. Large, glacial erratics lie scattered around as decorations on the landscape.

As you ski off the hogback, the trail—now only a path—jogs left across a small gully, but then it follows the contour to the right around Height of Land Mountain on your left. The path is hard to follow; don't take any of the several apparent paths that lead downhill. Keep going left, slightly uphill. In this area it is possible to see the track of a fisher, a large animal (males can be nearly four feet long) that resembles a black fox with shorter legs and a skimpier tail. The track can be identified by five toe prints, each with a claw mark. The fisher's track is usually paired, but will show a variety of patterns as it ranges cross-country.

One hour and twenty minutes after leaving the car, you should be heading about 300 degrees magnetic. Ten minutes later your course is almost west into the sun; the mountain with the ledges is at your back. You will still be climbing gradually (it will seem wrong, but you are still a long way from the pond) through a lot of hobblebush. Two hours after starting, you enter an extensive blowdown area that continues almost to the pond. The trees are difficult to ski around, but eventually you can find a way. The path is recognized by blue ribbons and occasional red paint dabs on trees. You swing gradually to the right downhill, bearing north and then northeast briefly. In about 2 hours and 10 minutes you reach a dense balsam, red spruce, and yellow birch setting on the Second Pond shoreline at 2,241 feet, 50 feet lower than the trailhead.

Ski out on the snow-covered ice to the island straight ahead, with the admirable vastness of Gore Mountain to your right. The island is a nice place for lunch, especially if an afternoon sun casts bright, warming rays.

On a cloudy day there is shelter behind some red spruce. Edges of the island and shoreline are bordered with leatherleaf (*Chamaedaphne calyculata*) and sweetgale (*Myrica gale*). A rock on the island has a chain attached to it, a relic that relates to fishing or logging.

Another trail comes over the shoulder of Gore Mountain from the Highwinds Ski Touring Center, and, if you have left a car there, you can go out that way. It is better, however, to plan a round-trip from Highwinds, as described in Trip 12.

The trip back, after the 20 minutes it takes to get through the hobblebush and blowdowns, is fun and fast. There is a lot of gentle downhill as you follow the contour around Height of Land Mountain. In 50 minutes you cross the short gully and start over the hogback. The run down the spine is too fast to notice the beautiful open woods of large beech, yellow birch, and hard maple; it is a 50-foot drop from the top of the hogback to your car. As you cross the Chatiemac Brook outlet, just under two hours after leaving the pond, blinding rays of the late sun shine down the draw, capping the enjoyment of a rough but satisfying excursion into the Siamese Ponds Wilderness.

12. Highwinds to Second Pond

■

4.0 miles round-trip
Skiing time: 2 hours
Advanced
USGS Thirteenth Lake 15' or 7.5' x 15' metric
Map—page 75

The beginning of this trip is at the Highwinds Ski Touring Center. It can be skied as a short round-trip, if you want an advanced downhill run and a steep climb back. You can ski it one way to Second Pond and out to Chatiemac Road. It can also be an extension of Trip 11 into Second Pond that finishes at Highwinds.

The road to Highwinds is described in Trip 6. You must pay the day rate for skiing at Highwinds and pick up their trail map. Starting at the ski shop, ski to the Sheepskin Brook Trail and start down it. After a steep drop leading into a turn across a bridge, you bear right along a level section then swing left. Here another trail goes left up a steep hill; a sign indicates this is the route to Second Pond. You are only about six minutes from the ski shop.

You climb about 200 feet up a fairly steep, but wide, old road. Highwinds packs it with a snowmobile as far as a ridge; from there it is all downhill. The trail is brushed out in the private land section, so, while steep, there are places for wide turns and telemark stops. Be careful, however, because about halfway down you enter Forest Preserve land and the trail becomes narrow and challenging, with blowdowns and hobblebush making it hard to turn. About 20 minutes after starting your descent, the trail levels out, leaves the attractive hardwoods, and enters a grove of balsam fir and spruce. The trail winds right through dense woods and abruptly emerges onto the pond, about 45 minutes after you started. You come out on the north side of the extreme northeast portion of the pond. Turning left to explore the inlet, you will cross the remains of an old beaver dam. This end is choked with leatherleaf, and gorgeous black spruce (*Picae mariana*) dot the shallow cove.

As you gaze up the pond, there is a small island in the center that is not on the topographic map. Usually there is a strong wind gusting over the pond into your face as you pole and stride to the island. The summit of Gore Mountain, marked by a fire tower and radio antenna, is directly behind. When you reach the island, look to your left for an opening in the woods. As you ski into the opening, you should see a camping spot and fire rings; this is the beginning of the trail out to Chatiemac Road (Trip 11). If you ski past the island to the outlet end of the pond, there are some spruce logs to sit on for lunch. This secluded spot in the wilderness is a beautiful place to catch your breath.

If you are coming in from Chatiemac Road and skiing out to Highwinds, ski almost all the way down the northeast end of the pond toward Gore Mountain. There are several large, dead spruce and balsam trees as you reach the bog area. Ski past them for at least 100 yards. Then look for the opening in the woods on your left. There is no sign, but it is an obvious camping spot. This is the beginning of the trail over the shoulder of the mountain to Highwinds. It will take 7 or 8 minutes to ski through the balsam/fir thicket, and 25 minutes to climb the 360 feet to the groomed trail. As you schuss down the other side there is a distant view of Mount Marcy through the trees. The drop to Sheepskin Brook Trail takes less than 10 minutes. You are at the ski shop in less than one hour after leaving Second Pond. A round-trip, including lunch and some exploring in the bog, is an easy 2½ hours.

13. Nate Davis Pond

▪

3.6 miles round-trip
Skiing time: 1 hour and 30 minutes
Beginner
USGS Thirteenth Lake 15' or Bakers Mills 7.5' x 15' metric
Map—page 82

If you want a short trip into a small glacial pond with a lot of snow, this is it. The trail is unmarked, except for old hatchet blazes, but is easy to follow until the very end. After struggling through some young hemlock and over a low spruce-covered ledge, suddenly you are there. Solitude prevails. Paul Schaefer, who summers on Edwards Hill Road and has done much to preserve the Adirondacks, "discovered" the pond during one of his sojourns in the woods. It is listed here thanks to his daughter, Evelyn Greene, who visits it for birding and late winter ski trips.

Drive west from Bakers Mills on NY 8 for 0.95 mile from the intersection with Edwards Hill Road. Turn left (south) on Bartman Road, go 1.1 miles to a fork, and turn right where a sign points to Bartman Trailhead. Go 1.3 miles farther to Bartman School Road

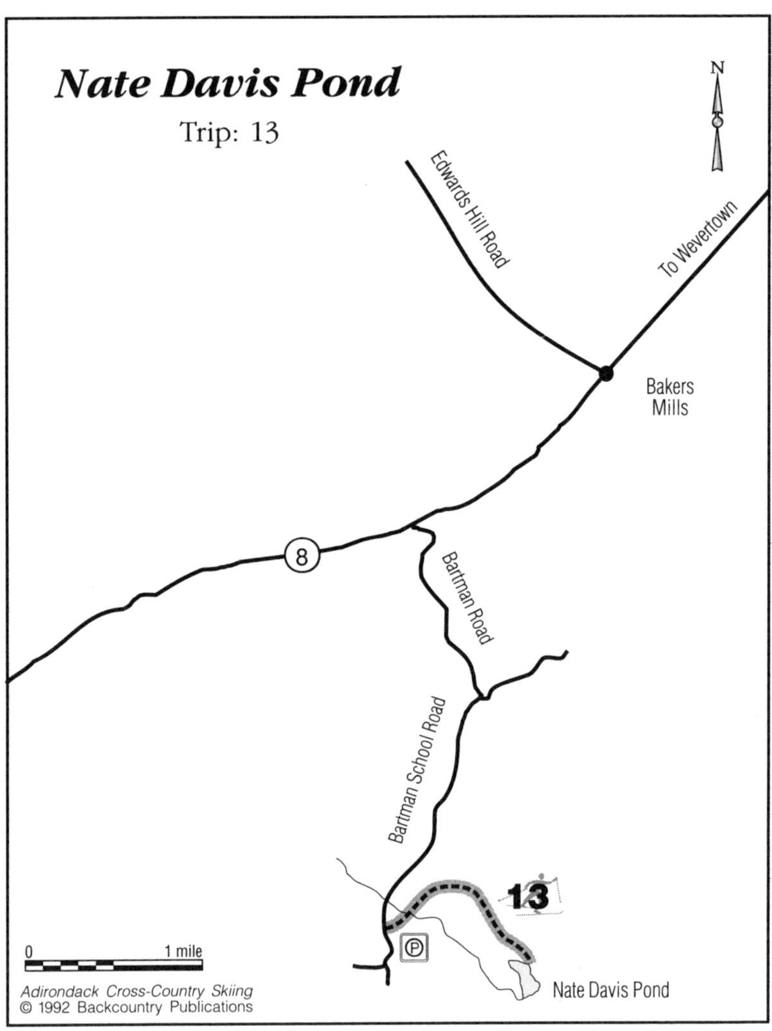

turnoff (unplowed) and park in the wide parking area. You are at 1,934 feet and the snowbanks on the narrow roadway are high. Ski back down the road for two minutes (0.1 mile) and look for an old road angling off to the right. There is no sign or marker but the opening of the trailhead is obvious.

In a few minutes the old tote road and trail cross a brook on a wide bridge spanning the outlet of Nate Davis Pond. A white-pine plantation darkens each side of the open road that passes several large maples, probably the site of a farm. A gradual rise through former pasture is followed by a dip, another height of land, and then a smaller stream crossing. A nice stand of white birch marks the edge of the pines. Forty minutes after leaving your car, as you come to a beaver meadow, the old road disappears. Look sharply for the hatchet blazes along the right side of the dammed area. The blazes lead into a small hemlock grove, and you bear right around it. This leads you to another beaver meadow, which you also skirt on the right. Then follow blazes that angle slightly right over a small ridge. On the other side lies the pond, reached in 50 minutes of fast skiing.

Nate Davis Pond is an unusual, long, frozen expanse. The edges are decorated with luxurious growths of leatherleaf (*Chamaedaphne calyculata*), sheep laurel (*Kalmia augustifolia*), and pale laurel (*Kalmia polifolia*). The pond was created by glacial action, not by beavers. It is surrounded, except for the eastern outlet end, by small hills. Nate Davis was a sawyer and blacksmith who lived on Bartman Road in the early settlement days.

The glide back is mostly downhill and, except for a couple blowdowns, is great fun. Within ½ hour from the pond you are putting skis back on the car. Try it for a late spring trip when the snow is too thin elsewhere.

14. River Road from North Creek to Riparius

■

3.0 miles one way
Skiing time: 1 hour and 30 minutes
Beginner
USGS North Creek 15'
Map—below

An easy beginner's track starts from North Creek and continues for three miles on an unplowed town road. There is a moderate hill that

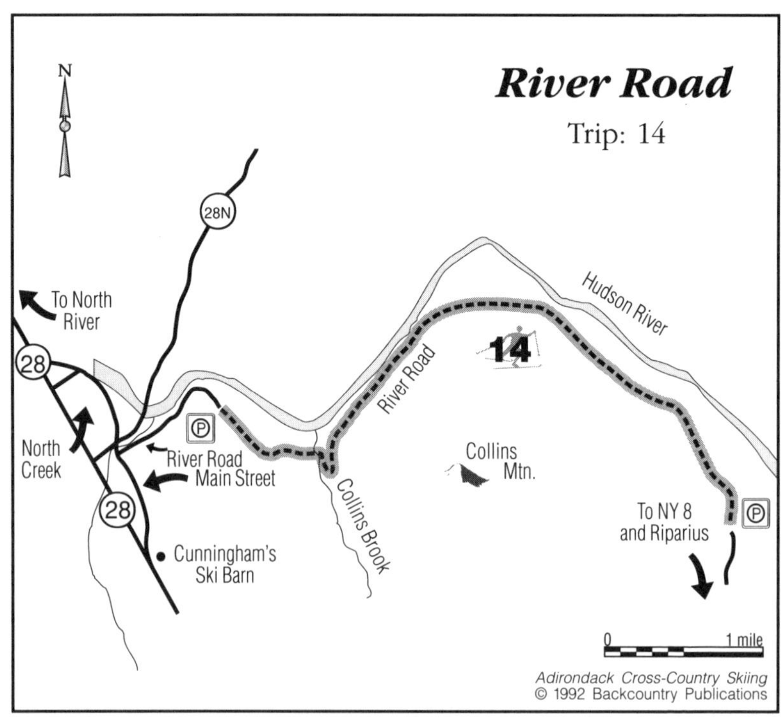

may trouble a complete novice if there is not a lot of snow, but otherwise it is a breeze. You can leave a car at the Riparius end for a one-way jaunt, or ski in as far as you wish and turn around.

To reach the start go southwest on Main Street in North Creek past the town hall and over a small bridge (not the NY 28N bridge over the Hudson River). Turn left immediately after the bridge on River Road and drive 1.15 miles to where the snowplow stops, and park. If you want to ski through, drive shuttle cars 5 miles south of North Creek on NY 28. Turn left toward Riparius at the flashing light in Wevertown on NY 8. About 2.85 miles from the light, turn left on River Road and drive 3.1 miles to the end of the plowed road, where you leave the shuttle car.

Starting at the North Creek end, you will find the trip is straight and level for five minutes and then turns left. When it bends right, there is a small hill that ends at a brook crossing. At the fork just beyond, go left; the right route takes you onto Cunningham's commercial trails. In 10 minutes you cross Collins Brook and swing sharply left up the steepest hill on the road. As you top the hill, there is a stunning view of the wide Hudson River, flowing directly toward you from the northwest. The granite base of Collins Mountain causes the river to veer northeast and your route follows it for over 1 mile. The road is 20 feet or more above the river, with the snow-covered railroad in between.

After a pleasant glide, the road swings right, away from the water. This is called the straight line by the railroaders because it cut straight across the hypotenuse of the river's right angle. You pass a large grove of black spruce and, beyond it, a planted area of red pine. The railroad is nearby on the left. You climb a small grade and swing southeast, away from the river and the rails. It takes 45 minutes to reach this point; if you turn around, you will be back to the car in 40 minutes.

Continuing, it is another 2 miles to the other end of River Road. This section climbs slightly, about 100 feet, through open fields and woods, without a view of the river. The North Creek end is by far the prettiest. One of the nice features of the trip is that it can be skied with a minimum amount of snow.

■

Opalescent River Trail: Trip 18

Newcomb Area
High Peak Views

■

Newcomb is the gateway to the southern high peaks of the Adirondacks. It consistently has some of the coldest temperatures in the region and generally gets abundant snowfall. You will find some of the earliest and easiest cross-country skiing at this center of the park. Although the trails slope gradually, some are long. You will remember them for the attractive destination ponds, the Santanoni Great Camp, and the sweeping views from many vantage points.

Newcomb stretches along a ribbon of road running east and west. The trailhead for Trip 17 to Goodnow Mountain is on the western end; closer to town is the Adirondack Park Visitor Interpretive Center. Trips 15 and 16 to Santanoni Great Camp and Moose Pond begin near the center of town. The Hudson River, small and tame at this point, flows under NY 28N at the eastern end. Farther east, near the health center, is a parking area with a stunning panorama of the massive mountain range. Driving south from here, on NY 28N, takes you to Trip 20 near Vanderwhacker Mountain.

East of Newcomb on NY 28N, a spur off the Blue Ridge Road takes you on a dead-end road to Tahawus. The Indians who summered here called the tallest peak *Tahawus* (He splits the sky). Trip 18 to the Opalescent River and beyond begins on this road just past the stone remains of a blast furnace beside the road. It may seem odd that there was industrial activity in this near pristine environment, but almost at the end of this spur road is the deserted village of Adirondac, once a prosperous iron-smelting community. A small blast furnace was operated by a water-driven compressor with wooden cylinders, a process depicted in a diorama at the Adirondack Museum in Blue Mountain Lake. At the end of the plowed road, trails for advanced skiers, not described in this book, lead to high passes in the heart of the mountains.

Past the Tahawus turn, the Blue Ridge Road continues east toward North Hudson. The trail to Lester Dam, Trip 19, begins near one of the overlooks along the ridge.

An excellent booklet, *Cross-Country Ski Trails in the Newcomb Area,* is available at the town hall. One trail listed is an old road called the Roosevelt Truck Trail on state land. (It is recommended by Walter Chapman, an avid cross-country skier who lives in Newcomb.) Other trails included, also not described in this book, are trails to Woodruff Pond, Bradley Pond, Lake Henderson, Chasson Road, and Linsey Marsh. Some of the trails traverse private land, and presumably the owners allow skiers to use them.

The Visitor Interpretive Center

A new Visitor Interpretive Center nestles on a forested mile-long peninsula in Rich Lake. Operated by the Adirondack Park Agency, the Center provides an introduction to the natural resources of the area as well as information on lodging, restaurants, and recreational opportunities in the park. The Center features 3½ miles of interpreted trails and a 6,000-square-foot building, open all year. It is adjacent to the Huntington Wildlife Research Forest of the College of Environmental Science and Forestry of Syracuse University. The extensive information collected by the college on the forest and ecological systems in the area—including the effects of acid rain—is incorporated into the Interpretive Center's program.

The Center has a winter trail system for cross-country skiing and snowshoeing. The Rich Lake Trail is an easy 0.6-mile loop and the challenging Peninsula Trail an additional 0.7-mile circuit. There are mountain vistas, scenic overlooks, a small but distinctive wetland, and an interesting 200-acre forest. The Center is adjacent to the Santanoni Preserve, and a skiing connection to the road to Santanoni Great Camp (Trip 15) is planned. For information write: Visitor Interpretive Center, Box 3000, Paul Smiths, NY 12970.

15. Santanoni Great Camp (Newcomb Lake)

▪

9.4 miles round-trip
Skiing time: 4 hours and 30 minutes
Competent Beginner
USGS Newcomb 15' & Santanoni 7.5' x 15' metric
Map—page 90

This long but easy trip probes into the southern edge of the High Peaks Wilderness Area. Its destination is Newcomb Lake and the Santanoni Great Camp, an impressive group of now-abandoned log buildings that grace the shoreline of the lake. An Adirondack great camp is like a small village with its main lodge, separate residences, dining buildings, game rooms, and staff quarters. At Santanoni Great Camp there were also stables, barns, and a boathouse. The main complex of the camp was designed by Robert Robertson for Robert C. Pruyn, and construction was begun in 1888. The barns and utility buildings and many of the servants' quarters were built in 1910 of native stone. The camp was enlarged by the Melvin family of Syracuse, who bought it in 1953. The entire complex is a premier example of the Adirondack style of rustic architecture.

On July 10, 1971, a young Melvin grandson wandered away from the camp. Over 650 people joined the largest search in Adirondack history, but Douglas Melvin was not found. This tragedy affected the owners so deeply that the camp and land were sold to the Adirondack Conservancy. In 1972 the conservancy conveyed the 12,500-acre estate

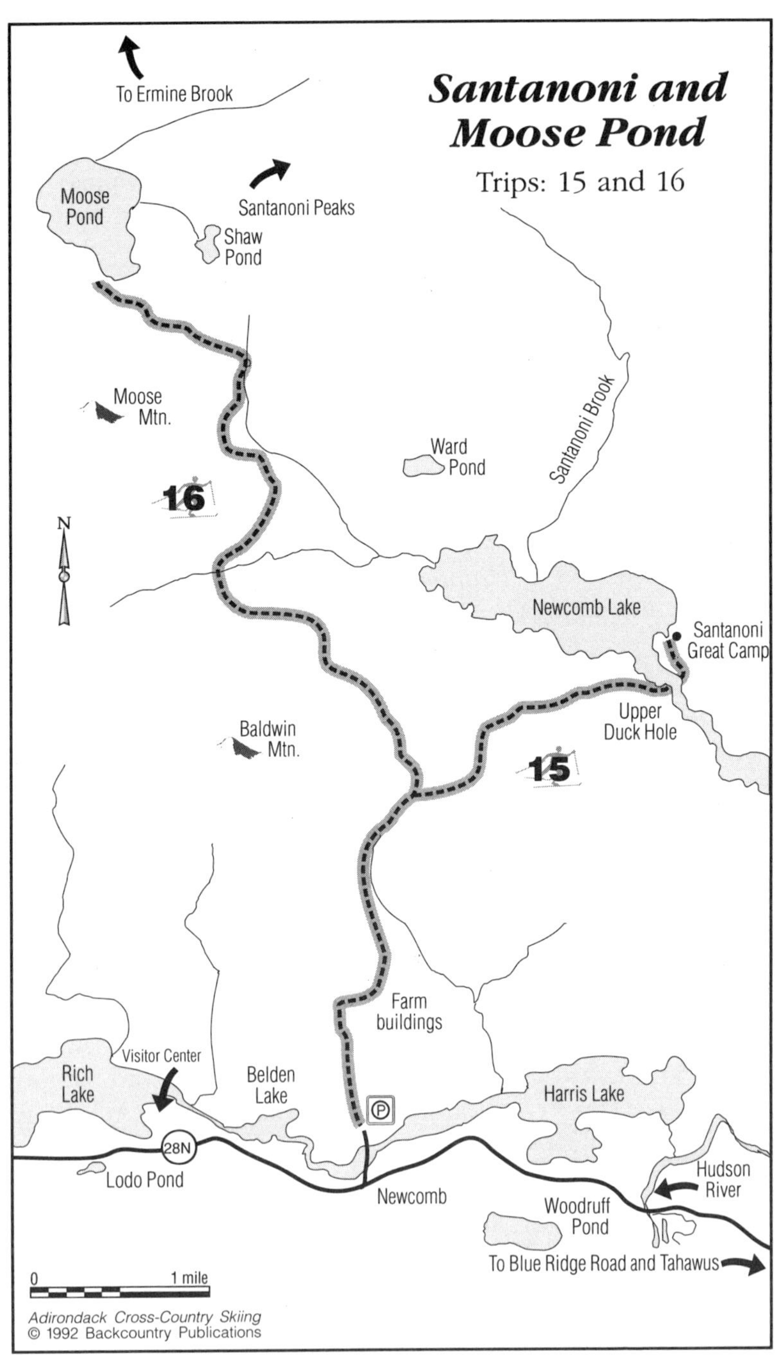
Santanoni and Moose Pond
Trips: 15 and 16
To Ermine Brook
Moose Pond
Santanoni Peaks
Shaw Pond
Moose Mtn.
Ward Pond
Santanoni Brook
16
N
Newcomb Lake
Santanoni Great Camp
Upper Duck Hole
Baldwin Mtn.
15
Farm buildings
Visitor Center
Rich Lake
Belden Lake
Harris Lake
28N
Lodo Pond
Newcomb
Hudson River
Woodruff Pond
To Blue Ridge Road and Tahawus
0
1 mile
Adirondack Cross-Country Skiing
© 1992 Backcountry Publications

to New York State. Following the Adirondack Park Agency Act, the land was divided: the farm buildings, about a mile from the trailhead, were made part of the Primitive Area; the main lodge buildings were placed in the High Peaks Wilderness Area. Today the main camp is in limbo because, under the act, there are to be no unnatural structures in wilderness areas. Many people have an attachment for this and other great camps because they represent an important cultural phase of Adirondack history and craftsmanship. Efforts continue to allow the camp to remain, and recently a plan has been announced that protects the integrity of the forest preserve while recognizing the importance of maintaining historic sites.

The trip lets you explore the excellent workmanship of the period and relish the expanse of Newcomb Lake, which lies like a white jewel in the setting of the Santanoni peaks. The trailhead is reached by turning north in the center of Newcomb on an angular street, running east. A sign by the road says Santanoni Preserve. Coming from the east, it is 1.9 miles west of the NY 28N bridge across the Hudson River; 1.1 miles from the Visitor Center, driving from the west. Within 50 feet, turn left (north) again, where another small sign says Santanoni Preserve. Drive across the narrow bridge that spans a stream from Rich Lake to Harris Lake. Go straight up the hill past maintenance-type buildings, then turn right 0.35 mile from NY 28N to a large, plowed parking lot. You will see the trailhead registration booth straight ahead before you make the turn for parking. The DEC trailhead sign gives mileage to Newcomb Lake as 5.0 miles, Moose Pond as 7.0 miles.

This trail is the place to practice your kick and glide. There are generally two tracks—one in and one out—and it seems natural to stay in them. The well-built roadway rises almost imperceptibly through a dense evergreen forest. After skiing 0.5 mile the road makes a wide, gradual right turn; in about 20 minutes (1 mile) you reach a large barn with a fancy turret. On the left is a small building, constructed entirely of stone except for the trim and roof; it was the milkhouse for the farm. The wide porch is a good place to sip some juice and enjoy the view. You have climbed almost 100 feet to this cluster of farm buildings.

The road then curves around to the left in a tight, level loop. Another small stone building, a springhouse perhaps, is on the left. After a slight glide you climb through an open hardwood forest. In another mile you will have gained another 100 feet. There are pretty dips with hemlocks in some areas, but maple and birch predominate, with evergreen spinulose wood ferns (*Dryopteris spinulosa*) peaking through the snow along the banks. At one open place there are some magnificent balsams with thick, heavy needles.

The trail forks just over an hour into the trip. Your way is to the right, 3 miles more to Newcomb Lake. The left trail goes 5 miles to Moose Pond (Trip 16).

The route from here rolls pleasantly up and down. There are some gentle glides and equally easy hills. As you approach the lake in a long, gentle downhill, there is an impressive view of 4,605-foot Santanoni Mountain. In about 2½ hours, a small hill takes you down to a bridge across the narrows of the lake, called the Upper Duck Hole. Across the bridge the road curves left to the great camp on the point.

Take time to look around. A complex roof system shelters the five cottages, which are connected by a wide porch that shades the front of the large log buildings. Most of the logs were cut on the site, and the construction work was done primarily by men from nearby villages. The exterior has a black stain set off by bright red window and door frames. Peering through the windows into the empty rooms, you can see the detailed workmanship, such as the split-sapling wainscoting. Massive stone fireplaces served the lounge and dining area.

Ski around the water's edge and examine the large boathouse. Most people who visit the Santanoni Great Camp believe that this grand example of log construction should be preserved. The buildings seem to blend into the wilderness rather than detract from it.

Newcomb Lake is at 1,736 feet (529 meters), and the parking lot is at 1,600 feet. There is a gradual climb for about one hour as you start back, but the last part of the trip is mostly downhill. Beginning skiers will find it a long but interesting and rewarding day.

16. Moose Pond

■

14 miles round-trip
Skiing time: 5 hours and 45 minutes
Competent Beginner
USGS Newcomb 15' & Santanoni 7.5' x 15' metric
Map—page 90

The easy grades and wide, brush-free road make this trip appropriate for a competent beginner, but good conditioning is required to go the distance. Two things can make it easier: if the trail has been broken by someone else and if the snow is just right for a good kick and a long glide. Pick a sunny day and start early, and you will be rewarded by a magnificent view of Little Santanoni and massive Santanoni peaks from the shores of this isolated wilderness pond.

The directions for reaching the trailhead for Moose Pond are the same as for Trip 15. The trailhead sign indicates that Moose Pond is 7.0 miles; your altimeter should read about 1,600 feet. The first 2.2 miles of this trip, until you reach a marked left fork, follows the route to Santanoni Great Camp. You reach the fork in less than 1 hour, and a DEC sign points you left to Moose Pond. After the fork the route continues in a long, gradual climb. The open, small hardwoods show this land was once private and lumbered in the past 20 to 30 years. The route heads around to the northwest and climbs gradually to almost 2,000 feet on the northeast shoulder of Baldwin Mountain. There, about ½ hour from the fork, there is a splendid view ahead of low but picturesque Moose Mountain.

From this point there is a long but gradual run to the valley. If the snow and your wax are in tune, it is a great glide without the risk of gaining too much speed. At 1,800 feet the trail swings right, to the northeast; the magnificent snow-covered summit of Santanoni dominates the scene ahead. This lowland area west of Newcomb Lake was apparently some of the farmland of the Santanoni Great Camp, as there are still open areas fringed by balsam and red spruce. Surprisingly there are no signs of deer. The sun beats into this cleared area, and it is a good place for lunch, standing in the trail.

After the meadow, you ski in a roughly northerly direction. There is a brook valley nearby on the right, and you climb very gradually as you follow it. About 15 minutes from the clearing, the trail turns sharply west and begins to climb steeply, from 1,800 to almost 2,000 feet in a short distance. This is the steepest part of the trip and the only place where, returning, you may start skiing too fast. Look it over on the climb to see where you need to snowplow and slow down. From the saddle it is a short drop to a fork, with Moose Pond showing through the trees ahead. A sign indicates that Ermine Brook and Cold River are to the right; Ermine Brook is about 1.5 miles, and Cold River is much too far to reach in one day. The trail to the left leads to a large opening with two campsites back from the water. From here a short, skiable path ends at a tent site 20 feet from the shore.

As you walk down the steep bank to the ice, a breathtaking panorama of mountains emerges. From the 1,780-foot-high shoreline, high peaks loom close in the northeast; on the distant northwest horizon the Seward Range appears. The tallest summit is Santanoni with a large, continuous, ribbonlike snow gash down its side, marking Ermine Brook. The mass of this mountain is stupendous and its bulk exaggerated by a frosty coating. Closer and to the left of the higher peak is Little Santanoni Mountain. No slides mark this lower, 3,500-foot peak, but a white open area appears on the side with a dark ledge in the center, resembling the white eye of a husky.

The slopes of Little Santanoni screen the 4,000-foot peak of Couchsachraga, the 44th highest peak in the Adirondacks. Russell Carson, in his informative book, *Peaks and People of the Adirondacks,* describes the origin of the name. *Couchsachraga* was one of the great hunting grounds of the Iroquois. According to Carson the first known ascent of the remote peak was in 1924 by Robert and George Marshall and Herbert Clark, the indomitable climbing trio of the high peaks. The peak was originally called Cold River Mountain but was changed to the more appropriate name that commemorates the Iroquois hunting grounds in the "great and dismal wilderness."

Savor the view, but don't tarry past 2:30 P.M. or you will be skiing out in the dark. It takes more than three hours to ski in, but the trip back will take less time if all goes well. You will be back in the meadow in 45 minutes, in time to catch the low rays of the sun, which is sinking rapidly. After the long climb up the lower slopes of Baldwin Mountain you will begin to be tired, but the darkening woods will spur you on. In 1 hour and 45 minutes you will be at the fork; from there you will reach your car in 45 minutes.

17. Goodnow Mountain

▪

3.0 miles round-trip
Skiing time: 3 hours and 15 minutes
Advanced or Snowshoeing
USGS Newcomb 15' or 7.5' x 15' metric
Map—page 96

A fire tower and a sweeping panorama of the high peaks are the destination—and the reward—of this short, strenuous trip. The tall metal-and-glass tower, rising from the eastern shoulder of the 2,685-foot peak, can be seen from several spots along NY 28N. It appears close and accessible, but it is a 1,055-foot climb and fairly rugged going. The 1.5-mile trail is steep and narrow. If you are going to try it with skis, climbing skins will make it much easier. Except for advanced skiers, it is better to make this two-hour ascent on snowshoes.

The trail begins 5.2 miles west of the Hudson River crossing of NY 28N, as you drive toward Long Lake. A small sign on the left (south) side of the road reads: Goodnow Mountain Trail—Summit 1.5 miles, SUNY-ESF, Open to the Public. This trail is owned by the SUNY College of Environmental Science and Forestry and is well maintained. The trailhead is 0.3 mile west of the Visitor Center; a small parking area is plowed.

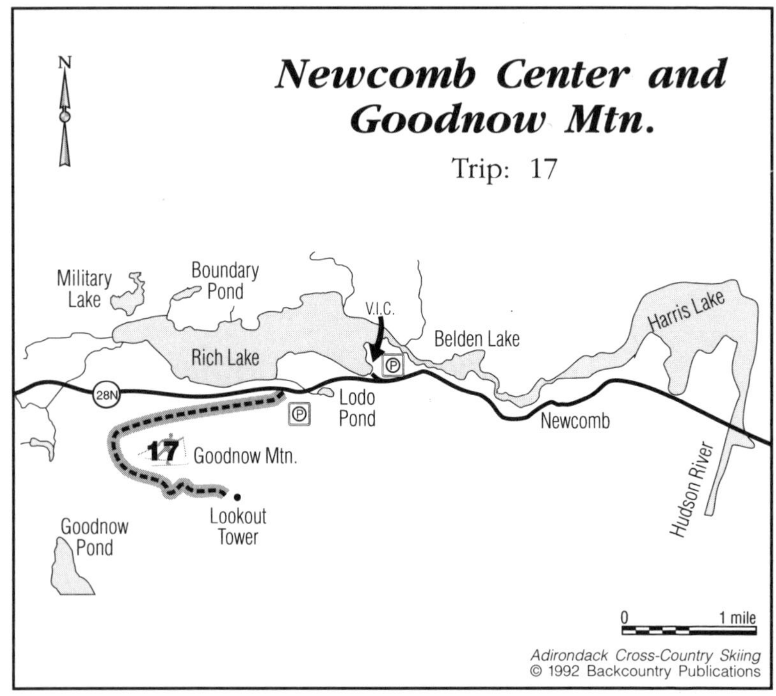

At the start a cable bars the way to vehicles, but step over it or ski around it for 100 yards to a sign-in register. From here the trail climbs up a wide and gradual jeep road in a southerly direction. This beginning rise is not difficult, but after climbing 200 yards, the trail gets steeper. If you are skiing and do not have climbing skins, it is all herringbone. You wish for a switchback through the woods to enable you to avoid this steep section, but the surrounding beech thicket is too dense for skiing.

In about Z\x hour the trail gets even steeper and gullied; this is the most difficult portion. After puffing up this rise, the trail mercifully swings right on a contour for a short way, then cuts left and climbs again. Pause here (you should feel the need) and enjoy the northern vista of the magnificent high peaks, less than 10 miles away. After one hour, now climbing more westerly, you pass over a narrow, rocky section of trail. Seepage from the ridge above freezes and coats the gray rock outcrop with layered ice. Spruce and balsam crown the ridge above, adding to the beauty. After 1½ hours, you cross a narrow plank bridge and start up again in a looping, left turn. Steep sections and gradual climbs alternate through the conifers in pleasant contrast to the beech, birch, and maple woods below. On the right, the foundation of an old cabin juts out precariously over the crest, providing an impressive view of the lower mountains to the southwest.

Another steep section with a switchback brings you to an old fire-warden cabin and a well. Through the trees you see the fire tower to the east. You have climbed for almost 2 hours and the tower is still 20 minutes away. It is not much higher than you are, although there are several abrupt sections on the final approach.

The tower offers a double treat. Seemingly straight down lies the mile-long Rich Lake peninsula—site of the Visitor Interpretive Center. Raise your eyes and there is a panoramic view of the high peaks! The 2¼-hour climb is well worth this scenery. In the future a shelter may be placed here for hikers and skiers; but for now, if it is a cold and windy day, you will not tarry long on this exposed crest.

The trip down is obviously very sporty, but experts can ski it if there is enough snow to cover rocks in the gullies. Extreme caution is necessary, and several sections should be sideslipped or skied slowly with frequent runouts. Skiing down takes about one hour if you use caution; it will take less time if you bomb it with tight, frequent telemarks in heavy snow. Opt for the slower run, and enjoy it.

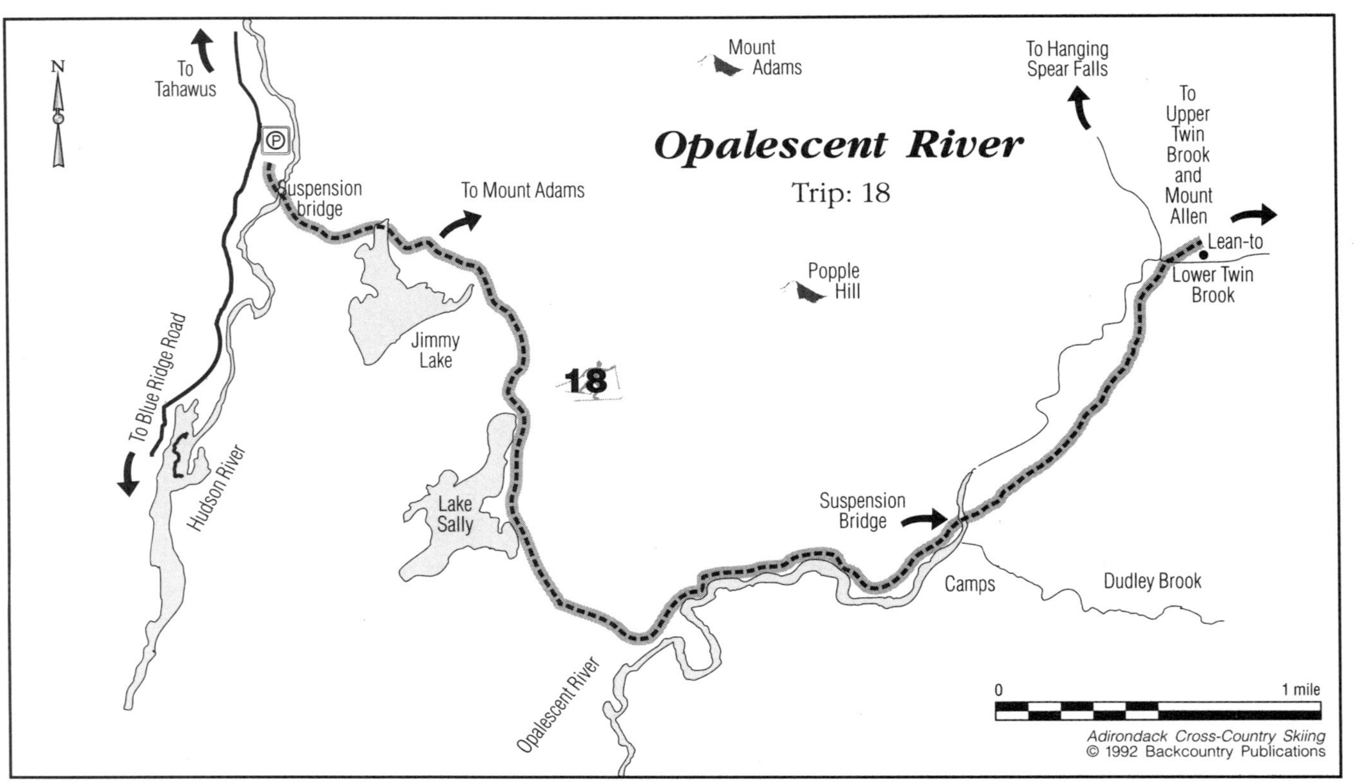

N
To Tahawus
Mount Adams
To Hanging Spear Falls
To Upper Twin Brook and Mount Allen
Opalescent River
Trip: 18
Suspension bridge
To Mount Adams
Lean-to
Popple Hill
Lower Twin Brook
Jimmy Lake
To Blue Ridge Road
18
Hudson River
Lake Sally
Suspension Bridge
Camps
Dudley Brook
Opalescent River
0
1 mile
Adirondack Cross-Country Skiing
© 1992 Backcountry Publications

18. Opalescent River and Twin Brook Lean-To

■

10.2 miles round trip
Skiing time: 5 hours
Competent Beginner
USGS Santanoni Peak 7.5' x 15' metric
Map—page 98

There are many challenging expert trails in the high peaks not covered in this book. Several easier trips into the higher mountains are included, however, to introduce you to the area. This trek to the Twin Brook Lean-to is one of them. You cross two streams on suspension bridges, ski through a variety of forests, and may meet snowshoers attempting a winter ascent of Mount Allen. It is a long trip, so start early. If you pick a clear day there are great views of distant peaks from the banks of the Opalescent River.

The trailhead is on the Tahawus road. From Newcomb, drive east for 5 miles on NY 28N; when the road forks, go left (east) on Blue Ridge Road toward North Hudson. Just over 2 miles from the fork turn left (north) to Tahawus. In 0.5 mile, go left following a sign for High Peaks-Calamity Brook. At 6.4 miles from Blue Ridge Road, take another left; at 9.2 miles look for the large plowed parking area on the right (it is 0.2 mile beyond the old MacIntyre Iron Works ruins). There is a wooden sign by the road. After parking you must climb over the snowbank to locate the trail sign and the sign-in register. The sign reads: Marcy 10.45 miles, Twin Brook Lean-to 4.7 miles. There are also distances for Adirondac Loj, Flowed Lands, and Keene Valley, but there are more direct routes if you have an urge to visit those places on skis.

Ski down an old road and you reach the Hudson River in a couple of minutes. The Hudson is narrow here, before it is joined by the Opalescent, but it is not safe to ski across. Go right, and in 100 yards

Winter trek along the Opalescent River trail: Trip 18

there is a suspension bridge with steps up to it; carry your skis across. On the far side, yellow disks mark the route up a gentle hill, through dense evergreens. In 15 minutes you reach an arm of Jimmy Lake with a log-and-plank bridge across the shallows. Large rocks in this section of the trail make it easier if there is a lot of snow. In 20 minutes you reach the junction of the Mount Adams trail; a sign says this point is 0.6 mile from the parking area, but it is probably longer.

Go right following the Mount Marcy sign and the yellow markers. After a slight drop you reach a frozen brook that you can ski across if the rocks are covered with enough snow. The trail now borders a dense cedar thicket with a number of uprooted trees. The trail has been maintained here, however, and there are no blowdowns to climb over. As you ascend, the trail narrows to a path with many large rocks; if there is not enough snow you will have to walk this stretch. Forty-five minutes from the start you reach a level road; the marked trail goes right to the south-southeast. In seven minutes it turns left down a short, steep hill, then makes a sharp right at the bottom. You can see Lake Sally through the trees to your right, but the trail avoids the lake and swings around to the southeast.

In 1 hour and 40 minutes you reach the Opalescent River. It is wide and meandering, with snowmobile tracks on the ice along the side. The entire area through which you have skied is owned by NL Industries and is leased to the Sanford Lake Rod and Gun Club. The snowmobiles, however, come from a small community of camps, downriver on other private land. The ski trail follows the riverbank north, sometimes ducking through dense balsam fir thickets. It is narrow and no snowmobilers use it. You should not have to break trail because this is a snowshoe route for Mount Allen and other high peaks.

In 2 hours and 20 minutes from the start, surprisingly, there is "civilization" across the river in the form of two decrepit trailers. A hand-painted sign says the lean-to is 1.6 miles, and the footbridge 100 yards, ahead. The suspension bridge across the river is skewed and difficult to cross. Carry your skis and poles across; the bridge sways and tips, so you must hang on as you walk over. The banks are steep and the river narrow at this spot. If snowmobilers have been on the ice, it may be easier to climb down the bank and ski across. On the other side you pick up an old tote road with a slight upgrade. Twenty minutes from the bridge, you may see Mount Adams off to the west.

Three hours from the start you reach Lower Twin Brook and, shortly afterward, the lean-to. You have gained only about 200 feet in altitude since leaving the parking lot, but it seems like a long haul. There is a junction in the trail at this point, with the left fork going to Hanging Spear Falls and Flowed Lands. The trail begins to climb here, and it is hard to reach the impressive falls in a one-day round-trip. The right fork follows Upper Twin Brook and is used by snowshoers reaching trailless peaks.

The trip back to your car takes a little less time. You will reach the suspension bridge in 30 minutes. From there, with good snow, you can make it back in just over two hours.

19. Blue Ridge Road to Lester Dam

■

5.0 miles round-trip
Skiing time: 2 hours and 30 minutes
Competent Beginner
USGS Schroon Lake 15' or Blue Ridge 7.5' x 15' metric
Map—page 103

Take this trip on a clear, sunny day because it leads to a historic dam and a sweeping, distant mountain view. It is short, and even beginners can try it if the snow is deep enough to slow you down on a couple of hills. There may be blowdowns, and you may meet a few snowmobiles on the weekend, but do not let that keep you from this enjoyable outing.

The marked trailhead is on Blue Ridge Road, 12.6 miles west of I-87 Exit 29 at North Hudson, or 8.7 miles east of the Hudson River crossing in the town of Newcomb. (Driving up from Minerva it is 5.15 miles east of the fork where you turn right on the Blue Ridge Road to North

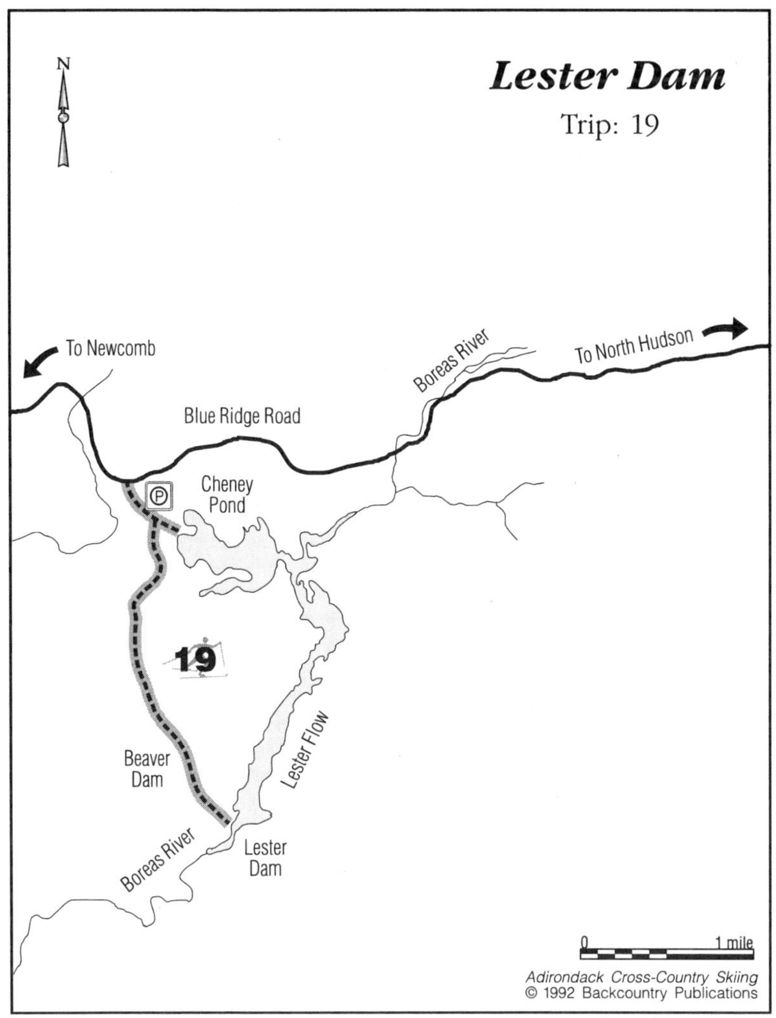

Hudson.) A plowed parking lot on the south side of the road holds five or six cars. The DEC sign reads: Trail to Irishtown 11.0 miles, Cheney Pond–Lester Dam–Minerva Stream. It is marked as a snowmobile trail.

The beginning is the steepest part of the whole trip so, if you can handle it, the rest is easy. There will probably be a snowmobile rut in the middle of the old road, but there is room to ski in the deep snow beside it. In five minutes you will drop about 100 feet, most of the total 165 feet to the dam. Take the first cleared route to the right; there is no sign. (If you want to see Cheney Pond, go straight for a few more minutes, and you are there.) Going right, within 100 feet you must ski around a metal barrier. The trail swings west here and climbs. A few wild cherry trees bent by an ice storm arc over the road, but you can ski under them. In a pretty evergreen glen there is an unusual stand of black spruce with very short needles and plentiful small, brown, round cones. Red spruce grows near it and you will notice the lighter green of the needles and the light brown, more pointed cones. Healthy, thick balsam fir also fringe the road. If these handsome conifers have a mantle of snow, the scene has unique beauty and charm.

Soon you swing south, climbing slightly; when the road tops the hill there is a gentle grade down. At the end there is a massive beaver dam six to eight feet high to the right of the trail. It is an engineering marvel that small animals can create such a huge structure. The beavers seem to have left this pond (there are few trees remaining) and built another downstream. It is a short way from here to the flow, which you reach easily in 1 hour and 15 minutes from the start.

The trail comes out above the dam, so bear left down the hill to the ice. If snowmobiles have been on the flow, you can ski across to the east bank. From here you can see the remains of the dam built in 1931 by Finch Pruyn and Company under the supervision of Jack Donohue, who lived in North River. It was a massive structure, over 30 feet high and 30 to 40 feet thick. It blocked the south-flowing Boreas River at this narrow neck of land and backed up the water for miles. Pulpwood was cut all winter and left upstream from the dam on the ice. In the spring, when Donohue decided the time was right, the water was released; pulpwood floated south down the Boreas to the Hudson River, and down the Hudson to the mill at Glens Falls. The last logs were sent downriver in 1951, and soon afterward the top portion of the dam washed out. This still left a sizable backwater that shows on the 1954 topographic map. Around 1980 the remaining timbers and rocks washed out, and the Boreas River is now back in its original channel.

A glance north reveals the beautiful Adirondack Mountains on the horizon. Easiest to recognize is the perfect, snow-covered cone of Mount Marcy, the highest peak. With a map you can pick out Boreas and Wolf Pond mountains in the foreground, beyond the long wide marsh that stretches before you.

There is a deep pool upstream from the dam. If you look carefully at the remains of the log crib, you will see animal tracks going to open water. Otter live among the timbers and fish the pool from this easy access.

It is possible to ski from Lester Dam to Irishtown but it is a popular snowmobile route, a long way, and (more important) an especially long shuttle.

The trip back takes about the same time as skiing in, making a round-trip of 2½ hours, not counting lunch.

▪

Otter's lair at broken Lester Dam

20. Vanderwhacker Mountain Road

■

5.2 miles round-trip
Skiing time: 2 hours and 30 minutes
Beginner
USGS Newcomb 15' or 7.5' x 15' metric
Map—page 107

This is a beginners' trail over a wide dirt road that in summer provides access to the several summer camps of the Moose Pond Club, a private inholding. Snowmobiles are permitted but, since it is far from houses and relatively short, you probably won't meet any.

The trailhead is a considerable drive on NY 28N from either Newcomb or Minerva, so plan to combine the outing with other short skiing trips in the area, such as Stony Pond or Linsey Marsh. You will note that NY 28N is designated the Roosevelt-Marcy Highway. The name memorializes Theodore Roosevelt's midnight dash by horse and wagon down a rough road on September 14, 1901. When Roosevelt arrived at North Creek, he learned that McKinley had died and that he had become president. A monument beside the road commemorates the event.

The skiing trip starts just north of the NY 28N bridge across the Boreas River. It is about 8.5 miles north of Minerva and slightly more than 8.5 miles south from the Hudson River bridge in Newcomb. A DEC sign at the trailhead reads: Vanderwhacker Mountain Firetower, ascent 3,385 feet. There are both orange snowmobile trail disks and red hiking trail markers.

Start west up the road with its stately border of large white pine and tall red spruce. The forest closes in on each side of the road so there are no views, but it is a pretty climb, especially after a heavy snowstorm. After about 35 minutes you reach Vanderwhacker Brook with an open wetland on the right. This is a good place for photographs of winter marsh scenes; there are rabbit and other animal tracks. Soon afterward you cross the railroad tracks.

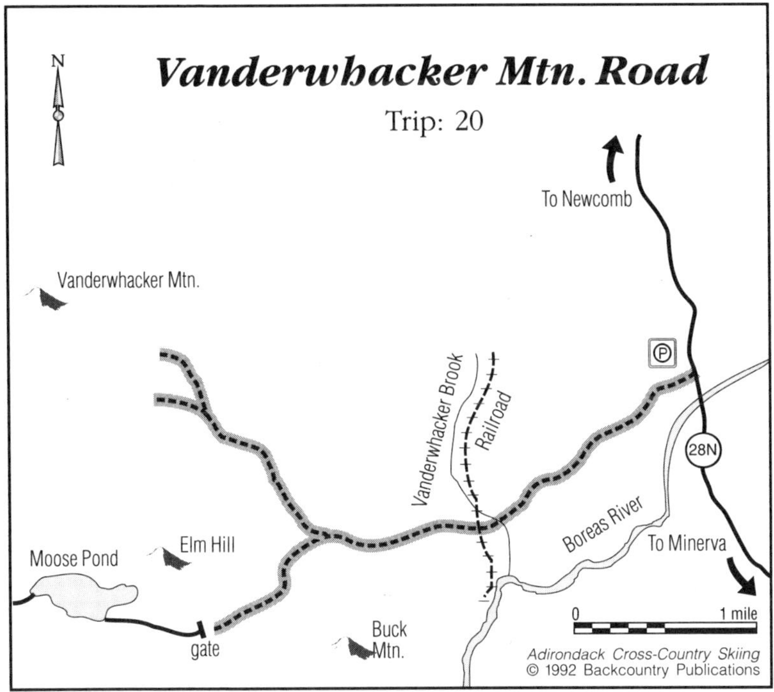

After the tracks the route is a little steeper, but it is wide and clear and easy to handle. You continue generally west through hardwoods for 35 minutes or so until you come to a fork, which marks the halfway point of this trip. A sign for the right fork shows a jeep road that continues up Vanderwhacker Mountain toward the fire tower. You can ski up it a way, but it eventually becomes too steep, except for snowshoeing. The left fork goes only a little way before reaching the gate of the private inholding.

Skiers generally turn around at the fork. It is about 1 mile (22 minutes skiing) back to the railroad tracks. In another 30 minutes, you will cover the remaining 1.5 miles to your car. With a group of beginning skiers it will probably take 2Z\x hours for the complete trip, but you can race up and back in less time. Don't rush it, this is a trip to enjoy the woods!

■
Blue Ledge in the Gorge: Trip 27

Schroon River Headwaters

Up Old Tote Roads

■

The five trips described here explore the eastern headwaters of the Schroon River that radiate out from the area around North Hudson. All of the trips are to ponds and lakes whose streams flow into the attractive Schroon River valley. Most of these trips are on old tote roads that follow the gradient of these stream valleys.

Trips 21, 22, and 23 are to ponds called Round, Moriah, Crowfoot, and Trout in the Hammond Pond Wild Forest Area. They are east of I-87 and easy to reach. They are described as round-trips, but if a shuttle car is left on the Tracy Road or North Hudson–Moriah Road trailhead, roundabouts can be skied. The more adventurous who are adept with map and compass may vary these loops by skiing the newer logging roads on private land southwest of Moriah Pond.

Beginners can take Trip 24 in this section to scenic Elk Lake to enjoy a panoramic view of high peaks. A main tributary of Schroon River called The Branch begins there. More experienced skiers can continue on Trip 24 toward Dix Mountain. The other trip in this section explores a more remote source of Schroon River; Trip 25 begins where The Branch crosses Blue Ridge Road and goes south through the Hoffman Notch Wilderness Area. This is a challenging trek through a beautiful and seldom traveled part of the Adirondacks.

Upriver from North Hudson to the west of NY 9 and I-87 are the peaks of the massive Dix Mountain Wilderness Area. Three large brooks feed Schroon River from these heights—Walker, West Mill, and Lindsay. The Walker Brook and West Mill Brook trails have informal blazes on trees and are the easiest to follow, but they are not well cleared and so are not described in this book. For those who like to explore and don't mind some blowdowns, the directions to these trailheads are in *Discover the Northeastern Adirondacks* by Dennis Conroy and others (see Sources and Suggested Reading). You might check them out first on snowshoes.

To the southeast, not far away, is the Pharaoh Lake Wilderness Area with additional trails but less snow. Contact the Schroon Lake Chamber of Commerce (telephone: 518-532-7675) for a cross-country ski trail map that shows other trips to Crane, Gull, and Spectacle ponds. The Pine Tree Inn in North Hudson (telephone: 518-532-9255) is a nice bed and breakfast to enjoy the winter experiences in this area. There are no commercial trail systems.

21. Round Pond and Moriah Pond

■

10 miles round-trip
Skiing time: 4 hours and 30 minutes
Intermediate
USGS Witherbee 7.5' x 15' metric
Map—page 111

It is hard to beat this trip, and it might become a trek that you will repeat often. There is a bit of everything—distant views, isolated ponds, beaver dams and otters, a long flow with bog plants, and a fast run down a woods road. Start early and take a lunch, because the trip takes time and there are side routes to explore.

You begin at Sharp Bridge Campground beside the Schroon River. The parking place is on NY 9, between Exits 29 and 30 off I-87. Driving from the south, take Exit 29 east toward North Hudson; in 0.2 mile turn

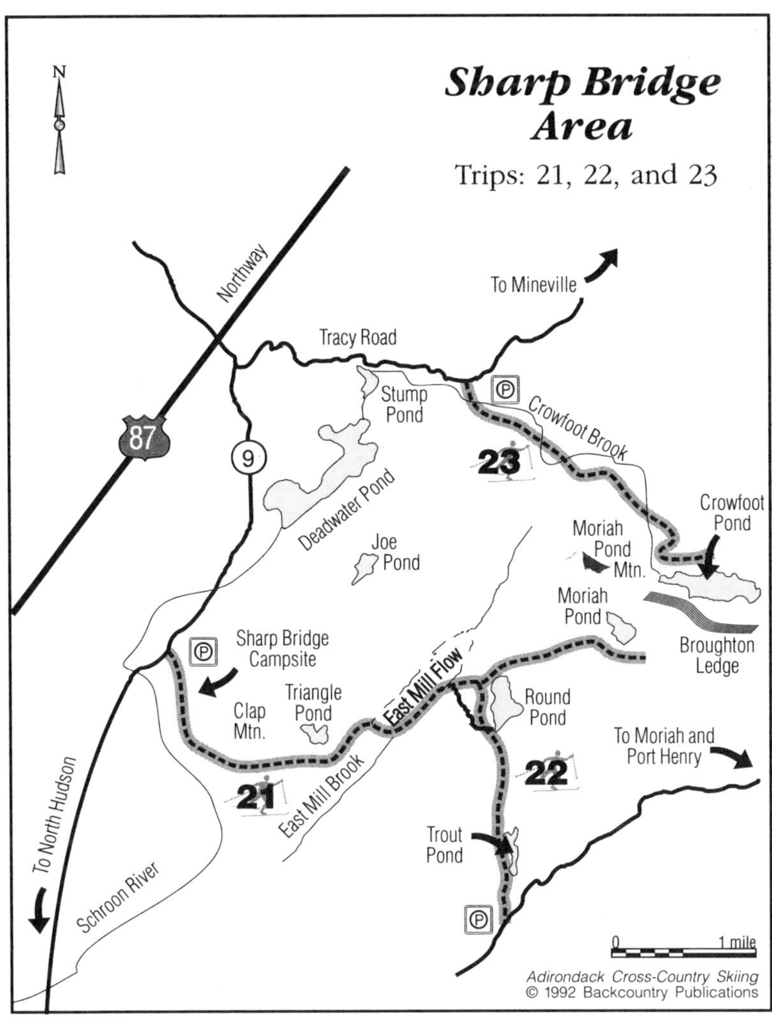

left on NY 9 and drive north for 7.0 miles. The plowed parking area is just north of the Schroon River bridge. From the north, take Exit 30 and drive south on NY 9 for 2.6 miles to the bridge.

The campground is on the hill amid tall, regal white pines. You can ski through it if you wish, but the actual trail starts below the pines near the stream. Ski east along a path with the Schroon River on your right. You will pass a DEC trail sign indicating (incorrectly) that Round Pond is 6 miles and Trout Pond is 7 miles (they are roughly 3.7 and 4.5 miles away). You cross several small ditches, with hard-to-ski logs spanning them; the stream is down the bank on the right. After skiing 20 minutes, the trail begins to climb up a steep, straight hill. You are following the old Moriah Road that came west past Moriah Pond to farming areas near the headwaters of the Schroon. After climbing 15 minutes, a gain of 320 feet from the campground, the trail levels off then swings left (northeast) around Clap Mountain. There is a pretty ledge and large rocks with polypody ferns poking their evergreen stems through the snow. Large hardwoods grow beside the trail; on the right the land drops off to a marshy area created by East Mill Brook. As the trail swings east, you can see a large open area ahead and will soon reach the beaver dam that causes it. One winter an otter had kept a fishing hole open and his tracks could be traced to the roots of a nearby cedar tree.

Cross to the other side of the East Mill Flow on the beaver dam and look for the trail that goes left (north). It follows the east side of the flow for 0.75 mile before it crosses the outlet brook of Round Pond. If the ice is thick on East Mill Flow, you can ski up it to this same small outlet brook.

Five minutes skiing from East Mill Flow you will see five red trail markers on trees that denote a trail going right. This is the route to Trout Pond (Trip 22). Go left to reach the shore of beautiful Round Pond, about two hours after starting. There may be snowmobile tracks on the ice, as they have access from the North Hudson–Port Henry Road, but it is unlikely that you will see any.

The old road to Moriah Pond goes left along the northern shore of Round Pond and up an obvious draw. You will be surprised to see a cabin on the right, near a small brook; it is one of the many inholdings you find in the park. After climbing 20 minutes from Round Pond, the trail levels off and reaches more private land. There are several logging roads to the left that can be explored and provide some nice skiing runs. (If you have a compass, you can follow the main road north and then bushwhack to the Crowfoot Brook Trail in Trip 23.) Continuing on the old Moriah Road, which has been opened up by loggers, you reach

Moriah Pond in 30 minutes from Round Pond. It appears to be a shallow pond in the middle of a large marsh. To the north is low Moriah Pond Mountain with a notch to the right of the peak. (This is the notch mentioned in Trip 25 and, climbing it, you can ski to the Crowfoot Brook Trail and down to Tracy Road.)

The most enjoyable way out is to ski back the way you came. It is a fast run back to Round Pond and the flow. (After passing the dam, you can look for Triangle Pond on the topographic map and try a side jaunt to this hidden basin under the ledge of Clap Mountain.) All too soon, you will be back at the top of the hill, listening to the screams of the skiers ahead as they gain speed down the straight schuss. From Moriah Pond it is a 1¾-hour trip back to your car.

22. Trout Pond to Sharp Bridge

■

5.5 miles one way
Skiing time: 2 hours and 30 minutes
Intermediate

Trout Pond to Round Pond

■

3.0 miles round-trip
Skiing time: 1 hour and 50 minutes
Competent Beginner
USGS Witherbee 7.5' x 15' metric
Map—page 111

This trip should be made after a heavy snow because you are in the lower elevations of the park, at 1,000 feet or less. The trail is well marked and clear. Intermediate skiers should bring two cars in order to make a through trip that starts at 1,140 feet (356 meters) and ends around 944 feet (295 meters). Huge white pines, two lovely ponds, and a beaver dam with otter tracks will make this one of your favorite trips!

To ski through, leave a car at Sharp Bridge Campground as described in Trip 21. Drive back on NY 9 toward North Hudson for 4.2 miles and take a left (east) on the road to Moriah. Drive along winding North Hudson–Moriah Road for 6.4 miles from NY 9. A green, metal signpost on the north side of the road marks the almost invisible trailhead; it reads: Trout Pond 0.7 mile, Round Pond 1.3 miles, East Mill Flow 2.5 miles, and Sharp Bridge Campground 5.2 miles. Park as far off the road as possible.

Start up an old tote road through an evergreen grove. In about 200 yards you ski across a small stream, the outlet of Trout Pond. Look right at this spot for three tremendous white pines, the first of these handsome trees that grace this short valley. In 15 minutes, following a relatively clear and wide trail, you reach the outlet end of long, narrow Trout Pond. Many large conifers border this western shore; it is somewhat unusual to find white pine, white cedar, and hemlock thriving together. After traversing the edge of this little gem, the trail gradually gains height and passes more ancient pines. It levels off for a way and then drops, skirting a marshy area with a nice stand of cedar. The route is easy to follow with frequent red disk markers.

As you mount another small rise, the sharp rock ledges of Trout Mountain rise on your right. There are more large pines—the bed of this valley must contain sandy soils on which they thrive. The slightly rocky trail now drops abruptly into another marsh, this one an alder thicket. It then goes steeply up to the right to avoid the marsh, and you may need to remove your skis for the climb. Twenty feet up, notice the three large white birches with bark badly singed by lightning. Walking, go up and over this hill and down to Round Pond. It takes 50 minutes from the car to reach it, a distance of about 1.5 miles.

Round Pond is a large, impressive expanse with a rock outcrop across to the right. Snowmobilers sometimes come in from the North Hudson–Moriah Road on private land; if they have been on it you will know that it is frozen and safe to ski. But you are near the outlet and it is best not to trust the ice there. The trail turns left and crosses the outlet on two logs, best negotiated on foot. From here the trail continues back from, but parallel to, the pond, bearing a little west of north. Within 10 minutes you reach the trail that goes left to Sharp Bridge and right to the other shore of Round Pond and Moriah Pond (see Trip 21). If you are returning to your car on the North Hudson–Moriah Road, it will take less than one hour from this junction to retrace your tracks down the narrow, pine-studded valley.

Intermediate skiers going through to Sharp Bridge should go left and follow along the right side of a streambed. Soon you are at East Mill Flow. The marked trail takes you above the southeast side of the flow, but skiers can go out and ski left down it. East Mill Brook meanders through it, so be cautious and stay near the edge of the open area, particularly as you get near the south end. The flow is squeezed by small hills, and beaver have wisely chosen this spot for a dam. Otter often fish this deep water, and their tracks may be seen. Crossing the beaver dam, the trail swings to the south and then southwest around Clap Mountain. When it bears west you start down, dropping over 200 feet in less than a mile! It's a wide, straight tote road, but steep. The last mile or so along the upper stretch of the Schroon River is gradual and delightful. It takes about 1½ hours to ski from the intersection near Round Pond down to Sharp Bridge. Allow 2½ hours for the whole trip from North Hudson–Moriah Road.

23. Up Crowfoot Brook to Crowfoot Pond

▪

5.0 miles round-trip
Skiing time: 2 hours
Competent Beginner
USGS Witherbee 7.5' x 15' metric
Map—page 111

An old wagon road once ran west from Moriah Center, past Crowfoot Pond, and on to Deadwater Pond and other settlements. It is now a marked snowmobile trail from Tracy Road up to Crowfoot Pond, but it is not heavily traveled and makes an excellent cross-country ski trail.

The trailhead is on Tracy Road, which runs from NY 9 to Mineville and Witherbee. Go east from I-87 Exit 30 onto NY 9 south; in 100 yards take Tracy Road (no sign) left (north) toward Mineville. Drive 1.7 miles to where the road swings left uphill and look for snowmobile tracks or an opening on the right (east) side of the road. Park as far off the road as you can.

The trail heads into a clearing with Crowfoot Brook on the right. Ski in and bear right to a Forest Preserve sign and a log bridge across the brook. After crossing the bridge, go left and climb gradually through the dense hemlock that shelters the trail. The road climbs steeply with Crowfoot Brook on your left. In 20 minutes you cross the brook on a solid bridge. Continue on the old road, which was well built and has not washed out, as it rises gradually to the southeast. In five minutes or so you cross the stream on a sound masonry bridge.

The road now passes between two hills: Stiles Hill on the left and Moriah Pond Mountain on the right. In this level stretch a trail has been cut to the right (southwest at 220 degrees magnetic) into the notch between Moriah Pond Mountain and Broughton Ledge. (The cleared path ends in the notch, but you can climb down the steep far side to Moriah Pond and go out through Round Pond to Sharp Bridge. Making this circuit would require that a shuttle car be left at the Sharp Bridge Campground.)

Continuing past this spur, you reach the outlet of Crowfoot Pond in 1 hour and 10 minutes from your car. There is an unmarked path to explore across the outlet, but it disappears on the ridge. You can continue on the old road up the north side of the pond to the end of state land, about 2.5 miles from the car. Beyond that are summer camps on private land. Scenic Crowfoot Pond lies between the rocky hills; the shore is a pleasant place for lunch.

Now comes the satisfying downhill return—the reason you came! The easy grade of the road gives a pleasant rhythm to your stem turns. If you ski fast it will take only 30 minutes to get back to your car. Except for the last steep stretch, the road is a steady and congenial gradient that will soothe the nerves and create a sense of well-being. Give thanks to the settlers who built such long-lasting roads and bridges.

24. Elk Lake and the Dix Trail

▪

8.0 miles round-trip to Slide Brook
Skiing time: 3 hours and 55 minutes
Competent Beginner

Elk Lake

▪

4.0 miles round-trip to Elk Lake
Skiing time: 2 hours and 55 minutes
Beginner
USGS Mount Marcy 7.5' x 15' metric
Map—page 119

The 4-mile round-trip into Elk Lake from Clear Pond is an excellent one for beginners. The lake is in one of the most attractive settings in the Adirondack Park, rimmed by towering, snow-covered peaks. Nippletop and Dix mountains are the two most conspicuous, but the entire panorama is spellbinding. Wait for a sunny day and bring your camera. The Dix Trail starts near Elk Lake and is difficult in some places; it reaches two lean-tos before it becomes too steep to ski. There are vistas of the slides on Macomb Mountain as you glide along.

The trailhead for the trip is reached from Exit 29 off I-87 at North Hudson. Drive west for 4.1 miles on the Blue Ridge Road, then right on Elk Lake Road. In winter the road is usually plowed to Clear Pond, 3.2 miles up Elk Lake Road. You will find a large parking area, as this is a popular place to snowshoe into the high peaks.

The trail is along a wide, cleared roadway with electric poles and other signs of civilization. Both sides of the road are private. The route lacks a feeling of wilderness but is pleasant and moderate. It is better if skiers make their own tracks rather than follow the snowshoers; the snowshoe track is uneven and causes a subtle strain on a skier's legs that is very tiring. It is about 2 miles into Elk Lake and less than one hour to the top of a hill where you have a view of the mountains. At this point a signpost on the right shows the Dix Trail going right (east) through a balsam grove.

Continue on the main road down the hill toward the lake. Leaving the parking area you will come to a large stream, called The Branch. It is the outlet of Elk Lake and the main source of the Schroon River. Elk Lake Lodge is closed and posted in winter, but there are easements that permit use of any marked trail. You can ski around on them in search of good places to photograph the mountains.

If you wish to ski along the Dix Trail, go back to the top of the hill

■

Adirondack lean-to on Dix Trail: Trip 24

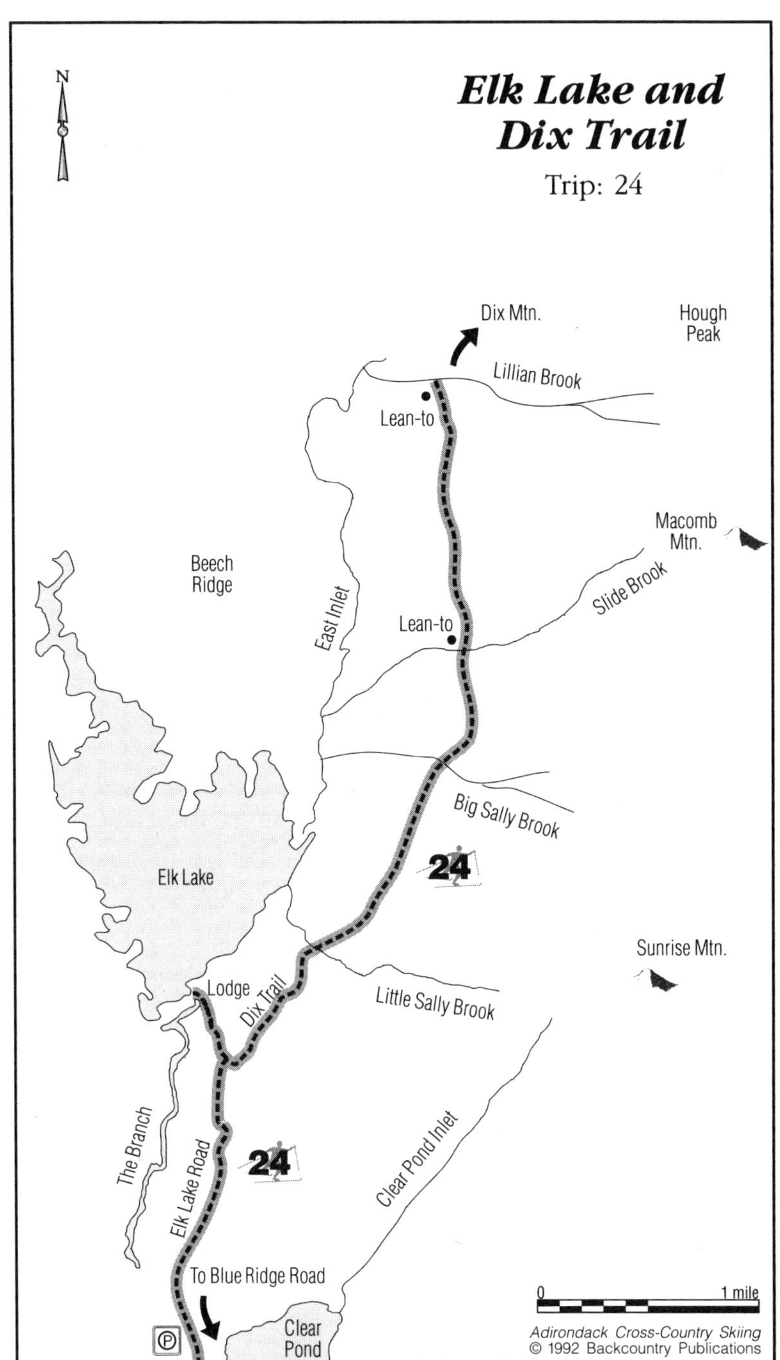
N
Elk Lake and
Dix Trail
Trip: 24
Dix Mtn.
Hough
Peak
Lillian Brook
Lean-to
Macomb
Mtn.
Beech
Ridge
Slide Brook
East Inlet
Lean-to
Big Sally Brook
24
Elk Lake
Sunrise Mtn.
Lodge
Dix Trail
Little Sally Brook
The Branch
Elk Lake Road
24
Clear Pond Inlet
To Blue Ridge Road
0
1 mile
P
Clear
Pond
Adirondack Cross-Country Skiing
© 1992 Backcountry Publications

to the signpost. The trail ducks into a small opening in dense balsam fir. In 10 minutes the forest changes to red spruce and white birch. The trail is very narrow and there are several blowdowns, so be careful on the run out. After 20 minutes you reach a wide logging road and turn left (north). You cross Little Sally Brook flowing through a culvert. The route continues on this wide road for another 20 minutes. There is one long, gradual climb prior to a wonderful view of the slides on Macomb Mountain.

The road narrows to a path through open hardwood forests. The view of Macomb dominates the scenery, with occasional glimpses of Hough and the south side of Dix. Big Sally Brook is reached and crossed easily, as the stream is frozen. After a level stretch in open hardwoods, you reach another stream and a lean-to. Slide Brook has steep sides and you will need to take off your skis to cross it. It takes over one hour from Elk Lake Road to reach here, over two hours from your car. The trail continues on to another lean-to at Lillian Brook, another ½ hour or more. From there you will see views of some of the peaks to the west, but you may find that skiing in the snowshoe tracks is tiring.

It will take 45 minutes to ski back from the lean-to at Slide Brook to Elk Lake Road. The long hill is delightful, but the path through the spruce and balsam grove is tricky. It is gradually downhill from Elk Lake back to your car and will take only 50 minutes. The best part of this trip is the Elk Lake scenery on a sunny day.

25. Traversing Hoffman Notch from Blue Ridge Road

■

7.5 miles one way
Skiing time: 4 hours and 15 minutes
Intermediate
USGS Schroon Lake 15' or Blue Ridge 7.5' x 15' metric
Map—page 123

This is a wild, beautiful, and interesting trip for "notchbaggers." The route is isolated and seldom skied, so be prepared for the backcountry. Trip 29 describes the round-trip from Loch Muller into Big Marsh from the south (intermediate), and the through route from south to north (advanced). This traverse from north to south has more climbing but is the safest way to ski the pristine gorge the first time. You climb a deep valley with enormous erratics and a splendid rock-strewn stream. There are three ice-and-snow crossings without bridges, and they are hard to negotiate when it begins to thaw in late spring.

Leave a car at Loch Muller as described in Trip 28. (If you are driving from Schroon Lake travel on Hoffman Road for 6.4 miles west of NY 9, turn right on Loch Muller Road and go to the end.) Drive the other car with all your skis, poles, and gear back to Schroon Lake, go north on NY 9 through the town and get on I-87 north. Get off at North Hudson, Exit 29. Go left on Blue Ridge Road (no signpost) for 5.5 miles to a bridge over a large stream. Five feet on the other side of the bridge, on the left (south), there is a green signpost with no sign; this is the trailhead. Ski down the hill and look for a yellow disk trail marker and a DEC sign showing an easement over private land. Follow this yellow-disk-marked trail along the logging road until you come to Sand Pond Brook. There is usually a bridge there; the stream may not freeze, so if the bridge has washed out, you will have to look upstream for a beaver dam. (If you can't find a crossing, you will have to abandon the trip and return when the weather is colder.)

After crossing the bridge, follow the yellow disks as the trail meanders through the wet bottomland. Pick your way along, generally heading south, until you reach a heavily logged area and higher ground. The marked trail leads right along a bank to a cleared power line. The trail goes up the clearing, marked by disks on stakes, for 100 yards, and then jogs left (south) on an old woods road. After 0.25 mile on this well-marked but washed-out roadway you enter the Hoffman Notch Wilderness Area. In another 0.25 mile, 35 minutes after starting, you cross the Hoffman Notch Brook on snow-covered rocks.

The trail now follows a less distinct old tote road and starts climbing in earnest. The rock-strewn stream is on the left; the skim of ice on the pools cannot mask the gurgle of an active flow. You are in a narrow, steep canyon between the rugged cliffs of Hornet Cobbles to the left and the abrupt ledges of Washburn Ridge on the right. Climbing up the draw, 50 minutes from your car, huge boulders appear below Washburn Ridge, some as large as cabins. The hillsides close in steadily; it is cold in the gorge and multicolored icefalls cover the ledges. The second crossing of Hoffman Notch Brook is very steep and tricky; the path twists through a snow, rock, and ice jumble. Ten minutes later there is another rough stream crossing. You may see pure white snow crystals forming on black ice, displaying myriad delicate and intricate sparkling patterns. It is the last brook crossing in the notch; the stream does not drain Big Marsh but flows from the Blue Ridge Range on the east—between Hornet Cobbles and Texas Ridge. (What exquisite names—a treat after so many unimaginative ones.) In less than 1½ hours (and a 400-foot gain in altitude), you reach the top and move onto a sizable plateau with large old-growth trees. From here it is an easy 10 minutes to Big Marsh. You are almost halfway to Loch Muller when you get there and certainly have burned up more than half the calories you will lose on the trip.

Dead cedars rise from the ice on the north end of Big Marsh (actually a sizable pond). The snags provide a photogenic foreground for the slope of Texas Ridge, seen across the open snow. You can ski along the frozen pond, which lies at about 1,700 feet, to the southern end; here some stumps make sharp but dry seats for lunch.

Going south from Big Marsh (which is also the return leg of Trip 29), you ski beside an alder-choked beaver flow. The trail is not level, how-

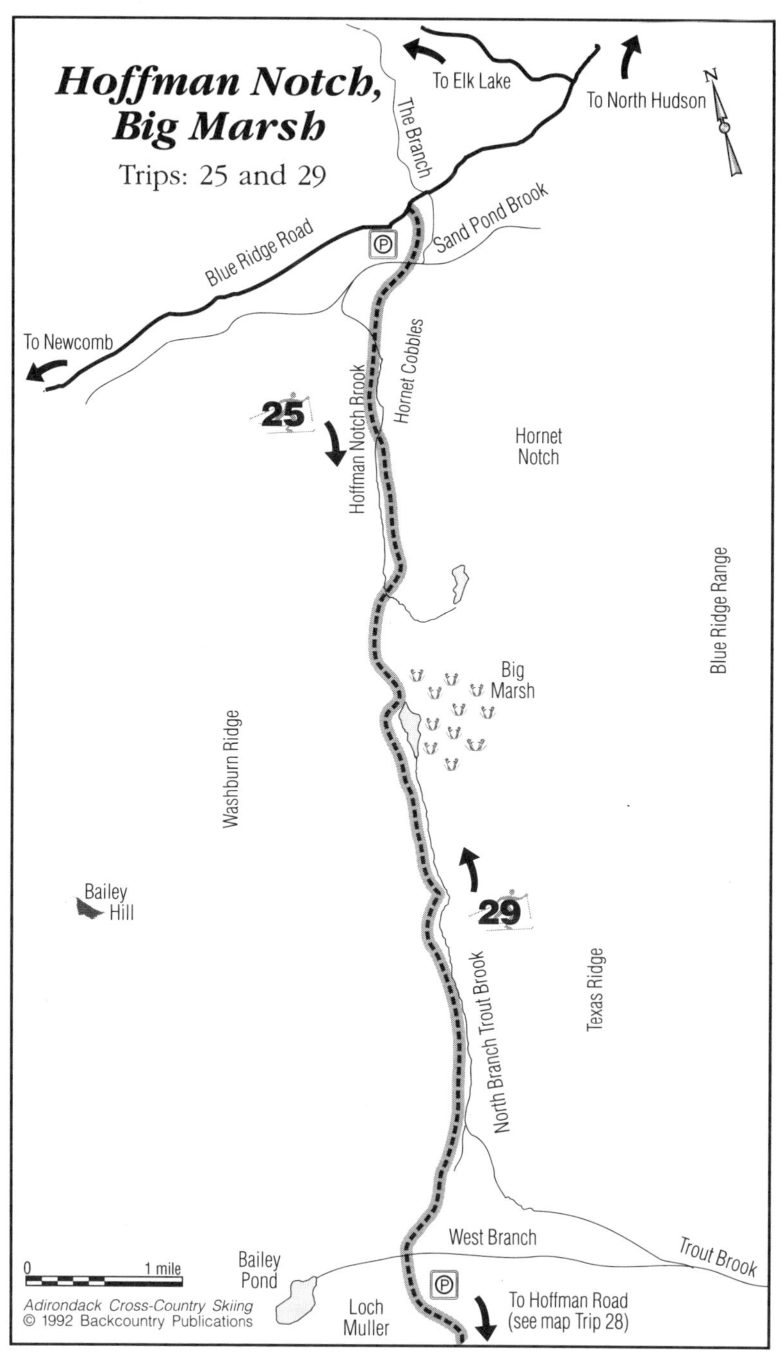

Hoffman Notch, Big Marsh
Trips: 25 and 29
To Elk Lake
To North Hudson
N
The Branch
Sand Pond Brook
Blue Ridge Road
To Newcomb
Hornet Cobbles
Hoffman Notch Brook
25
Hornet Notch
Blue Ridge Range
Big Marsh
Washburn Ridge
Bailey Hill
29
Texas Ridge
North Branch Trout Brook
West Branch
Trout Brook
Bailey Pond
0
1 mile
Adirondack Cross-Country Skiing
© 1992 Backcountry Publications
Loch Muller
To Hoffman Road (see map Trip 28)

ever, and you climb gradually for 15 minutes. After mounting a small hill, you ski back down to the frozen beaver flow. The trail continues for some distance in this fashion; ridges extend to the flow like spread out fingers, and you must ski up and over them as you continue south. This beaver flow is the drainage of Big Marsh, the beginning of the North Branch of Trout Brook. As you climb and glide south, the flow continues in a series of slightly descending terraces. A big rock marks the end of the

■

Icefall on Hoffman Notch Trail: Trip 25

beaver activity, which takes one hour to put behind you, and a gurgling brook emerges. Ice sparkles where it forms along the bank, but the stream is kept open by the tumbling water. The trail hugs the bank for a short distance until the brook falls away to the south. Now, the path angles higher to the right, away from the brook, and the well-marked trail again leads through open woods. Numerous boulders fractured off Washburn Ridge dot this side of the valley, one hour from Big Marsh.

This section of the trail is an exceptionally fine place to study nonflowering plants that are visible in winter. Interesting and varied species grow on the north side of large maples. The long, yellowish green mats at the base of the trees are feather moss (*Neckera pennata*). Decorating the same trunk is a yellow-green to brownish green liverwort, one of the *Porella* species. *Lobaria pulmonaria,* a large lichen, is a lunglike greenish gray; it grows only where the air is clean. On another tree is a different liverwort (*Frullania*), which clings to the bark with reddish brown tentacles.

A short while later the path descends to a clump of spruce; high in the tops you may hear the twittering of small birds flying quickly among the branches. They are hard to identify but are probably a flock of goldfinches or pine siskins.

A climb uphill is rewarded by a nice run down the other side. Deciduous trees give way to spruce and balsam before the slope ends at a solid new bridge crossing the outlet to Bailey Pond, another source of Trout Brook. Here you enter a wide tote road bordered with evergreens. The windup of the trip is a good tough climb.

A signpost at the edge of the clearing says you have come 7.3 miles from Blue Ridge Road. You cross the meadow, bear right, and soon join a wide road that you take left (south). You reach the shuttle car at Loch Muller about 2 hours after leaving Big Marsh, 4 hours and 15 minutes after leaving Blue Ridge Road. The trip involves considerable climbing: you start at 1,244 feet, climb to 1,700 feet, and, after many ups and downs, end up at 1,682 feet.

The magnificent notch, huge rocks, and diverse vegetation make this an especially enjoyable day. If you ski the trip from south to north (Trip 29), it is rated advanced because of the drop down the steep gully of Hoffman Notch Brook.

▪

Below Blue Ledge on The Hudson River: Trip 27

Minerva Area
Historic Clubs and Camps

■

The Minerva region epitomizes the social and economic evolution of the Adirondacks. The early settlers—farmers and lumbermen—opened up the land. They and their children then built the lodges for people from the city who discovered the beauty of the land and the sportsmen's bounty that existed in the ponds and forests. Hunters and fishermen used the logging roads. Today skiers travel many of these same routes into isolated places to enjoy the beauty of this unique wilderness.

The ski trails described in this section radiate in many directions. Two routes take you down to the deep valley of the Hudson River: Deer Creek (Trip 26) follows a wide roadway past cleared fields and old farmlands; and the Hudson River Gorge Trail from Huntley Pond (Trip 27)—steeper and more difficult to ski—reaches the most remote rapids.

As you drive the North Woods Club Road to the Huntley Pond trailhead you might contemplate the history of the club that lies at the end of the road. Thomas Baker and his wife moved onto this land in 1854, cleared it for lumber and farming, and opened an attractive but remote boardinghouse. Baker had been a minister with a church in nearby Chester. As a disciple of John Brown, he was opposed to slavery and was a key link in the Underground Railroad that smuggled slaves through to North Elba. This activity apparently caused his dismissal, or resignation, and he left the pulpit for the land. Later, city folks, impressed by the superb hunting and fishing, bought the Baker's Tract and the large boardinghouse. Thus the North Woods Club, as it eventually came to be known, was formed in 1886. The club attracted a large number of members and boarders. Year after year writers, painters, doctors, and other educated elite from the New York City area journeyed to these remote woods to enjoy life in the wild. Eliphalet Terry, a painter, built a log cabin not far from the clubhouse in 1889. It was to this cabin that Winslow Homer came almost every summer to paint. Homer's subjects were the guides, local workmen, and wildlife around the club as well as the landscapes of Mink Pond, the Hudson River, and Beaver Mountain. For many people, Homer's renderings of the distinctive cone shape of Beaver Mountain and the dark shores of Mink Pond became the very image of the Adirondacks.

Paintings and books by North Woods Club members give us a clear picture of the growth and development of a complex tourist "industry" in the early years. Jim Fosburgh and Clayton Seagers describe this lovely setting in books written in the 1950s and 1960s. Hugh Fosburgh, in his *A Clearing in the Wilderness* and several novels, has also captured the lumbering and building activities of this remote site.

Trips 28 and 29 begin at Loch Muller off Hoffman Road northeast of Minerva at the site of Warren's Hotel. The lodge was popular with fishermen and hunters until a few decades ago. In front of the sturdy frame building with its wide porch is a large pine tree, planted in 1845 by Paschal P. Warren when he and the sapling were both 12 years old. The tree still thrives beside the deserted hotel that was the scene of many stories of hunting and fishing successes and failures. Guest books in the Adirondack Museum library record the people who came here in the early days, when it was called Bailey Pond Inn, and describe the plentiful supply of white-tailed deer and brook trout. In addition to Trip 28 beginners will enjoy Trip 30 to Hoffman Cemetery and Trip 31 to Big Pond that start from trailheads along Hoffman Road.

The NY 28N road north of the North Woods Club turn has a trailhead for three trips. Trip 32 takes you to scenic Stony Pond on a delightful in-and-out trail for competent beginners. Intermediate skiers can continue on Trip 33 to the Hewitt Pond Road if you first leave a shuttle car there. The Hewitt Pond Club is a small group of buildings on the north side of the large pond. The site started out as the backwoods home of Collins Hewitt. The Hewitt family farmed, logged, and guided fishermen and hunters. Eventually wealthy people from Albany bought the land and cabins were built. In 1910 the Hewitt Pond Club was formed and the land along the east and north sides of the pond was posted. Michael Cronin and his wife Lillian owned nearby Aiden Lair Lodge, a log building that stood a little north of the present deserted one. Cronin wanted hunting and fishing access to the pond for his guests so he cut a trail from the Hewitt Club road to the southern part of the pond that avoided posted land. This is the northern end of Trip 33.

A long intermediate run from Stony Pond (Trip 34) takes you past other upland ponds and down a challenging logging road to Irishtown where you must first leave a second car.

Snowfall is generally ample in the area although it is not as deep as at higher altitudes; the trips in this area are best skied in midwinter. There are no commercially groomed trails. The area is large and a number of maps are needed if you want details of the topography.

26. Deer Creek

■

6.0 miles round-trip
Skiing time: 2 hours and 50 minutes
Competent Beginner
USGS Newcomb & Thirteenth Lake 15',
Dutton Mountain 7.5' x 15' metric
Map—page 130

There are some long, continuous runs on stretches of this delightful trip, but the trail is a wide road so novices with an ability to hold a snowplow can handle it. The road leads past old farms and a hand-hewn log cabin—all private property—and there is a good chance you will see a deer. Pick a sunny day, pack a lunch, and try this excursion with your family. It will become one of your favorites.

From North Creek take NY 28N north toward Minerva for 7.0 miles, then turn left (west) on Fourteenth Road. Drive 1.4 miles from the turn and bear right at the Y for another 0.4 mile to where the

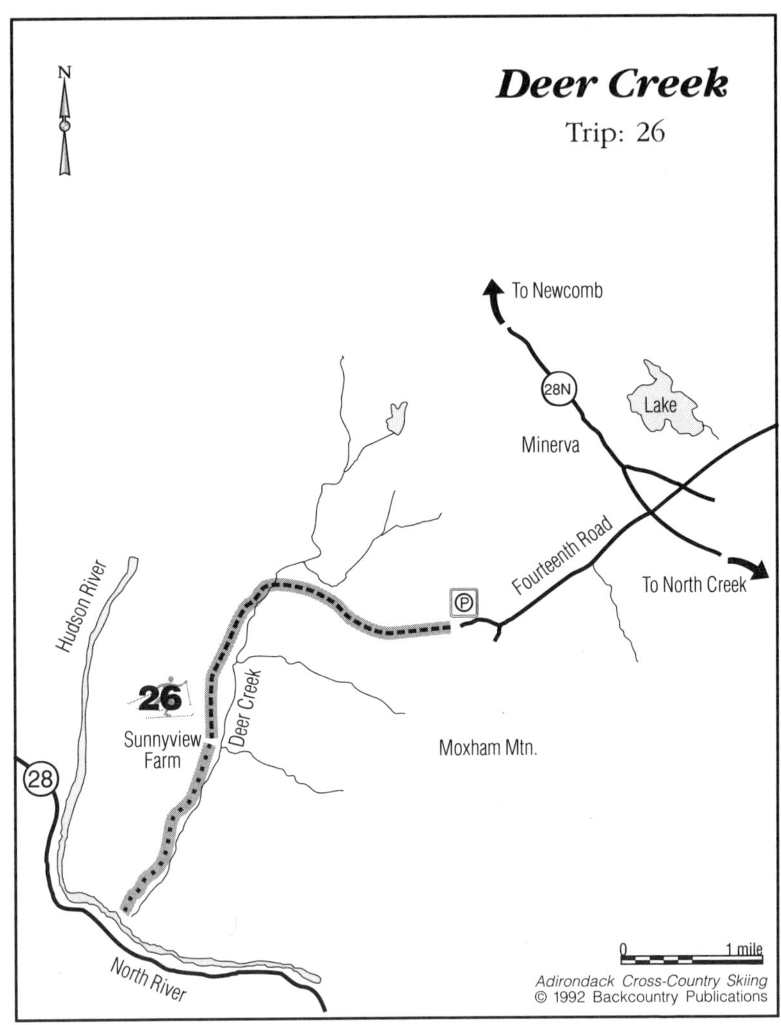

plowing ends (unless someone is logging farther on). Park your car out of the way so others can turn around.

Start skiing down the wide two-lane road that has probably been packed by snowmobiles. At the bottom of the hill continue straight across (avoiding the open area and logging roads on the left) and up the other side. The road curves around to the right as it rises. Within 200 yards you enter Forest Preserve land. Along here the one-track road is easy skiing through beautiful open hardwoods, with clumps of hemlock in the moist flat areas down the hill. After 10 minutes the road descends gently but steadily for a long, delightful run. You can pick up a lot of speed so keep under control. The run out is in an open valley with a clear bubbling brook. It will take 25 minutes to get from your car to the bridge over Deer Creek.

Now the road turns left and winds through old fields and private land. There are deer tracks around the scraggly apple trees. One camp of considerable vintage has an incongruous octagonal window. Private roads veer off to old farms, but it is easy to follow the main road as it goes up and down enough to be interesting but not difficult. Twenty minutes from the brook you reach a hand-hewn log house; from the field there are sweeping views of the rocky outcrops of Moxham Mountain. Striding and poling down the road for 10 more minutes you pass through a balsam grove on public land. You may hear the raucous croak of a raven from the nearby rocky cliffs; occasionally one flies close enough for you to see its spade-shaped tail as it swerves through its acrobatics. The snow is scuffed where deer have dug for moss and ferns and tree buds have been nipped.

Fifteen minutes from the log house (more than one hour from the start) there is a turnaround with a track to the right, which went to abandoned Sunnyview Farm. From here the road continues to the Hudson River another 1.5 miles. Deer Creek is close by on your left as the trail drops over 300 feet. The trail is narrow and difficult—and there is the climb back up so it is hardly worth it unless you crave a view of the Hudson. It takes over one hour to make the round-trip to the river from the turnaround and the whole trip becomes a long 9 miles.

It takes about 1Z\x hours of continuous skiing to get from the turnaround back to your car. About half the return is a gradual climb and if the snow is good and you have waxed correctly, it is not difficult. The road is public and open to snowmobiles. It is not used extensively, however, and it is unlikely that you will meet one.

27. Huntley Pond to Hudson River Gorge

▪

5.0 miles round-trip
Skiing time: 3 hours and 15 minutes
Intermediate or Snowshoeing
USGS Newcomb 15', Dutton Mountain 7.5' x 15' metric
Map—below

An old-growth forest with magnificent trees is the added benefit of this trip to the Hudson River across from the impressive Blue Ledge, usually reached by canoe, kayak, or raft; this trip on skis or snowshoes is the only way to reach it in winter.

The drive to the trailhead is long and hilly but well plowed. From

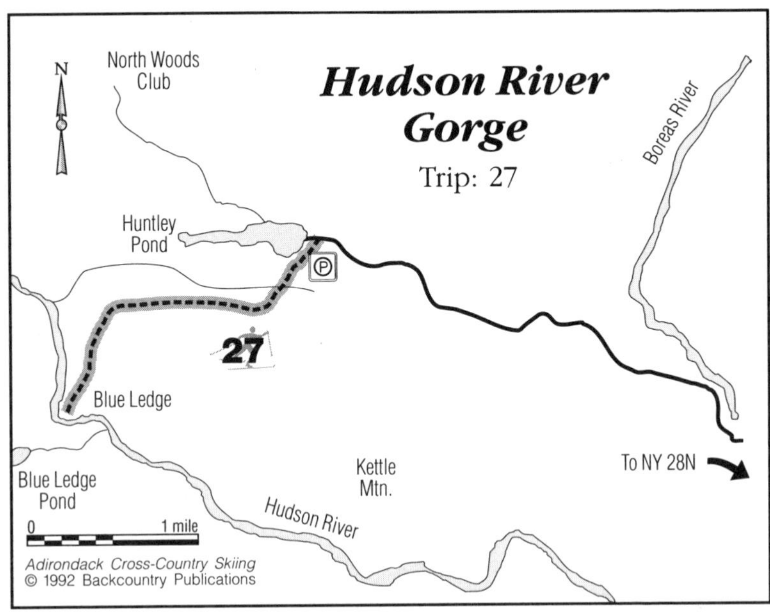

Murdy's General Store in Minerva drive north on NY 28N for 1.9 miles to the top of Minerva Hill. Take a left (west) on North Woods Club Road. Initially you pass houses and summer camps and then, entering the Hudson River Gorge Primitive Area, you drop 550 feet to cross the Boreas River. On the other side of this swift-flowing stream you go up 600 feet and drive gradually down to the trailhead. There is parallel parking on each side of the road just before Huntley Pond, which you can see ahead on the left. The sign reads: Trail to Blue Ledge on Hudson 2.5 miles. It has blue disk markers. (The plowed road is posted beyond the pond.)

A two-log bridge spans a small brook at the start of the trip. You angle right through evergreens on a narrow rock-strewn path that needs a fair amount of snow to be skiable. Making your way slowly to avoid rocks and tree roots, the trail skirts the edge of the large frozen pond, which lies at 1,580 feet. After 12 minutes you climb away from the pond through an extensive yellow birch grove. Large, rough-barked, limbless tree trunks are topped by a tangle of small branches, brownish yellow against the blue sky. Deer tracks are numerous, forming a casual pattern as they browse tips off the hobblebush (*Viburnum alnifolium*).

Still climbing slightly, you lose sight of the pond and enter a woods with some large hemlocks. Moss-covered erratics are scattered about, their greenish gray masses capped with snow. After 30 minutes the path drops steeply into a valley. Part of this slope can be skied but sidestepping down between trees and rocks is safer. At the bottom, logs span a stream that drains a huge marsh to the east. The path swings right, parallel to a former beaver pond. Blue markers are frequent but there may be blowdowns that require a scouting detour. The old dammed area is extensive. There is a logging road on the other side, and it is possible that, in logging days, this flow was artificially dammed. Logs would have been skidded onto the ice in winter and flushed down to the river in the spring.

In 55 minutes you reach the posted signs of the North Woods Club and the trail crosses through a corner of their property. As you bear left, you will see a spruce-fir marsh on the right; gradually you climb over a knob. Deer and coyote tracks cross the trail and a red fox has walked daintily in it. After 1 hour and 15 minutes you will hear the river and see it far below through the trees. The path is narrow and goes in and out of several gullies parallel to, and 300 feet above, the river. At one point, beside some huge white pines, you will have to carry your skis up a bank. You can leave them and walk from here to the river if the snow is not too deep. The next gully contains a small brook that shows on the topographic map. The rest of the way is a gradual—and skiable—0.25 mile down to the river.

If the sun is shining you will know you are almost there because the 300-foot-high Blue Ledge masks the sun's rays. The pool below Blue Ledge is frozen and quiet; below it open water appears where the river runs fast. On the far side otter tracks are seen running into and out of the deep pool. But the most impressive sight is the towering rock face of Blue Ledge. Complementing the general blue-gray sheen of the rock are a variety of hues: light blues, pinks, yellows, and purples show above the cedars at the base. Near the nest of a raven, marked by a triangular opening, bright orange splashes cover the rock, as though brushed in by an abstract painter. Deep silence pervades the shadows, lifeless until spring.

It is too cold near the water for lunch so hike back up the trail to a sunny spot. If you have left your skis at the steep bank, it will take almost ½ hour to walk back to them (cross-country boots are not made for uphill hiking). Enjoy the woods; there are some really magnificent old pines, roughly 130 to 150 years old.

The ski back is generally downhill and you can get in some nice glides, cutting corners of the trail for a faster straight track. In 35 minutes you are back to the empty beaver pond and the posted sign. This flat stretch is slower; you reach the head of the flow and the log bridge in just over one hour. Climbing the hill takes 10 minutes, and then there are some more nice runs down to Huntley Pond. Skirting the pond again (it is not wise to trust the ice as there are springs and thin patches) you easily reach your car in 1 hour and 35 minutes from the river.

The hill halfway along the trail and the walk down to the river detract from the ski trip, but the huge trees and the wonder of Blue Ledge make it a must excursion. If you are worried about skiing the hills, it is an excellent trip on snowshoes.

28. Bailey Pond and Beyond

▪

2.0 miles round-trip to Bailey Pond
Skiing time: 1 hour
Beginner to the pond, Intermediate beyond
USGS Schroon Lake 15' or 7.5' x 15' metric
Map—page 136

Loch Muller is the site of Warren's Hotel—still there, but closed. Beside it, at the end of the road, a 156-year-old white pine graces the southern entrance to the Hoffman Notch Wilderness Area and two excellent cross-country skiing trips. The tote road into Bailey Pond is excellent for beginners. Intermediate skiers can continue for another mile or more up the old road toward Washburn Ridge.

Loch Muller is reached by driving north from the four corners in Olmstedville on Irishtown Road, which becomes Hoffman Road. It is an attractive winding road that forks three times; you go right at each fork. At 6.9 miles from Olmstedville the Loch Muller Road goes sharp left (north). Drive up about 6.0 miles to the end and park where the snowplow turns around. If you are coming from Schroon Lake, the Loch Muller Road is 6.4 miles west of NY 9 and 1.5 miles west of the junction with Trout Brook Road.

The start of the trip is an unplowed continuation of the road, passing in front of a summer residence on the left. The sweeping mass of Hoffman Mountain rises across the valley. Ski along the road past a deserted camp with a beautiful stone chimney, and glide down a small hill. As you climb the other side go right at a fork, ski out to a clearing, and then bear left to a gap in the woods. A new DEC signpost shows Bailey Pond to the left at 1.0 mile and Blue Ridge Road straight ahead, 7.3 miles. No snowmobiles are allowed.

As you start toward Bailey Pond, there is a small hill that an absolute beginner might have trouble climbing, but it is short. As you top the rise there is a summer home on the left and a level old road that goes right; beginners will enjoy the clear wide track. Stunning

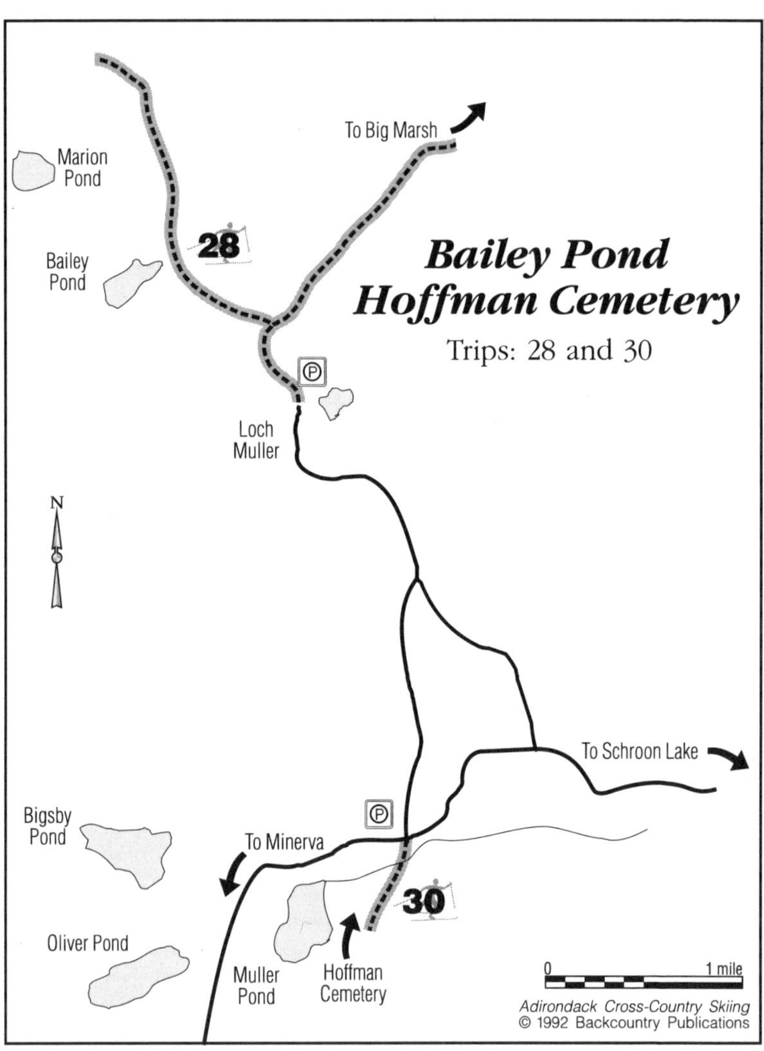

views of Hoffman Mountain appear through the open woods as you glide down a slight grade. Twenty minutes from the car you cross a little bridge and the remaining trail is practically level. Several washed out culverts must be negotiated, but you are able to ski in and out of the gradual dips without falling. Frequent blue disks mark the entire route that leads past white pine, beech, and white birch.

In 35 minutes (going slowly) you reach a flowing stream without a bridge. Fifty feet before the stream there is a narrow path to the left, and you can see Bailey Pond through the woods. Two minutes on that path and you reach the outlet, which may not be frozen over. The pond is shallow at this end, however, so you can ski around the edge and explore the boglike area. It is likely that there will be otter tracks near the pond—recognizable as troughs in the snow with distinct rear paw prints. The steep ledges of Hayes Mountain rise picturesquely from the far shore. If you wish to ski farther, cross the outlet on the narrow beaver dam and bear right through the woods to pick up the tote road. The trail climbs quite steeply after Bailey Pond Brook, so the extended trip is only for intermediate skiers. You can go on for another mile or more, climbing about 200 feet from 1,656-foot Bailey Pond. The inlet brook to Bailey Pond creates an impressive gorge on the left and there is a slope on the right as you ascend a steep ridge. The open track ends after climbing over 1 mile from Bailey Pond. It is difficult to actually reach Marion Pond, as the path is narrow and hard to find. The run back down to the crossing is very fast.

The easy glide from Bailey Pond back to Loch Muller will take only 30 minutes. Although the area is only about 1,650 feet in altitude, it gets a lot of snow. The trip can be skied, however, with a minimum snow cover.

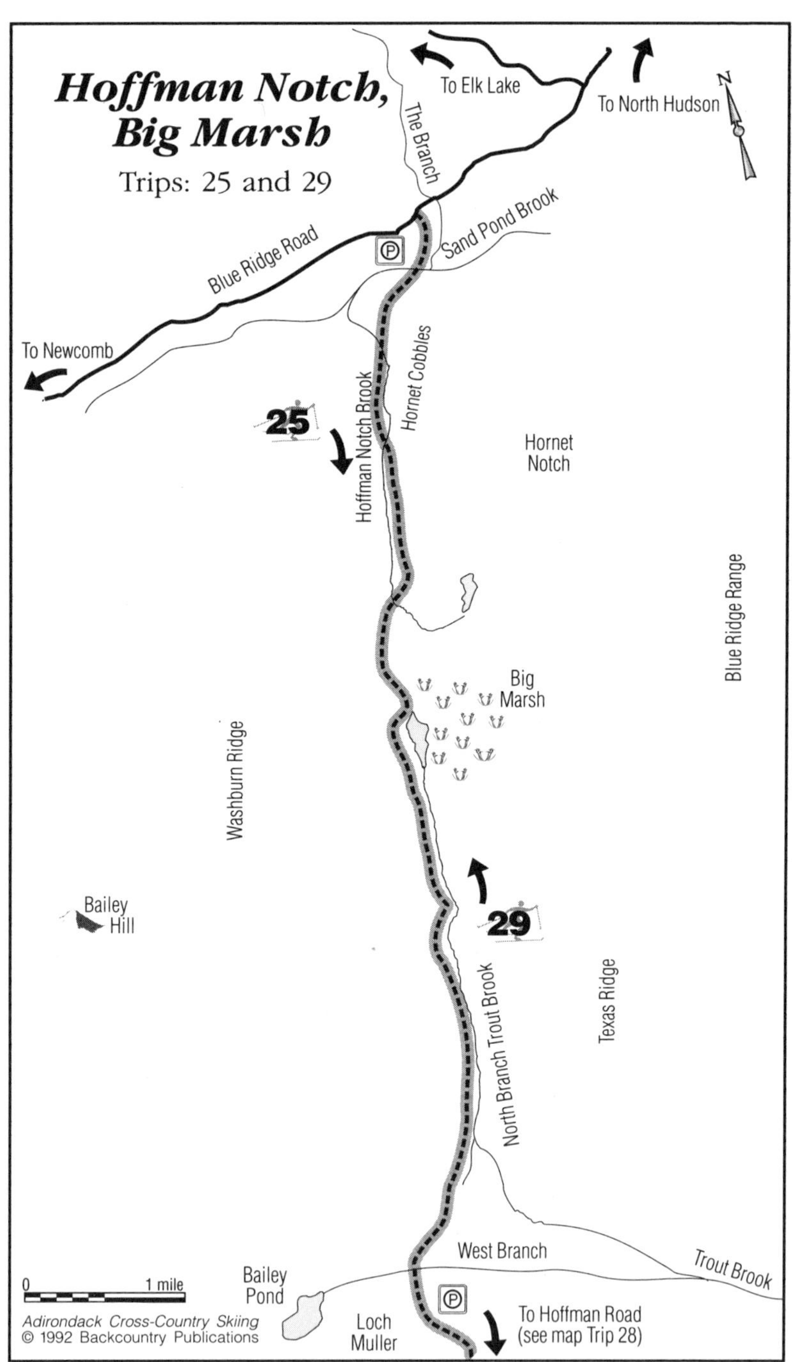

Hoffman Notch,
Big Marsh
Trips: 25 and 29
To Elk Lake
To North Hudson
N
The Branch
Sand Pond Brook
Blue Ridge Road
P
To Newcomb
Hornet Cobbles
Hoffman Notch Brook
25
Hornet
Notch
Blue Ridge Range
Big
Marsh
Washburn Ridge
29
Bailey
Hill
North Branch Trout Brook
Texas Ridge
West Branch
Trout Brook
0
1 mile
Bailey
Pond
P
Loch
Muller
To Hoffman Road
(see map Trip 28)
Adirondack Cross-Country Skiing
© 1992 Backcountry Publications

29. Loch Muller to Big Marsh and Beyond

▪

7.0 miles round-trip to Big Marsh
Skiing time: 3 hours and 45 minutes
Intermediate

7.3 miles to Blue Ridge Road
Skiing time: 2 hours and 40 minutes
Advanced—through trip
USGS Schroon Lake 15' or 7.5' x 15' &
Blue Ridge metric
Map—page 138

This round-trip enters Hoffman Notch from the south and travels along the North Branch of Trout Brook as far as Big Marsh. If you continue for a through trip to Blue Ridge Road, there is a difficult 400-foot drop down a valley (described in Trip 25). The round-trip is interesting and varied and skis very well in either direction. You will be passing through an isolated area with few other skiers on the trail, so be prepared for wilderness emergencies.

The trailhead is the same as for Bailey Pond (Trip 28). Park and ski to the signpost inside the woods after crossing the meadow. Follow the route marked with yellow disks that goes straight (north) to Blue Ridge Road (7.3 miles ahead). The initial part of the trail does not show on the 1954 topographic map.

The route starts gradually downhill from the signpost but soon drops steeply, about 100 feet in 0.25 mile. After a fast 10-minute run you reach a solid bridge over the West Branch of Trout Brook, the outlet brook of Bailey Pond. The old road passes through a beautiful evergreen forest, especially attractive after a fresh snowfall. Beyond the brook there is a gradual climb to the northeast, followed by a steep, demanding hill. In ½ hour you approach the spruce-filled valley

■
Cedar sentinels on Big Marsh: Trip 29

of the North Branch. Look for mosses, liverworts, and lichens on the trunks of the huge maple trees in the mature forest. Large, room-sized rocks are scattered around, the result of the glacial scouring that toppled them from the slopes of Washburn Ridge. In about one hour the easy-to-follow trail reaches the edge of the North Branch. The brook falls steeply enough for water to be visible, but don't drink it as there is extensive beaver activity upstream.

Skiing beside the stream is especially enjoyable, and you leave it reluctantly. Now a series of ridges begins, and the stream becomes a series of multileveled beaver ponds. A gentle climb up a ridge is followed by an easy run back to the flow. For 45 minutes after leaving the stream this up-and-down pattern is repeated—again and again. The path is relatively clear, with few blowdowns, and the open hardwoods on the hillside to your left are handsome. The last 15 minutes before arriving at Big Marsh is level, alongside an extensive beaver flow.

Big Marsh is a misnomer; it is a good-sized pond. The outlet is choked with alders but the trail reaches the ice just beyond it. Stumps make a satisfactory lunch stop as you enjoy Texas Ridge to the southeast, Hornet Cobbles to the northeast, and the summit of massive Hoffman Mountain in the distant east.

It will take a little longer to ski back to Loch Muller as it seems to be more uphill, particularly toward the end; actually Big Marsh is close to 1,720 feet in elevation and your car is at 1,680 feet. Returning, you follow the beaver dams and the stream down to 1,600 feet before veering to the southwest for the climb back to Loch Muller.

If you are an advanced skier and want to ski through to Blue Ridge Road, it will take some planning. Don't start the trip unless you are sure there is a way across the stream at the northern end. To do this take a shuttle car to Blue Ridge Road (as described in Trip 25) and walk or ski down the trail to see if a bridge or beaver dams provide a way to get across.

The trip down the notch from Big Marsh to Blue Ridge Road is steep and narrow. There are three brook crossings that appear suddenly during the 400-foot drop; there may be trees across the path and little room to maneuver. Tight turns and quick stops are essential. If you can handle this kind of skiing, then try it. You will have a great run!

30. Hoffman Cemetery

▪

1.2 miles round-trip
Skiing time: 30 minutes
Beginner
USGS Schroon Lake 15' or 7.5' x 15' metric
Map—page 136

At the turn off Hoffman Road up to Loch Muller (Trip 28) there is a sign on the south side of the road that says: 1808 Hoffman Cemetery. Park beside the road and ski down a short run to a narrow but sound bridge that crosses the outlet of Muller Pond, which flows east into Trout Brook. Beyond the bridge the old road leads uphill through an attractive and dense grove of white pine. On the gradual climb up the straight track you move into hardwoods.

In 15 minutes, just over 0.5 mile from the start, the open roadway turns right at a sharp angle. Follow it 200 yards to a small cemetery. The clearing is formed by the canopy of two magnificent white pines. The headstones mark the resting place of the Oliver and other families—early settlers in this area. Flags indicate that many were Civil War veterans. You may wonder why this resting place was located so deep in the woods. The trail you have traveled was actually the original road from Irishtown to Loch Muller. The road south and west of the cemetery is overgrown, but if you can follow the old road, you will come out near Oliver Pond.

The nice long glide from the cemetery back to the road will take only 10 minutes. This short ½-hour trip can be added to other short excursions in the area, such as Trip 31.

31. Big Pond

▪

3.0 miles round-trip
Skiing time: 1 hour and 20 minutes
Beginner
USGS Schroon Lake 15' or 7.5' x 15' metric
Map—page 143

The trip into Big Pond is short but worth it. There is a huge beaver dam, an extensive white cedar grove, loads of deer, and a large lake as your destination. Combine it with excursions to Hoffman Cemetery (Trip 30) or Bailey Pond (Trip 28) for a nice, easy afternoon.

The trailhead is on the north side of Hoffman Road, 2.8 miles east of the intersection with Trout Brook Road, and 2.1 miles west of NY 9 in Schroon Lake. There are some barrier posts, a Wilderness Area sign, and a No Vehicles notice. Park off the road as far as possible.

The trip starts with a gradual rise through a mixed forest. Soon you

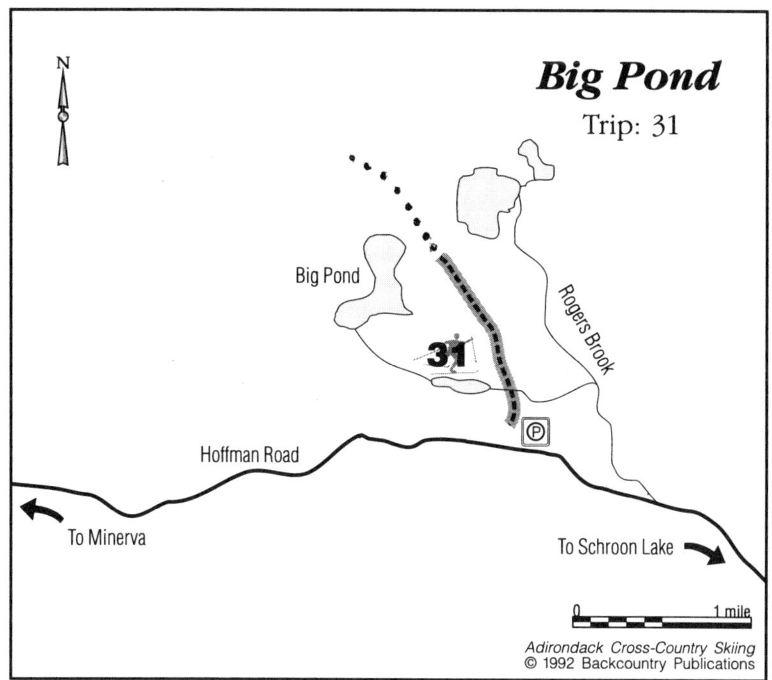

enter a reforestation area of large red pine, uncommon in the Adirondacks. The trail is wide and clear, with blue trail markers. Rounding a small hill there is a large beaver pond ahead. A short glide brings you to Rogers Brook, but keep your speed under control as you might take a bad fall if you don't make a sharp left turn onto a sturdy bridge. A high solid beaver dam blocks the stream just up from the bridge, forming an exceptionally large pond. Frost-covered evergreens form a backdrop for the spikes of dead trees that poke through the ice. This dam is less than 15 minutes from the road.

After the dam, the trail climbs slightly before you enter a very extensive white cedar grove. Many seedlings grow under the wide sweeping branches. Deer tracks dot the snow; it is obvious that white-tailed deer relish the succulent cedar shoots in the winter. The trail passes a very large erratic, and other sizable rocks are scattered about the mixed forest. Several varieties of fungus grow on dead trees. In a stand of hemlock, chickadees sound their cheerful call. These winter friends seem to congregate only in this area, so these trees must harbor seeds and the egg clusters of insects.

Shortly after this hemlock grove the roadway narrows to a trail. You can see the large pond through the woods ahead on the left. The trail continues over the hill, past the pond, but becomes steep and narrow. Before the hill, look for a way to ski through the open woods to a small bluff near the shore of the pond. You will reach it in less than 50 minutes from the start.

The trail climbs only about 80 feet, so you enjoy a gentle glide back that will take about 30 minutes.

32. Stony Pond and Center Pond

■

4.0 miles round-trip to Stony Pond
Skiing time: 1 hour and 50 minutes
8.0 miles round-trip to Center Pond
Skiing time: 3 hours and 50 minutes-
Competent Beginner
USGS Schroon Lake 15' or 7.5' x 15' &
Dutton Mountain metric
Map—page 145

There is a pleasant ambience to this trip—the trail is wide, scenic, and varied and leads to a lake with a lean-to and an interesting bog area. The bays of Stony Pond can be explored (you are sure to see otter tracks), and you can ski over toward tiny Center Pond if you want to explore the bog.

The marked trailhead leading to Stony Pond is on NY 28N 3.8 miles north of Murdy's General Store in Minerva. There is a plowed area for parallel parking by the trail sign that says: Stony Pond 2.0 miles.

The beginning of the trail rises gradually through balsam and spruce and soon changes to open but relatively young hardwoods. After about eight minutes skiing you will see a track to the right. This

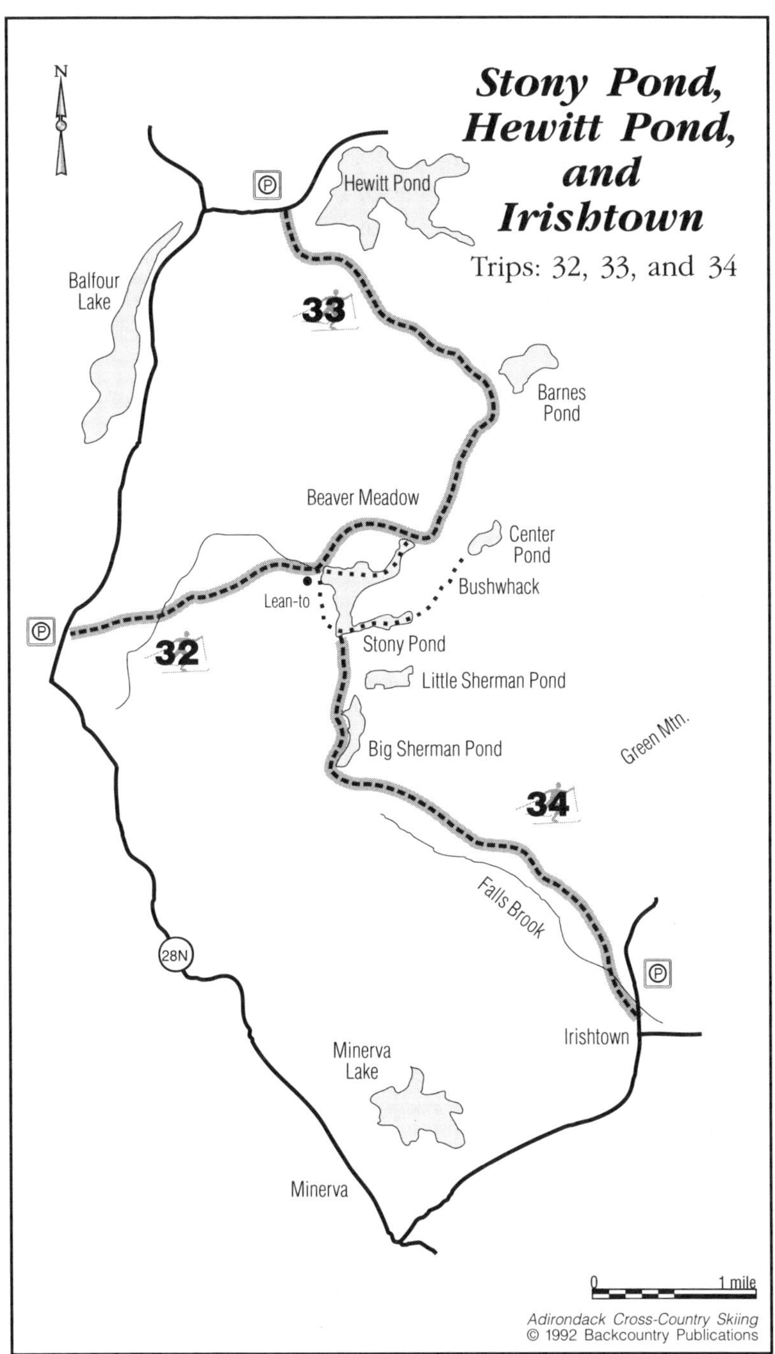
Stony Pond, Hewitt Pond, and Irishtown
Trips: 32, 33, and 34
N
Hewitt Pond
Balfour Lake
33
Barnes Pond
Beaver Meadow
Center Pond
Bushwhack
Lean-to
32
Stony Pond
Little Sherman Pond
Big Sherman Pond
Green Mtn.
34
Falls Brook
28N
Irishtown
Minerva Lake
Minerva
0
1 mile
Adirondack Cross-Country Skiing
© 1992 Backcountry Publications

goes to small Twentyninth Pond and private land. At this point the old tote road swings a little left (north of east). After cresting a hill there is a long, delightful glide down a slope that ends in a sharp dip at the remains of an old beaver dam. The dam is breached, but a large beaver meadow extends north from it.

A half hour into the trip you climb gradually up a hill. Notice the huge hemlocks. Fifteen minutes from the beaver dam there may be red spruce blowdowns. Skirt the end of a beaver meadow, go up a short rise, and you are at the Stony Pond lean-to. The 2 miles takes 1 hour to 1 hour and 10 minutes to cover.

The traditional Adirondack lean-to is situated handsomely at the western end of the pond. Assuming the pond is frozen (there should be tracks of snowmobiles that come in from Irishtown), go right (south) down the pond to the end. Look for an opening on the left that goes into a large bay. Head east into that bay to explore its remote winter stillness. If you continue straight through the marsh you can reach Center Pond. It is level and about 1 mile from the end of the bay, about 2 miles from the lean-to.

It will take 1 hour to return to the lean-to but only about 40 minutes to drop the 64 feet from the 2,078-foot altitude at Stony Pond to your car.

33. Stony Pond and Hewitt Pond Roundabout

■

7.0 miles one way
Skiing time: 4 hours
Intermediate
USGS Newcomb & Schroon Lake 15' or 7.5' x 15' metric
Map—page 145

This long excursion takes you beyond Stony Pond, past Barnes Pond, and out to the Hewitt Pond Road and will require that a second car be left there. Some difficult sections make this a challenging trip and it may not be brushed out; check with the ranger in Olmstedville for the status.

The route to the trailhead for the trip to Stony Pond is described in Trip 32. Since you ski from south to north to reach your shuttle car, pass the trailhead with both cars and continue north on NY 28N for 2.8 miles (6.6 miles from Murdy's General Store in Minerva). Turn right on the road for Hewitt Pond and drive in 0.6 mile. There is a DEC sign and a small parking lot just before the gate. The sign says: Hewitt Pond to Stony Pond via Barnes Pond 5.0 miles. Another sign says Stony Pond is 5.0 miles, Irishtown 9.0 miles, and NY 28N 7.0 miles. Park a car and return to the Stony Pond trailhead.

The 2-mile trip to Stony Pond lean-to takes a little over an hour. If the pond is frozen (check for snowmobile tracks), go up the left shore. Otherwise, go left (north) across the outlet on flat rocks and pick up the red-disk-marked trail. The trail goes east for a way, parallel to the shoreline, with some easy ups and downs. Thirty minutes from the lean-to, away from the pond, you come to a steep part, hard to climb, and perhaps with dead spruce across the trail. As you ski down the next ridge, you see Stony Pond, then, turning away, you climb again. Eventually, you ski down to a beaver flow, cross the outlet, and turn left. (As you cross the outlet of this beaver flow you are near the extreme northeastern bay of Stony Pond—if you had skied along the shoreline for 0.5 mile you would reach this point and pick up the trail.)

Now the trail goes north through a spruce grove with the beaver flow down to the left. There may be blowdowns along the trail so it is better to ski up the beaver meadow. At the head of the flow, the marked trail dips to the meadow and the two routes join and continue northerly.

In 1½ hours from the lean-to you reach a height of land in a young forest. From here the trail drops 340 feet in about 1 mile to Barnes Pond. It is an old logging road, but hobblebush prevents easy turns. You will need to drag your pole tips and stop frequently. Barnes Pond is scenic, with large standing dead trees. At the pond turn left (west) and follow a better trail used by fishermen. After skirting a marshy area, the trail turns north across a log bridge. In 2½ hours from the lean-to you see

Hewitt Pond. The trail goes left (west) up a very steep hill to avoid posted land. It is too steep to ski and you must scramble up, holding trees and shrubs while carrying your skis. It is almost as steep going down the other side. You then ski through a marsh area, partly on flat log paths. You are happy to see your car! This trip is recommended only if it is brushed out and cleared, otherwise there are better places to ski.

34. Stony Pond and Sherman Pond to Irishtown

■

7.0 miles one way
Skiing time: 2 hours and 30 minutes
Intermediate
USGS Newcomb & Schroon Lake 15' or 7.5' x 15' metric
Map—page 145

This trip is a more difficult extension of the popular trip to Stony Pond (Trip 32). After reaching the Stony Pond lean-to the trip continues in a wide loop past hidden ponds deep in the Forest Preserve and drops 800 feet to a place called Irishtown. You will need two cars for the fairly short shuttle. Snowmobiles are permitted on the segment from Irishtown up to Stony Pond. The end of the trip crosses private land, but you are permitted to ski through.

Irishtown appears on the 1953 USGS Schroon Lake topographic map east of Minerva. During logging days it was a sizable settlement, but it is now a few scattered houses. To get there drive southeast on NY 28N from Murdy's General Store in Minerva for 1.65 miles to an intersection. Go left (northeast) on a dirt road called Town Shed Road, cross an intersection, and continue on the dirt road past the road to the Minerva beach. At 2.0 miles there is a road to the right, but go straight ahead on what is now called Long Hill Road. At 2.3 miles from NY 28N look for a trail coming out of the woods on the left just prior to crossing a brook.

(If you miss it you will reach the end of the road at a farmhouse in 200 yards.) Leave a car beside the road where the trail emerges from the woods, and drive back to Murdy's Store in Minerva. Continue north from the store for 3.8 miles to the beginning of the trip to Stony Pond.

Follow the directions in Trip 32 for the 1-hour-and-10-minute trip to the lean-to at the western end of Stony Pond. Plan to lunch at the lean-to as it is a beautiful setting. The Stony Pond-to-Irishtown segment of the trip begins by skiing right (south) from the lean-to down the pond to its southernmost tip. The pond should be frozen in the middle of the winter, but if there are no snowmobile tracks on it, don't take a chance. Follow the red-disked trail that goes southerly from the lean-to parallel to the shore.

At the southern tip of the pond there are no trail signs, but look for an obvious opening used by snowmobiles. In the woods the red-marked trail from the lean-to comes in from the right. After that, going south, there is a short but very steep hill that you might want to walk down—depending on snow conditions. After this drop there is a gradual descent to Little Sherman Pond, which you reach 30 minutes after leaving the lean-to.

On the topographic map the trail from here follows along the western shore of Big Sherman Pond. The woods are thick enough and there are enough alders that it is unlikely that you will catch a glimpse of it. If the pond doesn't materialize, don't feel that you are lost! About 15 minutes after leaving Little Sherman the trail swings east on the contour line following a path parallel to Falls Brook, which flows out of Big Sherman. The cleared trail hugs the hillside above the brook, and sometimes drops near it. At times it is narrow and rather steep as it goes from 1,900 feet down the slope of Green Mountain to the Minerva Stream valley at 1,200 feet. At the higher elevations there are open hardwoods, and toward the bottom there is a beautiful grove of conifers. At this point you are on private land but through skiing is permitted. The very end of the trip crosses a bridge over Falls Brook. From there it is short, level glide to the car, reached 1 hour and 20 minutes after leaving the lean-to.

This is a demanding trip, but if you are in the mood for a long, fairly challenging run down the side of a mountain, try it! It's a great way to spend 2½ hours on skis with very little climbing.

■

Elm Island Trail: Trip 38

Indian Lake Area
Wilderness and Snowmobiles

■

The town of Indian Lake has two winter worlds. To the south, the lovely, secluded hills and ponds of the Siamese Ponds Wilderness Area are easily reached. Northerly, starting at the outskirts of the town, trails fan out into the Blue Mountain Wild Forest. Snowmobiles can use some of the Wild Forest public lands. While it is unpleasant and unsafe to ski on major snowmobile routes (such as the high-speed thoroughfares that link Indian Lake with Inlet and Speculator), skiers can comfortably share the narrow, winding trails with snowmobiles.

Competent beginners can begin by trying two loops on either end of the village (Trip 35). Three more trails start at the Indian Lake landfill. Trip 36 takes you beside beautiful Cedar River, with its quiet falls, on a competent beginner's trail to McGinn Mountain—where it gets steep. Remote Unknown Pond is reached on a narrow snowmobile trail by Trip 37; another competent beginner trail (Trip 38) leads to distant Elm Island at a bend in the Cedar River.

Farther west on NY 28 intermediate Trip 39 drops steeply to Rock River; Trip 40 is a beginner run to Rock Lake. On the other side of NY 28, Trip 41 is a snowshoe hike to an overlook on Sawyer Mountain. You must share Trips 37 to 40 with snowmobiles. The local snowmobilers respect skiers on the trail—and generally run only on weekends—so this is not as bad as some people think. After a heavy snowstorm there is an advantage to skiing in such snowmobile trails as the town of Indian Lake grooms them, and this makes the going easier.

Trails to the south of Indian Lake enter the Siamese Ponds Wilderness Area. Trip 42 to scenic John Pond is a family-type trail, and the lean-to at the destination makes it a wonderful spot for wilderness camping. A varied and beautiful series of intermediate cross-country trails starts farther out on Big Brook Road at Kings Flow. As you approach Kings Flow, a marvelous view of twin-peaked Humphrey Mountain is seen over the sweep of ice. At one time, old maps reveal, there was a stream, probably dammed by beavers, called Joe King Flow. Eventually a cement dam was built which flooded the flow and the name was shortened. The land surrounding the flow, except for the northern tip with cabins, is the Siamese Ponds Wilderness. (The owners of the cabins permit access to the public trails and provide a place to park for the charge of $1 per car.)

There is a difficult loop to Puffer Pond with Trip 43. Competent beginners will enjoy easy Trip 44 to Round Pond on the old stagecoach track called Kunjamuk Road. The Kings Flow Loop (Trip 45) is a long, intermediate, cold-weather trek because it crosses three unbridged streams. Once in the woods the wilderness closes quickly around you and the beauty of the forest and mountain ponds can be enjoyed with peace and quiet. An added gift is that it has not been "discovered," and you will often ski without meeting anyone.

Wilderness Lodge is a convenient place to stay while you are skiing in the area; the food is excellent and the portions sufficient for the largest, outdoor-acquired appetite (telephone: 518-648-5995). The Indian Lake, Blue Mountain Lake, and Thirteenth Lake topographic maps cover most of the area. There are no cross-country commercial outfits with groomed trails.

35. Indian Lake Loops

▪

3.0 miles each loop
Skiing time: 1 hour and 20 minutes each
Beginner
USGS Blue Mountain 15' or
Blue Mountain Lake 7.5' x 15' metric
Map—page 154

The town of Indian Lake has two small cross-country loops within minutes of the Grand Union supermarket. It takes a little over an hour to ski each one, and they are worth it if you want a short, easily accessible workout. The first loop described here is more enjoyable than the second; both are also useful for beginners who want to get acquainted with the conditions encountered on more isolated trails.

The first loop is near Geandreau's Cabins on land owned largely by them. Drive southeast from the center of Indian Lake for 0.5 mile. Pass Geandreau's Cabins and, at the point where a highway sign gives the mileage to North Creek, turn right down a steep road. Go straight past two houses on the left. At the entrance to a private drive there is a sign that says: X-C Ski Trail—No Snowmobiles Allowed. Park to the right, and ski down the private road. Within 100 yards there is a house on the left, but continue straight. Yellow cross-country ski disks show the way.

Within a minute or two you cross a bridge over Carroll's Brook. On the other side there is a trail map on a tree, and a small marker with number 1 indicating the first intersection. The outer loop trail goes to the right; it is marked by red ribbons on trees. It is easy to follow and kept clear by Indian Lake volunteers. The trail climbs slightly until you get to intersection 2. Here there is a view of Lake Abanakee through the yellow birch, red spruce, and balsam fir on your right. Beyond this intersection the forest floor has low-growing yews that are browsed by white-tailed deer. There are places in the snow where they have pawed and depressions where they have spent

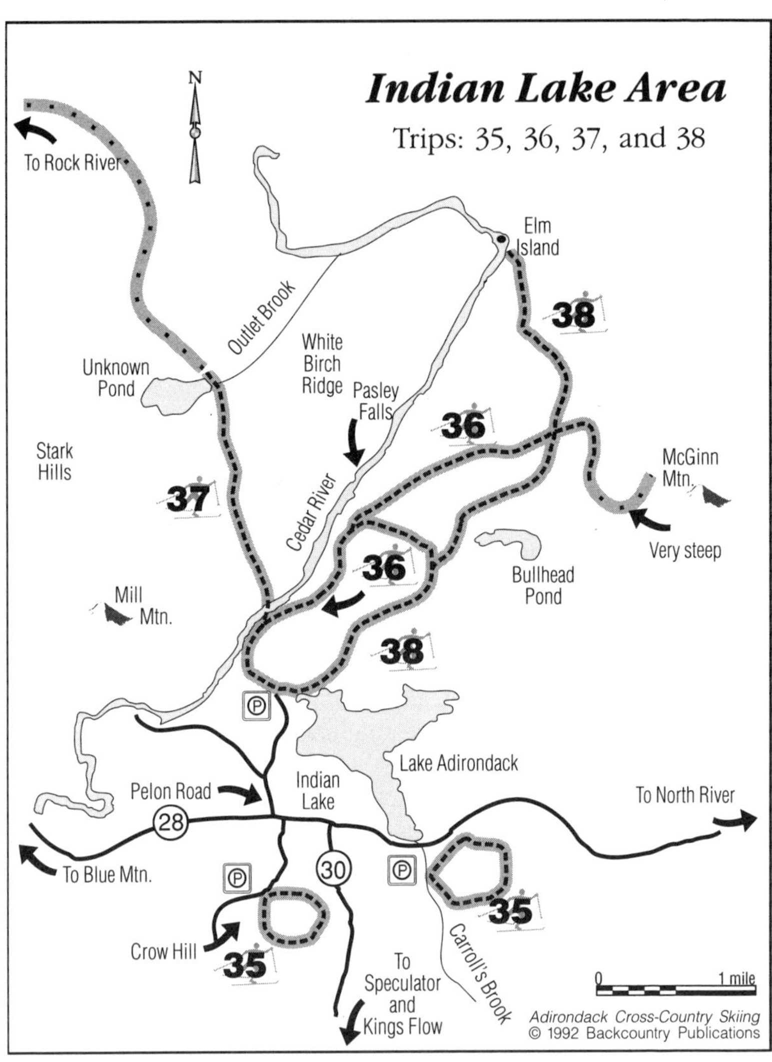

the night, about 20 minutes from the car. A few minutes later, intersection 3 is reached; here a yellow-flagged trail appears on the left. It is a crossover trail, readily seen on the trail maps posted at each intersection.

After intersection 4, two large, dead white birch grow a mammoth crop of large fungus on their trunks. The trail climbs slightly to intersection 5, which is reached in less than one hour. On this hill you will notice a clump of large, towering trees with heavily furrowed, straight trunks. Looking up 40 to 50 feet, you will see a scraggly topknot of short branches. On several of the trunks, fungus knobs show where branches have broken off. These trees are bigtooth aspen (*Populus grandidentata*), usually found in dry soils and in burned-over areas.

As you ski down from the knoll the trail passes close enough to the lake for you to make your way through the trees for a view. After this you swing to the left and pass near a field, where you can hear the traffic on NY 28. From this location there is a gradual drop past intersections 7 and 8. Soon you are back at the bridge over Carroll's Brook. Skiing slowly it will take about 1 hour and 20 minutes to make the loop. For more skiing you can take the yellow-flagged and the blue-flagged horizontal crossovers.

The other town-sponsored trail starts at either Crow Hill Road or the ski slope. To get to Crow Hill Road, drive west 0.3 mile from the center of Indian Lake on NY 28. Drive up Crow Hill Road (south) for 0.35 mile to where the trail begins on the left. Park beside the road.

This loop is not laid out well. The trail is 1.68 miles long and follows the fence line of a rectangular area. Most of it is narrow and steep. If some of the trail had been cut along a contour, avoiding the steep lower corner, it would be more skiable.

You can also get onto the trail from the top of the town ski slope and make a wide loop to the bottom of the lift; this is preferable to the rectangular section. There are trail maps at intersections to guide you.

36. Cedar River and McGinn Mountain Trail

■

8.0 miles round-trip
Skiing time: 3 hours and 45 minutes
Competent Beginner, Snowshoes for McGinn
USGS Blue Mountain & Newcomb 15' or
Blue Mountain Lake 7.5' x 15'
Map—page 154

This trip follows a marked cross-country trail that meanders beside the smooth ice and tumbling falls of the Cedar River, not far from the village. A beginning skier with some experience can handle the first 3.5 miles to the point where it crosses the skiable snowmobile route to Elm Island (Trip 38); the last stretch up McGinn Mountain is much more difficult, and it is better to use snowshoes. The entire trip avoids snowmobile trails. This run is meant for skinny ski devotees who enjoy the quiet.

The trailhead for this and the next two trips is inauspicious—it starts at the town landfill. To reach it, drive west from the intersection of NY 30 and NY 28 in Indian Lake village for 0.3 mile. Turn right (north) on Pelon Road, follow it for 0.2 mile, then take the right fork. Continue for 0.5 mile until it deadends at the landfill. Park outside the gate and walk in through a side opening.

On the right there are two trails; one goes straight ahead to Unknown Pond and the other goes to the right to Elm Island. The Unknown Pond route leads to the cross-country trail. It goes straight ahead (northwest) down a wide trail for 0.3 mile to the Cedar River. There are yellow cross-country skiing disks along with orange snowmobile markers. At the river turn right and follow the trail marked (for snowmobilers) Unknown Pond/Rock Pond/Blue Mountain, which you will leave in about 400 yards. When the snowmobile trail drops down the bank onto the river's ice, look to the right for a small sign and a yellow cross-country marker on a tree 20 feet from the river's bank. Do not cross the river.

The marked ski trail follows along the east bank of the river for about 1 mile. This stretch is quiet, gentle, and relaxing. Cares slip away as you enjoy the solitude found surprisingly close to civilization. The trail is brushed out, but there may be trees across it. If so, make your way around them but keep the yellow disks in sight.

After skiing about 1 mile, the riverbank becomes steeper and heavily wooded. The trail veers away from the river, up over an evergreen-covered knoll, and then drops back parallel to the silent river. After you have skied 2 miles (perhaps 1 hour), the river is compressed between steep, rocky walls. The sound of water falling over large boulders heralds another climb away from the river. You are coming to Pasley Falls; if you take off your skis you can get near enough for a view of the small gorge.

At this point there is a trail to the right, marked with a small sign, to Lake Adirondack. It goes over the hill, crosses the red-marked snowmobile route to Elm Island (Trip 38), and then follows the orange snowmobile trail to the lake. If you are short of time you can use it as a cutoff—although it has numerous blowdowns—and race back to the landfill on the red-marked snowmobile route.

At Pasley Falls, however, the official, marked cross-country trail to McGinn Mountain continues downriver. It loops around and over a tall, spruce-covered knoll above the falls. You have to look sharply for the yellow disks. Make sure you follow them, as you can get lost in spruce thickets if you get off the track. After climbing around the knoll there is easy going through a very extensive stand of white birch, away from the steep banks of the river.

The trail bends gradually to the right. About 45 minutes after leaving Pasley Falls (1.5 miles), skiing easterly, you intersect the snowmobile route to Elm Island. The narrow, cross-country path joins the wide, groomed snowmobile track for 100 yards as it drops into a hollow and goes partway up the hill on the other side. The ski trail then turns right (east) up the draw toward the rocky, south-facing cliffs of McGinn Mountain. There are trail markers up this draw, but the trail has numerous, huge poplar blowdowns; you must work around them through the open, mature woods. The going soon becomes steep and is only for experts. Although the yellow disks go all the way to the top, the last 200 feet up is not skiable. You can walk through the deep snow with difficulty or, better yet, carry a pair of snowshoes to reach the summit. The view of Indian Lake, Snowy Mountain, and the range of the Siamese Ponds Wilderness is stupendous. To the right, you can see the Blue Ridge Mountain range, with the Stark Hills closer by. On the left, completing the panorama, are the distant peaks and rock ledges of Moxham Mountain, beyond the Hudson River.

You can either ski back on the red-marked snowmobile trail and complete a loop or retrace your tracks. It is as pleasant returning as it was skiing in, and a little faster because there is more downhill. You should be back at your car in about 1½ hours if you glide along in your fresh tracks. It is hard to imagine a more perfect way to enjoy a half-day outdoors in the winter.

37. Unknown Pond

■

4.0 miles round-trip
Skiing time: 2 hours
Competent Beginner
USGS Blue Mountain 15' or
Blue Mountain Lake 7.5' x 15' metric
Map—page 154

One wonders who the hunter or fisherman was who named this large, isolated beaver-dammed body of water—and why. It is remote, but so are hundreds of other ponds in the Adirondacks. This wayward area is now reached by a wide, clear swath through handsome woods. The route is not traveled frequently by snowmobilers so you can enjoy it on skinny skis.

The beginning of this trip is the same as for Trip 36, Cedar River Trail. Read those directions for getting to the landfill and starting on the Unknown Pond Trail. After 10 minutes skiing, take the snowmobile trail across the ice on the Cedar River, which is 100 feet wide and shallow at this point. There obviously has to have been enough cold weather for the ice to hold you, but if snowmobiles have crossed you don't have to worry.

Ski up the bank on the other side of the river and follow the marked snowmobile trail as it goes northwest. The trail stays on the contour with little change in altitude. To the right (north) there is a large swampy area. From its far side rises aptly named White Birch Ridge. If you look closely, you can see the stark, gray face of McGinn Mountain through the trees across the swamp to the right.

Since it has been packed by snowmobiles, the route is fast. In less than one hour you approach a marshy area, with the outlet brook meandering through it, downstream from the pond. Before reaching it there is a sharp, steep drop. Beginners may have trouble running this short hill, although it is straight and has a good runout on the frozen marsh.

Circle downstream until you find a place where the brook is filled in by snow. On the other side, ski toward the pond, then follow the snowmobile trail up a small hill into the woods. On top of the first rise, go left and you will reach a sheltered area above the pond. This a good place for lunch. You can ski down the bank onto the large, 38-acre surface: if you ski up the right shoreline, there are sweeping views. Stark Hills, a desolate and formidable wall of rock, is clearly identifiable. In the distance is the familiar shape of Blue Mountain.

This snowmobile trail runs northwest until it meets Rock River, then winds east to Rock Lake. It is a long way and not described as part of this trip. If you want to ski the loop, it is better to start from NY 28/30, as described in Trip 39, and end at the Indian Lake landfill. That way you avoid climbing a steep hill at the end of a 10-mile trip.

Before going back, ski around the large marsh northeast of the outlet. This huge, wetland area is in the middle of the southern portion of the Blue Mountain Wild Forest Area. It is an isolated wilderness and in the summer is a prime habitat and rookery for waterfowl and herons.

The trip back to your car will take about one hour. You must climb the steep hill after leaving the marsh below the pond, but after that it is pure joy.

38. Elm Island

■

8.0 miles round-trip
Skiing time: 4 hours
Competent Beginner
USGS Blue Mountain & Newcomb 15' or
Blue Mountain Lake 7.5' x 15'
Map—page 154

Some people abhor the sound of machines and the smell of exhaust so much that they refuse to ski a snowmobile trail. But, if the snow is very deep and you don't feel like breaking trail, try this one. Chances are that in the middle of the week you will see or hear few snow machines, and the groomed wide track makes for wonderful skiing; you may meet more people with skis and poles than with goggles and felt-lined boots.

The beginning of the trip is at the landfill less than a mile from the center of Indian Lake (see directions in Trip 36). Start into the woods to the right on the snowmobile trail. It winds through a thick conifer grove at the start. In less than 200 yards, go left, thus avoiding the spur to town. Soon the trail emerges into open hardwoods and climbs gradually. After about 1 mile, you are 100 feet higher than the 1,700-foot altitude at the landfill. The trail follows the contour around the northwest side of a hill. In the open forest it is hard to believe that you are within a mile of the village. If you should meet snowmobilers, they are probably local residents and will politely slow down when they pass. At the crest of the shoulder of the hill, there is a long, moderately winding grade into a draw. The glide down is much fun and wide enough to use stem turns to keep your speed under control.

Now you begin another easy climb around the southeast slope of an unnamed hill. The clean, leafless forest mixes with conifers as you reach a junction. (An orange-disked snowmobile track goes right to Lake Adirondack in a primarily flat and uninteresting trip.) Continuing on the red-marked trail, you have a short run, then climb more steeply to 1,800 feet. The map shows Bullhead Pond on your right as you climb, but you don't see it. Topping the rise you swing west of north on level ground for 15 minutes. If you look carefully through the trees, slightly to your right, you can see the rock cliffs of McGinn Mountain, the destination of Trip 36. Again you mount a rise, then, with several up-and-down undulations, you descend toward Elm Island. At one dip, after you have skied about 1½ hours, you will notice yellow disks where the cross-country trail joins this Elm Island route and then goes right to McGinn Mountain.

From this point, going north, it is a long, gradual swing around the western side of McGinn Mountain. Cedar River hides in a steep gorge to your left as the trail rises and falls pleasantly. The woods are young white birch; appropriately, on the other side of the river stands White Birch Ridge. A long run takes you to 1,580 feet where you reach an open area and the river. Look up the frozen jumble of the Cedar River Gorge; after plunging over rocks, the river hits a rocky outcrop, downriver from where you stand, which forces it left. Just below the crook of this elbow lies Elm Island, a sediment bar in the middle of the river, so you won't see it in the winter.

You can ski across the river on the ice blocks if you are careful. The Indian Lake Recreational Trail Map (available at the Indian Lake Chamber of Commerce Information Office) and a composite topographic map (issued in 1984 by Plinth, Quoin & Cornice) show a snowmobile route from Elm Island to Unknown Pond, but it has been discontinued. It may be possible to ski through, if you have a map and compass, but it is a bushwhack and not recommended.

The trip back begins with easy climbing through handsome birch. A glide across a draw follows; it is up and down enough to be relaxing. In just under 1½ hours from Elm Island you reach the junction that goes to Lake Adirondack. At this point, an unmarked trail goes over the hill to the right (northwest) to Pasley Falls, described in Trip 36. If you keep on the red trail you can accomplish a nice kick-and-glide rhythm. There is a long climb that gets a bit tiring, but the final runout makes up for it. The entire trip back should take about two hours, the same as the trip in. For variety, you can make a loop by returning on the yellow-marked cross-country ski trail from the McGinn Mountain area, or by taking the Pasley Falls crossover. It will take several trips to explore this pleasant Cedar River area with its rolling hills.

39. Rock River

▪

6.0 miles round-trip
Skiing time: 2 hours and 45 minutes
Intermediate
USGS Blue Mountain 15' or
Blue Mountain Lake 7.5' x 15' metric
Map—page 163

This trip to Rock River is another one that follows a snowmobile track, taking you to the western end of Trip 37 past Unknown Pond. The trail is not heavily traveled during weekdays, but if snowmobiles have traveled it, some sections in the first mile will have a snowmobile "trough" that is hard to handle. Parts of the trail are fairly steep, and there are some sharp turns. The last 2 miles are enjoyable, however, and the lunch spot at the river is tranquil, making the whole trip worthwhile.

The trailhead is 4.65 miles west of the center of Indian Lake on the right (north) side of NY 28/30. There is a DEC trail marker indicating that Rock River is 3.0 miles following red trail disks. A parking area is plowed beside the road.

You start out at 1,950 feet; the trail climbs gradually as it winds through some second-growth hardwoods. After 10 minutes, you drop into the valley at a good speed on a trail that requires some tight turns. Through the trees to the right the rocky ledges of Stark Hills are seen. A

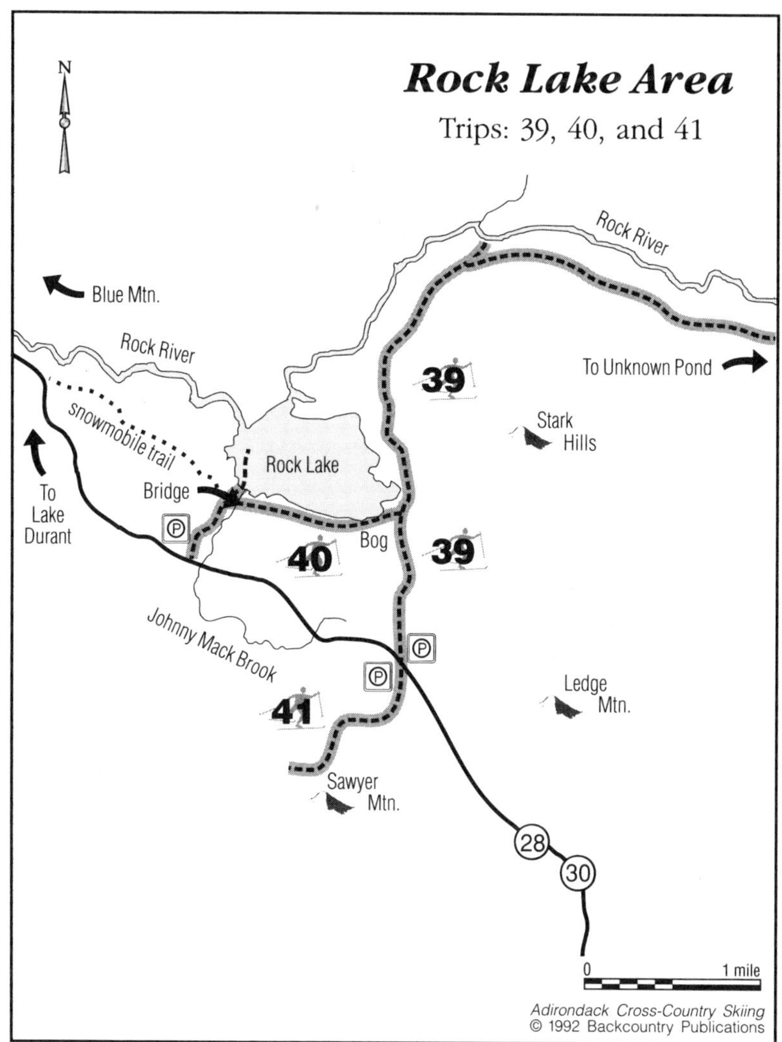

slight rise is followed by another good drop. At the bottom, just before the trail winds across a flat area at 1,720 feet, the snowmobile trail from Lake Durant joins this trail from the left. It is easy to miss; it enters just after you ski downhill under the broken-off top of a large tree.

Climbing slightly, ½ hour from the start, the large expanse of Rock Lake appears. The trail stays well back from the lake and it would be a steep bushwhack to get down to the shoreline. Going northerly, you climb gradually to 1,800 feet. The dense hardwoods block all views, but the trail is open and pleasant. After skiing one hour there is a fork: The right track, with no markers, goes east and is the main snowmobile trail to Unknown Pond and Cedar River; the left fork, marked with red metal disks, goes northeast to Rock River. After 10 minutes on this left trail, you ski down a small hill into a little clearing. Ski straight through the clearing. The rocky bluffs of some unnamed hills appear ahead slightly to the left. You should see a (misplaced) snowmobile trail disk on a tree straight ahead. Go past it, and sidestep down the steep bank. Hobblebush loops are everywhere, and they stop you quickly if you try to ski down on an angle. At the bottom of the hill keep going straight (you may see more snowmobile signs or some red flags) and you will soon reach Rock River at 1,600 feet. It is a pleasant place for lunch and pictures; the sun streams in on clear days, and there is a little log bench to sit on.

The trip back in the early winter afternoon is into the sun. There is a 100-foot climb up from the river, but then the trail levels. About 40 minutes after starting back there is a nice long run along a sidehill going southwest toward the lake. Approaching the lake, the trail turns sharply left. Soon it jogs again toward a bay of the lake, then again swings left to the south. One hour after leaving Rock River you reach the trail that goes west to Lake Durant (Trip 40). From here it is a long climb, about 25 minutes, back to your car. Notice the pretty vista of Stark Hills on your left, and think of the last five-minute glide down to NY 28/30 and your car. With a 15-minute lunch stop the entire trip takes three hours.

40. Rock Lake

▪

3.8 miles round-trip
Skiing time: 2 hours and 15 minutes
Beginner
USGS Blue Mountain 15' or
Blue Mountain Lake 7.5' x 15' metric
Map—page 163

There are two trails that go north to the vicinity of Rock Lake. The eastern one, which passes above the lake, is described in Trip 39. This western route is shorter and actually reaches the lakeshore. It can be used by beginners to get to the Rock River Trail described in Trip 39.

Drive west on NY 28/30 from the center of Indian Lake, where NY 30 joins NY 28, for 6.1 miles. There is a parking area and a DEC sign indicating that Rock Lake is 0.5 mile, with red trail markers. You park at about 1,770 feet, and with the lake at 1,713 feet, the trip is virtually level. The trail is marked for snowmobiles, but it is narrow and strewn with rocks, so it isn't used by them.

Beginners can manage this trail because it is fairly level, but it does require balance and the ability to glide on one ski as you lift the other to avoid rocks. The trail is easier if there is lots of snow to even out the bumps. Going in, Johnny Mack Brook is on the right, but there is little flow and you don't hear it. After 15 minutes of skiing along this rock-defined slalom course, you reach a snowmobile trail. Turn right, and then almost immediately, before a bridge, turn left toward the lake. The trail ducks through an alder thicket, but it is clear and well marked, and you can make it to the shore. Blue Mountain rises majestically to the northwest, identified by the ice-covered tower on the summit, and the snowy scars on its flanks. If the lake is frozen, you can ski toward the mountain and explore the large marsh at the western end, but avoid the thin ice where Rock River enters.

Back at the snowmobile trail, turn left (east) over the bridge. It is not the finest ski trail, because the snow machines tend to exaggerate the bumps, and there are numerous short ups and downs without long glides. It runs east, somewhat back from the lake. A saving grace is that the way is framed by snow-covered balsams that create picturesque winter scenes. Thirty minutes from the bridge the trail reaches the lake at a sharp drop; it is guarded by an immense, leaning white pine. Sidestep down this bank and across the opening, which leads into a bog area to the right. The trail goes up and into the woods and then bears right out onto the leatherleaf (*Chamaedaphne calyculata*) and grass-tufted bog. You can tell leatherleaf from the other acid-loving shrubs, such as labrador tea and bog rosemary, because the edges of the leaves are flat and not rolled in. The leaves are shiny and dark brown on top, point up, and taper to the tips. Rabbits sometimes eat the leaves and the seeds are common food for grouse. This is an older bog, almost filled with decayed matter, and red spruce are beginning to sprout on the drier hummocks. On sunny days this open area is the warmest place for lunch, because the trail is generally shaded.

The track through the bog bears left and into an opening to the right of two large white pines. The juncture with Trip 39 is reached in 12 minutes after leaving the bog. From here the trail goes north to Rock River. It is a relatively easy trip, and beginners will enjoy the longer runs if they are up to making the run to the river.

If you start back from this junction, it takes under 45 minutes to get back to the bridge. After crossing it, immediately look for your return trail on the left. It is easy to miss, and if you pass it, the snowmobile trail will take you to NY 28/30 at Lake Durant.

As always, bog areas and the damp areas along brooks are the best places to look for mosses and lichens. One tree beside the trail has a rich crop of tree lungwort (*Lobaria pulmonaria*); it is gray-green on top, and the whitish underside forms a convex, glabrous patch. This is the lichen that was widely used in the Middle Ages for treating lung diseases because of its resemblance to lung tissue. If you don't tarry long over nonflowering plants, you will be back to your car in less than 2¼ hours for the round-trip. It may be stretching the rating to label this a beginner's trip but, with the exception of a couple of hills to walk down, it can be skied by someone who has been out only a few times.

41. Sawyer Mountain

▪

2.2 miles round-trip
Climbing time: 1 hour and 50 minutes
Snowshoeing
USGS Blue Mountain 15' or
Blue Mountain Lake 7.5' x 15' metric
Map—page 163

This small, easy-to-climb mountain has two openings near the summit that provide intimate and pleasant views of Blue Mountain and the valley of the Cedar River. It is too narrow and steep in places for skiing but is well worth the climb on snowshoes.

There is roadside parking on the left (west) side of NY 28 30 as you drive from Indian Lake to Blue Mountain Lake. It is 4.5 miles northwest of the Indian Lake crossroads at the Grand Union supermarket. A DEC signpost indicates the peak is 1.1 miles; the trail is well marked with yellow disks.

The trail begins gradually through an open, hardwood forest. After climbing to the west, it sweeps around to the northwest to the crest of a small ridge. Here it swings west again and drops into a small col. Soon it begins to climb gradually, still in hardwoods. There are many large, dead, standing beeches that have been marked by pileated woodpeckers. You will see large cavities in the trees gouged by these birds as they probe for insects; the piles of chips on the ground are truly amazing. The live beech are still producing nuts that are scattered on the snow; black bear like them, but since they are sleeping you will not see any.

After snowshoeing less than one hour, you reach a slanting, rocky outcrop. This is difficult going with some kinds of snowshoes as, on the slope of the hill, they may slide sideways under the snow. Take your time; pause to look back at the glorious view of some of the high peaks. Three summits stand out: the massive cone of Mount Marcy is on the right, the tall summit of Algonquin on the left, and the smaller cone of Colden in between.

In a little over one hour the trail reaches one knoll of the summit. There is no view here, but you can go right, downhill, to a rock outcrop. The Cedar River valley stretches for miles to the west and southwest. The slopes of Metcalf and Wakeley mountains create the right wall of a notch; the left wall is formed by Panther Mountain. Take off your snowshoes (for safety because the rock is windblown and steep), walk down the slope 10 feet, and look right. The open-rock, white areas below the flat peak identify Blue Mountain. You can spot the fire tower on Blue Mountain and the one on Wakeley if you have binoculars. Between the two towers, below you, extends the 44,393-acre Blue Ridge Wilderness Area. Stephens and Cascade ponds, which you can ski to in Trips 47 and 48, are two white spots. You can visualize the route of the Northville–Lake Placid Trail if you have a topographic map; follow the route from the Cedar River, past Stephens Pond, to the right of Blue Mountain.

If your snowshoes are tightly attached to your boots, you can make the trip back in about 45 minutes. It is an extremely pleasant snowshoe trip for a family and well marked so you cannot become lost.

42. John Pond

▪

5 miles round-trip
Skiing time: 2 hours and 30 minutes
Competent Beginner
USGS Thirteenth Lake 15' or 7.5' x 15' metric
Map—page 169

A lean-to awaits you at the end of this easy trip into the northwest corner of the Siamese Ponds Wilderness Area. If you want to spend a night listening to coyotes and barred owls, this is as pleasant a place to do it as you can find. The woods are diverse and beautiful. The trail is easy enough to take the family.

The Unit Management Plan for this wilderness area called for this

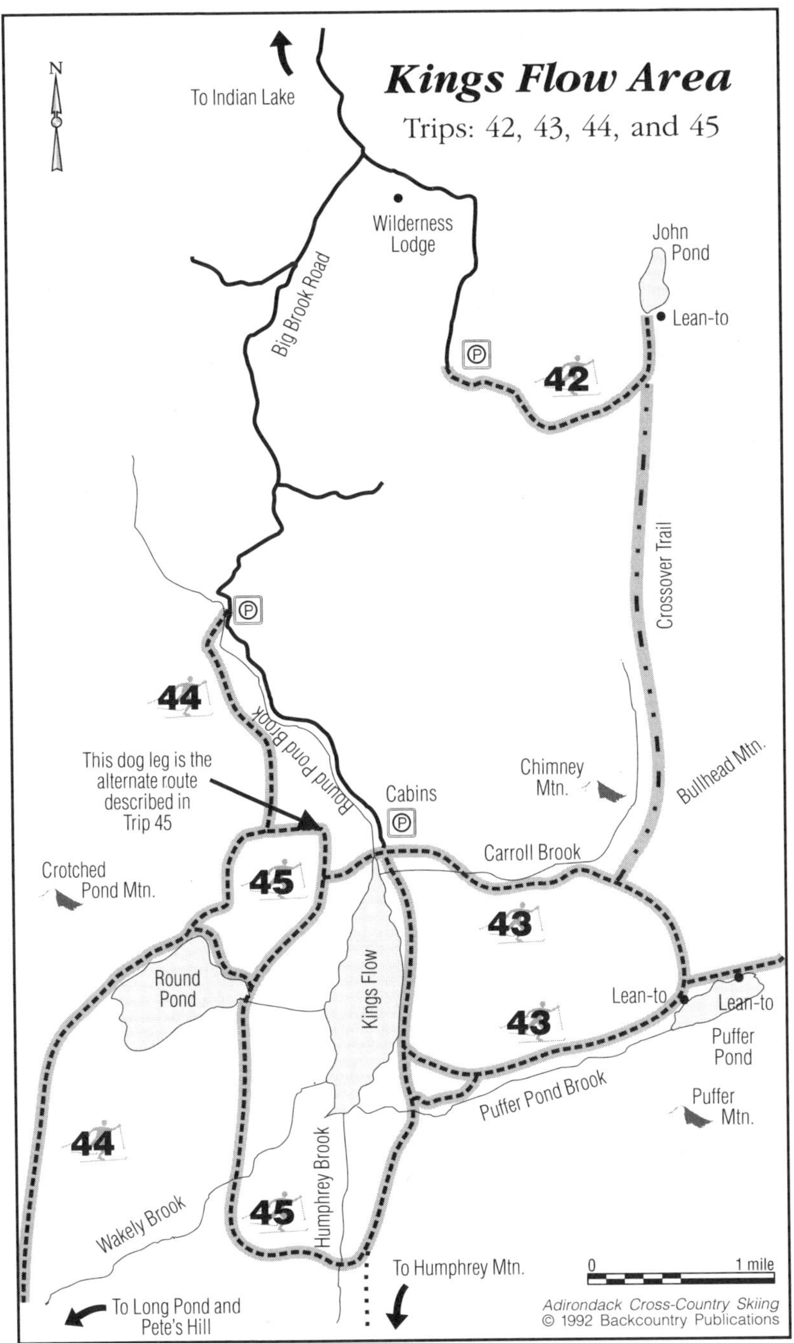
Kings Flow Area
Trips: 42, 43, 44, and 45
N
To Indian Lake
Wilderness Lodge
Big Brook Road
John Pond
Lean-to
42
Crossover Trail
44
Round Pond Brook
This dog leg is the alternate route described in Trip 45
Cabins
Chimney Mtn.
Bullhead Mtn.
Carroll Brook
Crotched Pond Mtn.
45
43
Round Pond
Kings Flow
Lean-to
Lean-to
43
Puffer Pond
Puffer Pond Brook
Puffer Mtn.
44
Humphrey Brook
Wakely Brook
45
To Humphrey Mtn.
0
1 mile
To Long Pond and Pete's Hill
Adirondack Cross-Country Skiing
© 1992 Backcountry Publications

Round Pond: Trips 44 and 45

rough, rutty route to be closed to vehicles and snowmobiles. A barrier has been placed near the wilderness line just beyond the trail register. You cross several small streams without bridges, so it is best not to ski this route late in the season after a thaw.

The trailhead is on the edge of a small subdivision off Big Brook Road. Drive south from Indian Lake on NY 30 for 0.5 mile; turn left on Big Brook Road, and cross the causeway of Lake Abanakee. At 4.0 miles from Indian Lake village, Big Brook Road bears right; take the left fork toward Wilderness Lodge. In 0.35 mile, the road forks right to the lodge; you bear left on Lakeview Drive. Continue straight on through the development and then right to a dead-end turnaround, 1.1 miles from Big Brook Road.

Park out of the way at the turnaround. Ski south (left) for 200 yards on an unplowed narrow road to a DEC register. A trail sign says: John Pond 2.5 miles, Puffer Pond 6.0 miles. Sign in, and if you plan to camp at the lean-to make a note to that effect. John Pond Brook is down the bank to the right of the register, but it winds through brush and is frozen. The ski trail continues south following the valley of the brook along a wide, old tote road. After skiing less than 1 mile, the route turns left (east) and climbs a small, gradual hill. Tracks may go off right to the meadow, but the main route is obvious; frequent blue trail markers show the way.

Especially attractive large spruce trees border the open areas to the south. There are frequent views through the trees of Bullhead Mountain. You may surprise small herds of white-tailed deer along the trail here. The road crosses the Hamilton–Warren County line about 1.8 miles into the trip. You will notice that the composition of the forest changes at the line; on the Warren County side you enter a reforested area, planted with pines. As you ski up a gentle hill through this cultivated area, you may see a narrow path up the hill to the left. At the end of it there is a small cemetery dating back many years; two small children are buried there.

Beyond the path to the cemetery, the trail swings gradually to the northeast. It meets the exit stream of the pond; crossing here requires some careful negotiating across large snow mounds along the downstream side of the road. Just beyond this crossing, about 0.75 mile from the pond, yellow ski-touring disks (together with blue hiking disks) lead south (right). This is a relatively new crossover trail that follows a valley with a small stream and then climbs a steep hill to Puffer Pond (see Trip 43).

You reach John Pond at its southern end where the lean-to is located. It lies at 1,828 feet, a climb of about 130 feet from the trailhead. Across the pond large cliffs rise from the shore, and after dark the ridge above seems to be a favorite spot of coyotes. Their sharp yips and tremulous howls punctuate the stillness of the night. The lean-to is in good condition, with a wooden floor. Nights are cold, however, and a good pad and a heavyweight sleeping bag is needed because the fireplace in front of the opening throws little heat. The 3-mile trip should take less than 1½ hours, so it is an easy day trip for a family.

43. Puffer Pond Loop

▪

5.0 miles round-trip
Skiing time: 2 hours and 30 minutes
Intermediate
USGS Thirteenth Lake 15' or 7.5' x 15' metric
Map—page 169

If you want a strenuous workout in a short time, this is the trip to take. You start out by climbing 620 feet in 1.6 miles (use climbing skins on your skis if you have them), then drop 176 feet to a lean-to on a beautiful pond, and then ski 1.6 miles with a drop of 444 feet. The trip back from the lean-to is the last leg of Trip 3 from Old Farm Clearing to Kings Flow (if you continue west after reaching Puffer Pond).

The round-trip starts at the privately owned area at the north end of Kings Flow. Drive south from Indian Lake on NY 30 for 0.5 mile, left on Big Brook Road across the causeway, then continue on Big Brook Road to the end at about 7.0 miles from Indian Lake. You will know you have arrived by the magnificent view of double-peaked Humphrey Mountain as you gaze down the flow. Drive left in an arc past the cabins and park at the far side of a garage, where there is a box to deposit the parking fee of $1 per car.

Ski east through the meadow toward a weathered barn; there is a DEC signpost marking the red-disk trail to Puffer Pond. Someone has penciled in 3.0 miles to the pond, but it is no more than 2 miles. Ski into the hardwoods to the southeast where the path immediately starts to climb. You cross onto Forest Preserve land in 10 minutes; in 20 minutes you ski out on an extensive series of beaver ponds along Carroll Brook. Ski left over a large beaver dam, then continue along the right side almost to the head of the pond. A red disk will show the trail that goes straight into the hardwoods to the southeast, continuing to climb. The path requires a herringbone or sidestep; if you have climbing skins, put them on at the beaver pond. After 40 minutes, the crossover trail from John Pond appears on the left; a sign says Puffer Pond is 0.8 mile away.

You reach the height of land at 2,360 feet in 1 hour and 5 minutes, gaining 620 feet in altitude on a shoulder of Bullhead Mountain. The beauty of the open col is glorious. An icefall glistens on a stunning rock ledge; artist's fungi (*Ganoderma applanatum*) grow profusely on a dead maple nearby. There is a steep drop as you start down to the pond, but the woods are open enough to zigzag around the steep part. After that it is open but fast skiing to the lean-to that sits 20 feet above the Puffer Pond shoreline. Puffer Mountain dominates the landscape across the white expanse.

Start the loop over to Kings Flow by skiing right (west) down the pond. The balsam fir along the shoreline are dead, and when you reach the outlet of Puffer Pond you will see why: a substantial beaver dam has raised the water level a foot or so, killing the balsam. As you reach the end of the pond, cut to the right around some tangled blowdowns, but keep going in an easterly direction. The outlet brook will be on your left, and you will soon reach a cleared woods road. Puffer Pond Brook drops into a deep, impressive chasm, and the old tote road starts downhill—it is steep enough to keep you occupied. The trail is fast but skiable if there is lots of snow; if it is icy you may want to walk down some of the steepest drops. Forty-five minutes after leaving the lean-to you will see a couple of ribbons marking where the path forks. The left fork follows the brook down; the right follows a contour around the slope that is less steep. Either way there is a significant drop to the loop trail around Kings Flow.

When you reach the loop trail go right (north) on the old road with Kings Flow on your left. It is possible to ski down the ice, but the wind blowing down the flow may make it more pleasant in the woods. It takes ½ hour from here back to your car. The road crosses the wilderness line about 10 minutes from the cabins. The trail takes you into the meadow, down across a bridge, and then up to your car, respecting the privacy of the cabins. The entire trip is either up- or downhill, except for the last stretch along the flow. It should be skied with a lot of snow because ice and crusty conditions make it very difficult.

44. Round Pond

▪

6.0 miles round-trip
Skiing time: 3 hours
Beginner
USGS Thirteenth Lake and Indian Lake
15' or 7.5' x 15' metric
Map—page 169

There are various crisscrossing trails to and around the Round Pond area. The route described here is the easiest way to reach this large, icy expanse; it follows the old Kunjamuk stagecoach route from Indian Lake to Speculator. The other way begins at Kings Flow, described in Trip 45 as the first part of the Kings Flow Loop.

▪

Sunset on John Pond: Trip 42

Drive south on Big Brook Road, as described in Trips 42 and 43. Two miles after the turn to Wilderness Lodge, 6.1 miles from Indian Lake, there is an unplowed bridge (and car barrier) to the right, over a brook. There is a place to park several cars in a plowed area beside Big Brook Road. Ski across the bridge and turn left (south) in about 300 yards, following a lightly traveled snowmobile route. After skiing for 10 minutes you will see evidence of recent logging by the International Paper Company.

The trail bears southeast and is easy to follow. In 20 minutes go left, avoiding the right fork up a hillside. After skiing south for 45 minutes (1.3 miles), bear left at a T; soon afterward the route veers right (southwest). At this right turn a trail cuts off to the left and joins the trail from Kings Flow to Round Pond (Trip 45). You turn right and continue on the old Kunjamuk Road, following snowmobile tracks. The logging area ends as you ski into the Siamese Ponds Wilderness Area. The forest changes to open hardwoods. In a little over 1 hour of fast skiing on the wide, level road you will see Round Pond on the left. You can ski out along the edge of the pond or stay on the road above it. This point on the trail can also be reached from Kings Flow by skiing to the outlet of the pond (Trip 45), then right (northwest) on the ice along the edge of the pond.

The old road follows southwest along, and slightly above, the lake. There are enticing views of the snow-covered pond and distant mountains through the white birch border. Round Pond is entirely on public land, but the land to the right (northwest) side of the road is a private timber area. When you get to the southern end of the pond go out for a magnificent view of Chimney Mountain to the left, large Bullhead Mountain straight ahead, and steep Puffer Mountain to the right. There are at least five beaver lodges on this end of the pond that are interesting to study. Look right for the nearly perfect cone of Kunjamuk Mountain to the west.

You can follow the road south from Round Pond toward the Kunjamuk River. In about 2 miles from Round Pond, the hut-to-hut tour people ski an old trail to the right that comes in at the north end of Long Pond. Straight ahead, old Kunjamuk Road will take you over Pete's Hill and eventually to the snowmobile trails that come up from

Speculator. The best way to explore this area for the first time is to sign up for the Adirondack Hut to Hut Tour described in the North River chapter. You will become familiar with several additional routes, as well as the area south of Long Pond.

By the time you explore the southern end of Round Pond, you will have been out for at least 1¾ hours; by the time you get back to your car, it will be a little over 3 hours. There is no easier or more enjoyable way for a beginning skier to enjoy the beauty at the edge of the wilderness.

45. Kings Flow Loop

■

5.5 miles round-trip
Skiing time: 3 hours and 30 minutes
Intermediate
USGS Thirteenth Lake 15' or 7.5' x 15' metric
Map—page 169

This circuit of Kings Flow requires that the lake be safely frozen and that there is enough snow and ice to cross Wakely and Humphrey brooks. There is a 200-foot climb up a steep hill, followed by a gradual drop of 300 feet down a narrow, partially cleared path; it requires the ability to make tight turns and to stop quickly. An alternative beginning to this trip originates on the Kunjamuk Road described in Trip 44; it is over a mile farther but avoids an ice crossing of Kings flow. For it, you need to leave a shuttle car at the fow, or walk back down Big Brook Road for 1.6 miles to your car.

Both loops begin at the parking area described in Trip 43. The trip begins by facing south toward Humphrey Mountain, skiing down across the meadow toward Kings Flow, then right to its narrow neck. Ski south along the shore for 50 yards until you come to a large rock, then cut across the ice to an opening in a conifer-covered point. Look carefully for the path into the woods that starts here.

■

Kings Flow and Humphrey Mountain vistas: Trip 45

The narrow ski trail rises gradually through hardwoods, climbing steadily after leaving the flow. It is marked by two-inch, unlabeled disks nailed to trees. You bear west, climbing, for 15 minutes until a trail comes in from the right. (The right trail comes from the Kunjamuk Road, if you start as in Trip 44; the crossover is unmarked and very hard to follow unless there are ski tracks.)

After this junction the trail swings southwest and levels off. You will see small, round clumps of green crisped moss (*Ulota crispa*) and dense clumps of a liverwort (*Porella*) growing on dead trees. The outlet to Round Pond is reached in 40 minutes from Kings Flow, 1 hour and 20 minutes if you come via Kunjamuk Road from Big Brook Road. One hundred feet below the outlet of the pond there is a two-level log crossing that can be negotiated on foot, but with difficulty. The best way to cross is to go to the right, and then traverse the beaver dam at the outlet. If you are sure the ice is safe you can cross on it, but keep well away from the thin ice near the outlet. (From this point you can also ski to the right (northwest) on the ice along the shoreline and join the Kunjamuk Road mentioned in Trip 44.)

After you cross to the south side of the outlet there is a small clearing near the shore. The loop trail around Kings Flow heads south uphill from this opening. It is a steep, 200-foot climb to a saddle between two small peaks. There is no name on the topographic map, but the loggers called it Pancake Hill because they needed a large breakfast of pancakes to get up it each morning.

You reach the col after a 15-minute climb. The route south to Wakely Brook is an old trail that follows a logging road. It has been partially brushed out and well marked with three generations of disks. It is easy to ski as it drops gradually through a forest of large yellow birch and red spruce. (If the snow is not deep, watch out for the section with hobblebush.) The crossing of Wakely Brook is reached in 45 minutes (over 1 mile) after leaving Round Pond.

Wakely Brook is a pretty setting; swift water creates openings in the ice and otter tracks are usually seen. You can cross on skis downstream from a large log that spans the brook if there is enough snow and freezing weather (this is not a late spring trip).

The trail now swings left (southeast), climbs briefly, and then drops to cross a small stream. This stretch between Wakely and Humphrey brooks has a large grove of red spruce, some dead. There are blowdowns of small spruce, but the trail can be followed if you look carefully for the disks. After a level stretch there are two massive dead red spruce with bark strewn underneath—a sign of three-toed woodpeckers. The trail drops steeply, but you can bear right on the contour and zigzag back in a wide traverse through the fairly open woods. The wetland around Humphrey Brook, which you reach in 1½ hours from Round Pond, grows a sizable amount of beautiful black spruce and thick balsam fir. Although shallow, the brook gets the sun and the ice is thin. The best place to cross is 50 yards upstream in a shady stretch created by a dense, mixed conifer grove. After crossing ski downstream along the bank until you come to the trail, which angles uphill. At this point you are headed northeast, because Humphrey Brook is as far south as the loop goes. The trail is not easy to follow as it climbs, but there are some markers. Look for the dense-growing liverwort (*Bazzania trilobata*) and mountain fern moss (*Hylocomium splendens*) on the rotting maple logs. Two hours and fifteen minutes from Round Pond you reach the main trail along the east side of Kings Flow, marked by a huge hemlock. A tree to the west has a large hawk's nest at the top. Now you ski north. You cross Puffer Pond Brook; the ice appears thickest 25 yards upstream from the trail. On the far side a trail comes down from Puffer Pond. After the brook, you climb slightly along a sidehill, with some pleasant ups and downs. Another trail angles down from Puffer Pond. Gradually you descend to Kings Flow and continue north, on the level, to the cabin area, about 2.5 miles from Humphrey Brook. When you come to rocky Carroll Brook you are almost around the loop. The trail leaves the woods, crosses a meadow and then a small bridge; the cabins are visible ahead. If you include a stop for lunch, the entire loop takes 3 hours and 45 minutes from the cabins at Kings Flow. It is 40 minutes longer if you start at the parking area for Trip 44 and use the Kunjamuk Road.

■
Blue Mountain in the clouds: Trip 49

Blue Mountain Lake Area

Mountain Views

■

One of the most impressive landmarks in the Adirondacks is 3,759-foot Blue Mountain. It dominates the vistas from trails in both the Blue Mountain and Indian Lake regions and is instantly recognized by the white slashes on its sides, created by snow-covered rock ledges. Two trips in this chapter describe trails around or up Blue Mountain. Intermediate skiers will enjoy Trip 50, which circles the mountain in a long roundabout past Tirrell Pond; competent skiers can also ski into the pond from the other end as a round-trip. Only advanced and intermediate skiers will want to tackle Trip 49, a challenging route up the mountain on the access road.

Another major skiing feature of this area is the Northville–Placid Trail as it traverses part of the Blue Ridge Wilderness. A popular summer hiking route, this section of the trail is equally enjoyable in winter. Trip 46 starts at Lake Durant and introduces the competent beginner skier to this wilderness on a 5-mile round-trip. Trip 47 for intermediate skiers starts at Cedar River Flow and ends up at Lake Durant, passing picturesque Stephens Pond on the way. Cascade Pond is reached by Trip 48 on a spur route toward the village of Blue Mountain Lake.

Each pond has a lean-to (Tirrell has two), and they are accessible enough for an overnight ski trip. March is a good month to try overnight camping because the nights and days are warmer than in midwinter. The mournful howl of coyotes or the eerie hoot of a barred owl will often disturb the stillness of your secluded camp. If you have a warm sleeping bag and a good pad, winter camping can be a memorable experience.

Another trip, not described in detail in this book, goes west from the north shore of Blue Mountain Lake. The 8.6-mile round-trip starts at the end of Maple Lodge Road, goes past Castle Rock, and ends up at Upper Sargent Pond.

There are no groomed trails in the area, and snowmobiles are not permitted on these trips. Metric topographic maps for Blue Mountain Lake and Deerland cover the entire region.

46. Northville-Placid Trail from Lake Durant

■

5.0 miles round-trip
Skiing time: 3 hours and 10 minutes
Competent Beginner
USGS Blue Mountain 15' or
Blue Mountain Lake 7.5' x 15' metric
Map—page 183

This section of the Northville-Placid Trail in the Blue Ridge Wilderness is a favorite. The route follows a gentle gradient through large, beautiful hardwoods, and the glide out is pure delight. You can increase the distance by skiing to either (or both) of two ponds, Stephens and Cascade, where lean-tos provide a dry seat to eat lunch. (The routes to these two ponds are described in Trips 47 and 48.)

The trailhead is located 8.7 miles west of the center of the village of Indian Lake, on the south side of NY 28/30. There is a plowed parking area beside the road, and a DEC sign reads: Northville-Placid

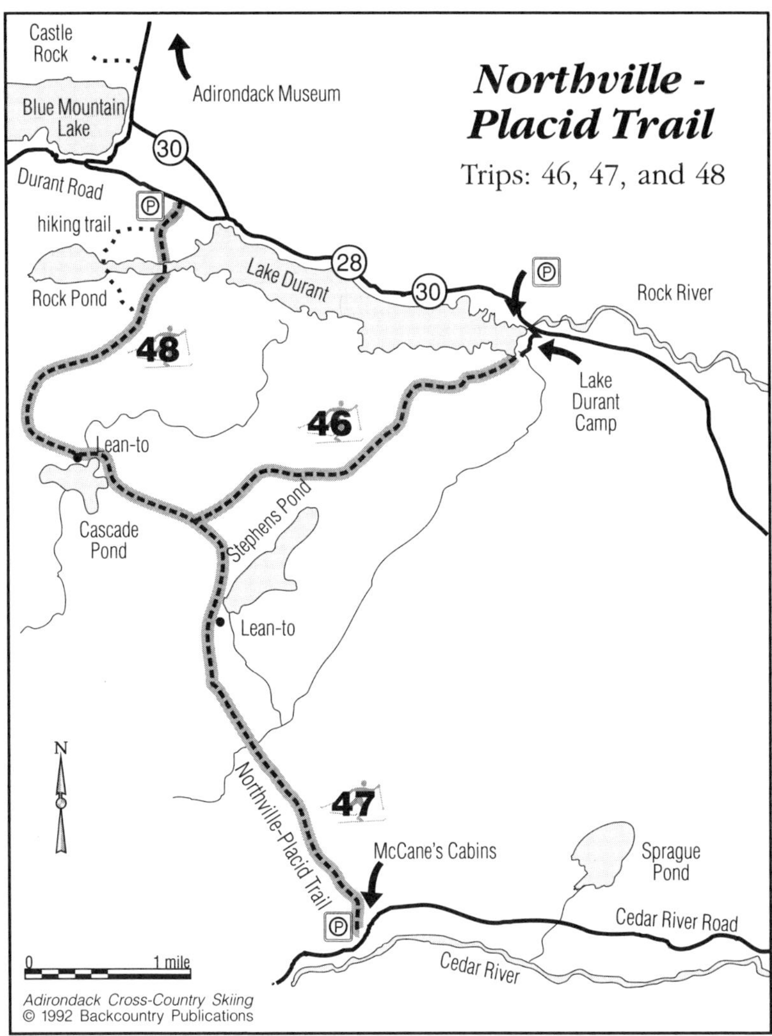

Trail, Blue Mountain-Cedar River Section; Stephens Pond Lean-to 3.1 miles, Cedar River Flow 13.25 miles. It is best to climb the high, crusty snowbank without skis on, as it is steep and icy.

Start the trip by skiing southwest through an open field, behind the forest ranger's house on your left. Cross a cement bridge—part of the main highway in 1950—that spans the outlet of Lake Durant on your right. The lake is the headwaters of the Rock River and is named for W. W. Durant, one of the leading entrepreneurs in this part of the Adirondacks in the 1890s. The lake was dammed to provide a head of water for release in the spring, so that logs could be floated down to the Hudson River—a practice that originated in the Adirondacks.

Harold Hochschild writes that this lake area was called 34 Marsh on the USGS Survey Map of 1900 but was known locally as 34 Flow. This was the lumbering domain of Jones Ordway, a hotel owner, farmer, and lumberman who lived in North River. According to Hochschild, Ordway "was known as one of the three best ox teamsters along the Upper Hudson." Ordway lumbered the hills and used 34 Flow as his "banking ground," the name used for the frozen surface of a headwater that was released after ice-out in the spring. Thirty-four Flow, two miles long, was held back by a log crib dam, now replaced by a cement one.

A head boom of logs was strung across the water above the dam to hold the logs back. At the time of the spring freshet, the dam's sluice gate was opened and water thundered into the bed of Rock River. When the water reached Rock Lake (Trip 40), the boom was released; the logs rushed down the flooded stream into Rock Lake. There another dam held them back and the process was repeated to the Cedar River. Log-driving days in Township 34 are described by Hochschild in his book, *Lumberjacks and Rivermen in the Central Adirondacks,* published by the Adirondack Museum in Blue Mountain Lake. Log driving ended in the Adirondacks in 1950, so today the level of Lake Durant is constant and provides all-season recreation. If the ice is thick enough, you will see the tip-ups of ice fishermen.

After skiing across the bridge you follow a wide road that swings around the shore of the lake to the right. Soon you pass between the cabins of a summer campground, with the swimming beach on your right. Continue past the camp buildings, down a small dip, and over another bridge. As you climb the small slope look right for a magnificent view of Blue Mountain with its snow-covered rock faces.

Ten minutes from the start there is a pine grove with picnic tables and fireplaces in individual camping spots. Look sharply for a small sign on a tree, with a blue disk marker, indicating the trail bears to the left. This is where the Northville-Placid Trail enters the Blue Ridge Wilderness. Another sign bans motor vehicles, so you do not have to worry about meeting snowmobiles. For the next 2 miles you ski west or southwest; in the early afternoon the sun will be warm and welcome. The trail is marked and easy to follow, with no blowdowns unless they are recent.

Initially the trail is a wide old tote road, and you glide easily along. After ½ hour there is a steep section in the old logging road that ends in a dry stream crossing; it can be rocky if there is little snow. Climbing out of that gully you top a small rise and glide on through young hardwoods.

After skiing for one hour, the route becomes steeper; water has eroded the tote road, creating a steep, rocky, uneven gouge. This is the trickiest section of the trail. Look it over carefully, and figure out how to ski it on the way back. After this you move easily through a magnificent old-growth forest of beech and yellow birch. When the wind hits these tall ancients, the trunks squeak and groan as if they are going to fall. Some trees have died of old age, yet they still stand as host to beetles and ants and an eruption of interesting fungi. Various lichens, mosses, and liverworts thrive. If you are interested in nonflowering plants, bring an identification book along. You can easily spot *Neckera pennata, Frullania selwyniana,* and *Porella platyphylla;* more types are found with a little searching.

One hour and fifty minutes of skiing brings you to a T in the trail. You have climbed 350 feet, and a DEC sign indicates you have come 2.5 miles from the Lake Durant campground. Stephens Pond lean-to is 0.6 mile to the left (southeast) along the blue-marked Northville-Placid Trail. Cascade Pond lean-to is 1 mile on the red-marked trail to the right (north). You can ski to either or both of the ponds before skiing back to your car. If you turn around at the T, you have a wonderful 1 hour and 20 minutes of skiing pleasure before putting your skis on the rack.

47. Stephens Pond and Lake Durant from Cedar River Road

■

5.2 miles one way
Skiing time: 2 hours and 30 minutes
Intermediate
USGS Blue Mountain 15' or
Blue Mountain Lake 7.5' x 15' metric
Map—page 183

This trip takes you from Cedar River Road, past Stephens Pond, over to a T, and down to Lake Durant. You can ski in the other direction, of course, but the gradients seem more congenial from south to north. The route is part of the Northville-Placid Trail and so is kept clear, although trees sometimes fall during a winter windstorm. The through trip requires two cars, but a round-trip (4.4. miles) to Stephens Pond from McCane's Cabins is very pleasant, if you have only one car.

To ski the one-way trip, leave a car beside NY 28/30 in the parking area near Lake Durant described in Trip 46. Drive east on NY 28/30 toward Indian Lake for almost 6 miles; turn right on Cedar River Road for a pretty drive along the river. In 5.6 miles from NY 28/30 you come to McCane's Cabins on your right. In front of the house there is a DEC signpost indicating directions and distances to various places along the Northville-Placid Trail. One arrow points up the driveway between the house and a shop. The McCanes have given permission for the trail to cross their property to reach state land to the north. Park beside the road without blocking any driveway.

Ski between the house and the shop, passing a full woodshed that will bring a gleam to any wood burner's eye. The trail enters woods within 100 feet and climbs gradually through a private woodlot. It is clear and easy to follow. After skiing 15 minutes, a tree in the middle of a fork has two handmade signs; the one marking the right fork reads Mountain, and that is the one to follow. There are a few metal-disk trail markers that you should look for regularly. Farther on there is an unmarked fork with a woods road angling to the right; keep straight ahead and look for the markers.

In 20 minutes you will see yellow blazes on trees marking the beginning of the Blue Ridge Wilderness Area. The trail generally climbs and occasionally levels off. There is a short rise to a knoll where you will see large trees with deeply furrowed bark and straight limbless trunks. They are big tooth aspen, a member of the poplar family. During two short, steep drops you must be prepared to stop quickly in case of blowdowns across the trail; these narrow, blind drops account for the intermediate rating for this trip. One of these drops brings you down into a beaver meadow with a small stream that is crossed on several planks.

After the marsh the trail continues through hardwoods, with some rise and fall, until you come to a small stream. With a thin snow cover you might have to detour to cross without getting your skis wet. In a little more than one hour you will see the ice-covered pond to your right. Go on for 150 feet to where another streambed is crossed, then look for a small path to the right. It will lead you to the lean-to with a commanding view of the pond; it's a great place to have lunch. It takes a little over one hour to ski the 2.2 miles and gain a vertical rise of 98 feet.

Continuing on the trail, you ski almost due north with a vertical rise of 100 feet, and then bear northeast for another struggle of 100 feet. This strenuous 0.5-mile climb brings you to the T in the trail. Ahead lies Cascade Pond, described in the next trip. Go right for Lake Durant; it is 2.5 miles downhill from here, with a vertical drop of 362 feet. From the T it will take about 1 hour and 20 minutes to reach your shuttle car beside NY 28/30. The entire trip from the Cedar River Road to Lake Durant should take about 2½ hours.

48. Cascade Pond Spur

▪

2.0 miles round-trip from T
Skiing time: 55 minutes
3.8 miles one way from T to Durant Road
Skiing time: 1 hour and 30 minutes
Competent Beginner (round-trip); Intermediate (one way)
USGS Blue Mountain 15' or
Blue Mountain Lake 7.5' x 15' metric
Map—page 183

From the 2,160-foot -altitude at the T, described in Trips 46 and 47, you can go west-northwest for a pleasant, fairly easy side trip to scenic Cascade Pond. Plan to lunch at the lean-to there. Skiing back to the T adds 2.0 miles to Trip 46. Alternatively, you can leave a second car on Durant Road in the town of Blue Mountain Lake, and continue down the very steep trail from Cascade Pond to the western end of Lake Durant and Durant Road. (If you have only one car, you can make a loop by skiing back along the Lake Durant shoreline to your car parked at the eastern end of Lake Durant on NY 28/30.) This route from Cascade Pond to Durant Road is a bit of a challenge; it requires a good snow cover and safe ice.

Drive west just over 2 miles from the parking spot for Trip 46 and turn left on Durant Road. In 0.2 mile there is a trail sign on the left for Rock Pond 0.75 mile and Cascade Lean-to 2.8 miles, and a place to leave a shuttle car. Drive the second car back and start on Trip 46. Ski 2.5 miles up to the T and turn right onto the red-disked trail.

The 1-mile trail from the T to Cascade Pond is wide and easy to handle, at least most of the way. Go northwest through an open, hardwood forest. In 15 minutes you will see the pond down to the left, but you continue parallel to it for 10 minutes more. Before you reach the pond there is a short, sharp drop, with a tight left turn at the bottom, so ski it carefully. A few feet farther, you face the problem of crossing the outlet brook from Cascade Pond. Do not ski out onto the pond as the ice is thin at the outlet. It is best to take off your skis and cross the small brook on the jumble of logs and rocks. The lean-to at the outlet is on a beautiful point. Behind it, look south across the pond for an awe-inspiring view of the Blue Ridge, for which this wilderness is named.

The red-disked trail continues west on the level for 10 minutes, then turns abruptly northeast. It climbs gradually for another 10 minutes to a height of land in a conifer grove. The descent along the wide trail is delightful until it is broken by a steep 150-foot drop to the left. In deep snow you might traverse this, but if there is too much brush, sidestep down. Another long run takes you down the brook valley going northeast. When the trail crosses the brook, leave it and continue down the valley through the trailless open woods. (The marked trail goes over a ridge with rocks and blowdowns, so don't try it on skis.) Lake Durant is narrow at this western end; go straight across it then ski right along the shore until you come to a large open area. A road leads out of this opening and will take you to your shuttle car. If you are without a second car, you can ski east along the shoreline of Lake Durant for 2 miles and complete a loop.

49. Blue Mountain Access Road

▪

6.0 miles round-trip
Skiing time: 3 hours plus
Advanced
USGS Blue Mountain 15' or Deerland 7.5' x 15' metric
Map—page 190

Telemarks and tailspins! This is the most difficult trip in the book. If you go all the way to the 3,759-foot mountaintop, the upper part of the trail is icy, windblown, and steep; it is only for advanced skiers, unless you are prepared to walk. Skins are a necessity for the climb,

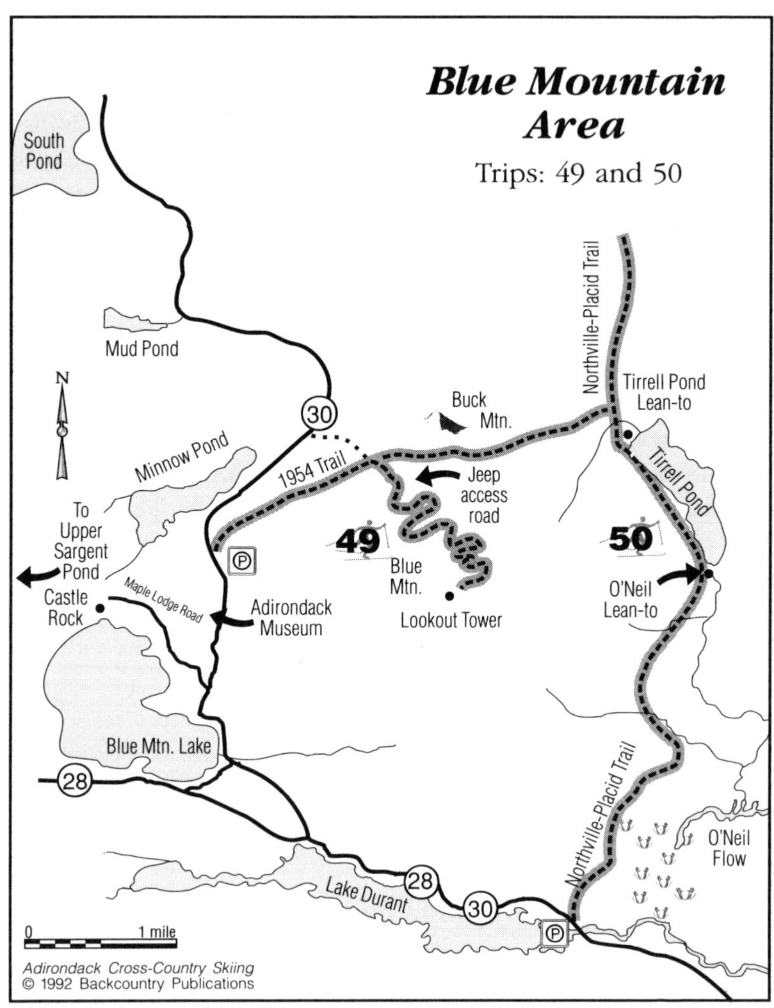

and some people leave them on to ski down the upper sections. The route is long and hard, but the views are stupendous and the sweeping panorama at the top is breathtaking.

The trip starts at the parking area for the hike up Blue Mountain, 1.4 miles west of the village on NY 30. At the crest of the hill, after driving past the Adirondack Museum, there is a large parking area and trail signs on the right. Do not take the steep hiking trail up the mountain. The trail you want has red markers and reads: Tirrell Pond Lean-to 3.2 miles, Lake Durant Campsite 7.9 miles. The first section of this ski route follows a contour northeasterly, with a 100-foot gain in elevation in 1.6 miles. At that point you reach the jeep access road up the mountain. The beginning of the access road is on NY 30, 1.45 miles west of where you parked, but there is limited place to leave a car.

This lead-in trail is delightful. It is clear, and with the exception of recent blowdowns, a joy for a beginner. Minnow Pond can be seen down to the left through the second-growth hardwoods; the area is private and has been logged, so all of the trees are relatively small. No sign of the logging remains, however, and the forest on a sunny day is beautiful. Going slowly, you will reach the intersection with the access road in about 45 minutes. Turn right. You have gained altitude gradually and are at 2,300 feet. The trail you were on, which shows on the USGS Blue Mountain Quadrangle (1954), continues on the other side of the access road to Tirrell Pond (Trip 50).

The access road, which does not appear on the 1954 topographic map but is on the new metric map, was constructed to erect a radar station on the mountain. The radar unit has been dismantled and the road, which is public but crosses private land, is maintained to service the fire tower and the communications antennas on top. The access road electric pole at this intersection is number 20; you can gauge progress as you climb, as the top pole is 103.

The wide and brush-free road is not steep initially but climbs constantly, with switchbacks. The sun is glorious to bask in as you pause. Looking back, Minnow Pond shows to the left. Farther to the right is narrow Mud Pond, and in the distance is the amoeba-shaped surface of South Pond, dotted with several islands.

At the first switchback a logging road leads off to the right, and just beyond that a wide tote road goes left. The tote road shows on the old topographic map; it led to an isolated farm on a brook that flows into Tirrell Pond. You continue up the access road with more switchbacks. If you have waxed correctly, or have waxless skis, you can still negotiate this lower slope. Most people put on skins at about 2,600 to 2,700 feet, after about 30 minutes of climbing; depending on snow conditions, you may get higher before you need them. Two hours after leaving the car the trees and wires become covered with hoar frost. The vistas are sweeping; the photo opportunities numerous. In this area you may notice a flock of ravens playing on air currents, cawing raucously as they tumble in the blue sky. By now the road is zigzagging up the northeastern flank, and you are often in shadow. Ice-encased spruce and stunted birch glow in the light. Now the trail narrows and becomes steeper. Wind-packed, it is icy in spots; the sides disguise deep drifts. The switchbacks are numerous. At pole 93 there is a small microwave dish; at pole 99 another small communications building. Finally, after numerous tight turns, you emerge on the ice-encrusted summit. A fire tower (manned in the summer) and an antenna stand starkly white against the azure sky, covered with rime ice. The fire observer's cabin is to the side, out of the wind. From the foot of the tower the 360-degree panorama is breathtaking. The summit is the logical place for lunch and a hot drink, but if the wind is strong you will not tarry long.

Unless you are an advanced skier, with telemark skis and boots, it is a good idea to leave the skins on your skis when you start down. It is exceedingly steep, icy in the center trough, and deep on the sides. Skins provide an uneven, clumsy glide, but they slow you down. Take the skins off when the trail widens, just after a sharp S-turn at about pole 88. From here to pole 65 it is steep but wide enough for telemark and stem christie turns. Deep snow at the sides of the trail often hide small spruce trees, which can snag a ski. Sometimes the drifts collapse as you turn, leaving you sitting in a snow tub; you must struggle to climb out. When conditions are right, it is an absolutely fantastic trip for telemark skiers.

It is a fast trip down, even though you reclimb some of the S-turns to try them again. In 45 minutes you are at the intersection with the Tirrell Pond Trail. Turn left and, zipping right along, you can be back to the car in 20 more minutes.

This trip is difficult and can be dangerous, so ski to the top only with other advanced skiers. If you are an intermediate skier, go ahead and try the lower sections, even if you know you can't make it all the way. Go as far up as you feel comfortable. Turn back when you feel your legs tiring, because you must have the stamina to make turns on the way down. Intermediate skiers can handle the trip down from about pole 70 without too much difficulty. That alone is a memorable and exhilarating trip.

50. Tirrell Pond Roundabout

■

7.9 miles one way
Skiing time: 4 hours
Intermediate
USGS Blue Mountain 15' or Deerland & Blue Mountain Lake 7.5' x 15'
Map—page 190

The northern end of Tirrell Pond is one of the most beautiful settings you will see in trips described in this book. It is remote, so you must be prepared for wilderness emergencies. Surprisingly, it is not skied often, and you may have to break trail. Lean-tos at each end of the pond provide shelter for a midtrip lunch or overnight camping. This one-way trip, which requires two cars, can be skied from either direction. It can also be a round-trip to the pond from the south, using only one car.

To ski from the north, leave a car in the parking area on the north side of NY 28/30 across the road from the parking area for Trip 46 (near the eastern end of Lake Durant); it is less than 3.0 miles east of the intersection in the village of Blue Mountain Lake. There is a steep bank on this north side, with a trail sign at the top reached by a diagonal path. The sign reads: O'Neil Lean-to 3.3 miles, Tirrell Pond Lean-to 4.3 miles. Load all your skis and gear into the other car and drive west into the village, then turn right on NY 30.

Go to the top of the hill and begin on the same trail as Trip 49; the sign says: Tirrell Pond Lean-to 3.2 miles (although it is more like 3.5 miles.) You start at 2,200 feet and follow the red trail markers. This section of the trail is used by snowshoers and skiers climbing the access road, so a track will probably be broken. In 45 minutes you cross the wide access road, easily recognized by the electric poles, and follow the red markers, going east. You climb slightly and then glide along the level col between Buck Mountain on the left and a ridge of Blue Mountain on the right. Attractive ledges on the left mark the end of the col; the summit of Blue, with the high antenna, looms high above your right shoulder. One hour and ten minutes into the trip, the trail descends toward Tirrell Pond, dropping 400 feet down in about 1 mile. The track is wide and the drop even, however, so it does not seem as steep as anticipated. If you are pushing new snow it will not be too fast. The red-marked trail meets the blue-disked Northville-Placid Trail at the end of the long slope. A sign at the intersection, pointing back, says: Hiway Route 30, 3.3 miles. Your trail goes to the right; the sign reads: O'Neil Lean-to 1.0 mile, Lake Durant Campsite 4.65 miles.

The trail skirts the edge of a large swamp as you head southeast toward Tirrell Pond. In about 0.2 mile on the level you reach a large conifer grove with an almost-new lean-to sited back from the pond. It takes 1 hour and 50 minutes to reach this stunning place. Ski out onto the ice and look around this evergreen-rimmed gem. Large cliffs of Tirrell Mountain sweep downward toward the shore on the east; the cliffs of Blue Mountain guard the other side. The snow-covered pond nestles between the two crests in a majestic setting.

The trail to O'Neil Lean-to follows closely along the western shore. Occasionally it dips to the shoreline and you can ski out to relish other views. You will pass a rustic campsite near the shore. The going is easy, there are few blowdowns, yet it takes about 35 minutes to ski the length of this long pond. You reach the O'Neil Lean-to at the southern end of the pond 10 minutes shy of 3 hours from the start. The outlet of the pond is not usually frozen solid; if you want to go onto the ice you must ski back up the trail for 200 or 300 yards to where the ice is safe. This end of the pond is also attractive, in a more quiet, subdued manner.

Continuing on the loop, the trail goes south. You climb from the 1,918-foot level of the pond, gradually but continuously. In 15 minutes a brook crossing may require removal of your skis to keep them from getting wet. This section of the Northville-Placid Trail is scenic as it was lumbered some time ago. Several lumber roads branch off, but the main trail is easy to follow. In a little over 30 minutes from the lean-to there is a height of land as you cross a major logging road. From here it is a good run down to O'Neil Flow, a 180-foot drop in less than 1 mile. As the trail skirts the flow, a huge boulder ledge appears on the right. You seldom see such huge rocks resting on top of each other, as though stacked by a giant stonemason. Twenty minutes later you are still skirting the large swamp; the trail actually crosses an arm of it so this is not a trip to take in late spring. You now climb over a knoll, have a short run, then climb another knoll. There are two long, fast runs with sharp turns, that are tricky if there isn't a lot of snow. On fast or thin snow this section requires intermediate ability.

About 4½ hours from the start, going slowly and stopping for lunch, you hear traffic. A large white pine marks the end of one of the loveliest trips described in this book. Skiing from north to south, you start at 2,200 feet and end up at 1,800 feet. This is deceptive, however, as there is still a lot of climbing. The trip could be skied from south to north, although at the north end there would be a 400-foot climb. Why not try it both ways? It's enjoyable enough for a repeat performance.

▪

Cliffs from Tirrell Pond

Speculator/Piseco Area

Lakes and Wilderness

■

An average of 150 inches of snow falls each year on this southwestern region of the Adirondack Park; sometimes the snow conditions are better than at higher elevations. The three towns of Speculator, Lake Pleasant, and Piseco are situated near several large lakes that attract many summer residents. Until recently most of the winter business came from snowmobilers, and you will see a number of them in town. Recently the community has made a successful attempt to develop trails for cross-country skiers.

Trip 52 starts in downtown Speculator and takes beginners on a long, pleasant cross-country loop near the Kunjamuk River. At Piseco, west of Speculator, another beginner's loop (Trip 51) starts at the airport (not used in winter) and tracks through a diverse forest. There are cross-country races on both loops on separate weekends in February. If you don't mind sharing a winding and pleasant trail with snowmobiles, Trip 53 takes you past Fawn Lake, through some handsome woods, and across several interesting vlys.

A gratifying experience for robust skiers is found in the nearby West Canada Lakes Wilderness Area. The West Canada Lakes and the Cedar Lakes are deep in the backcountry—far from the sights and sounds of civilization—and have a rich history. This was the territory of French Louie, a famous Adirondack character, who had a cabin on

West Lake for over 30 years. Louie Da Boy, as he called himself, hunted and fished and lived off the land. He trapped, made maple syrup, and traded the furs and syrup for supplies in Speculator. A fascinating account of the region and French Louie is found in Harvey Dunham's *Adirondack French Louie.* Trips 54 and 55 enable competent beginners to penetrate this wilderness to Pillsbury Lake and the Cedar Lakes on long day trips or for overnight camping at the lean-tos.

The Northville-Placid Trail crosses the area near the Piseco airport and also leads into this wilderness; the trailhead begins at the end of Haskell's Road on old NY 8 in Piseco. The route isn't described here but adventurous intermediate-to-advanced skiers can follow the old logging road 10 miles to Spruce Lake.

The trails (except for the wilderness area) are maintained by the town and there are no blowdowns. Ski conditions and trail maps can be obtained by writing: Office of Tourism, Speculator, NY 12164; telephone: 518-548-4521.

Lapland Lake

In a natural snow area to the south, near the beginning of the Northville-Placid Trail, an Olympic skier, Olavi Hirvonen, personally grooms a 35-kilometer cross-country trail system. The set tracks and skating lane will please skiers of all levels. An adjacent 10-kilometer ungroomed loop penetrates the wilderness area to Grant Lake. Write to Lapland Lake RD 2, Box 2053, Northville, NY 12134-9606; telephone: 518-863-4974.

51. Piseco Airport Nordic Ski Loop

■

6.0-mile loop
Skiing time: 2 hours and 15 minutes
Beginner
USGS Piseco Lake 15'
Map—page 201

A delightful loop through former Forest Preserve land begins and ends at the Piseco Airport. The trail is practically level, but there are enough variations in grade, and in the ecology of the woods, to make it interesting and charming. The trail was cut and kept open by Wilsey Waggoner, a forest ranger in the area for many years, and other volunteers.

You reach the loop by driving southwest on NY 8 from the crossroads in Speculator for 8.9 miles. Turn right (north) at the sign for Piseco Airport, drive 1.95 miles, then go right again. There are DEC snowmobile signs at this last turn, as well as at the airport, but no snowmobiles are allowed on the Nordic Loop. A small sign at the airport, which is not used for planes in the winter, tells you where to park.

The skiing begins by striding northeast along the side of the snowmobile-tracked runway, with trees on your right. After 0.5 mile, almost at the end of the runway opening, a small sign indicates the loop trail to your right. As you enter the woods there is a place to register and a sign reading: Piseco X-C Ski Trail 8 km to point of beginning, trail returns to airport. Sign the register, as it gives an indication of the amount of use and helps to justify maintenance and upkeep.

You glide away through a mature, deciduous forest on a path that winds through the open woods. About 25 minutes after leaving your car you will reach a huge hemlock tree that has been shattered by lightning, stark evidence of the brute force of a bolt from the sky. Shortly after the hemlock is a huge, dead yellow birch, greatly deformed by some mysterious fungus or insect that has created large burls at its base. Off the trail to the right you will notice the large, common artist's fungus (*Ganoderma applanatum*); other, smaller pore fungi are seen on decaying logs.

In just under one hour you reach the 2-kilometer point, marked by a small sign. You leave the hardwoods and enter a red spruce and hemlock thicket, a lower, wetland area where the forest ecology changes perceptibly. Here the grayish green tree lungwort (*Lobaria pulmonaria*) can be found and large clumps of crustose lichens cling to rocks and trees. The skiing is easy, and this helps form a more intimate bond with the forest than if you were careening downhill.

In 1 hour and 15 minutes you cross a bridge over a stream, just before the 4-kilometer mark. Ruby-crowned kinglets winter in these tall hemlocks, so pause and listen for their delicate call from the very tops of the trees. They are small, but you may get a brief glimpse of them as they flit between branches. On the right side of the trail you can find a log to sit on to enjoy lunch. In just under two hours you reach the 6-kilometer point.

Twenty minutes later, there is a sign pointing north (right) to the Northville-Placid Trail, 0.5 mile away; another sign points south to the airport, 0.25 mile away. In 2½ hours you reach the opposite side of the runway from where you started. Ski across it, then to the right, and in five minutes you are at your car.

This is a wonderful trail for beginners and families, although small children and people who have not exercised may find the entire loop somewhat long. The young and muscular can ski the 10-kilometer race the first weekend of February.

52. Kunjamuk Loop Trail

▪

5.0-mile loop
Skiing time: 2 hours and 30 minutes
Beginner
USGS Indian Lake & Lake Pleasant 15'
Map—page 203

The village of Speculator maintains an easy and attractive cross-country loop that starts and ends in the village behind the firehouse. On weekends it can be a little noisy, because snowmobiles run near some sections of the trail, but they are not on your track, and it is still an enjoyable trip.

The start is about 300 yards south of the four corners in Speculator on NY 30 and NY 8. There is a yellow firehouse, a skating pavilion, and a large parking lot on the left (east). Drive in past the firehouse, where there is an information desk and rest rooms. A big sign at the far end of the parking lot marks the start of the trail. Snowproof pockets on the sign contain a sign-in sheet and a map of the trail.

The first 20 minutes crosses a frozen marsh in the wide floodplain of the Sacandaga River. You glide past smooth alder (*Alnus serrulata*), dried brown leatherleaf (*Chamaedaphne calyculata*), and sheep laurel (*Kalmia angustifolia*). The frozen river is to the right and, between it and you, an occasional snowmobiler bounces past. In a few minutes you ski under the power line, where there is a well-marked snowmobile crossing. Shortly after there is a spur to the left that goes north a few hundred yards to the tennis courts on Elm Lake Road. After more frozen marsh, the trail enters the typical balsam fir swath that surrounds marshy areas in the Adirondacks. Crush a few needles in your hand for a woods perfume with memories of Christmas. There is another snowmobile crossing here but little traffic. A sign at an intersection, just inside the evergreen woods, points left to the Upper Trail and right to the Lower Trail. Go left, as the right trail goes back to the marsh.

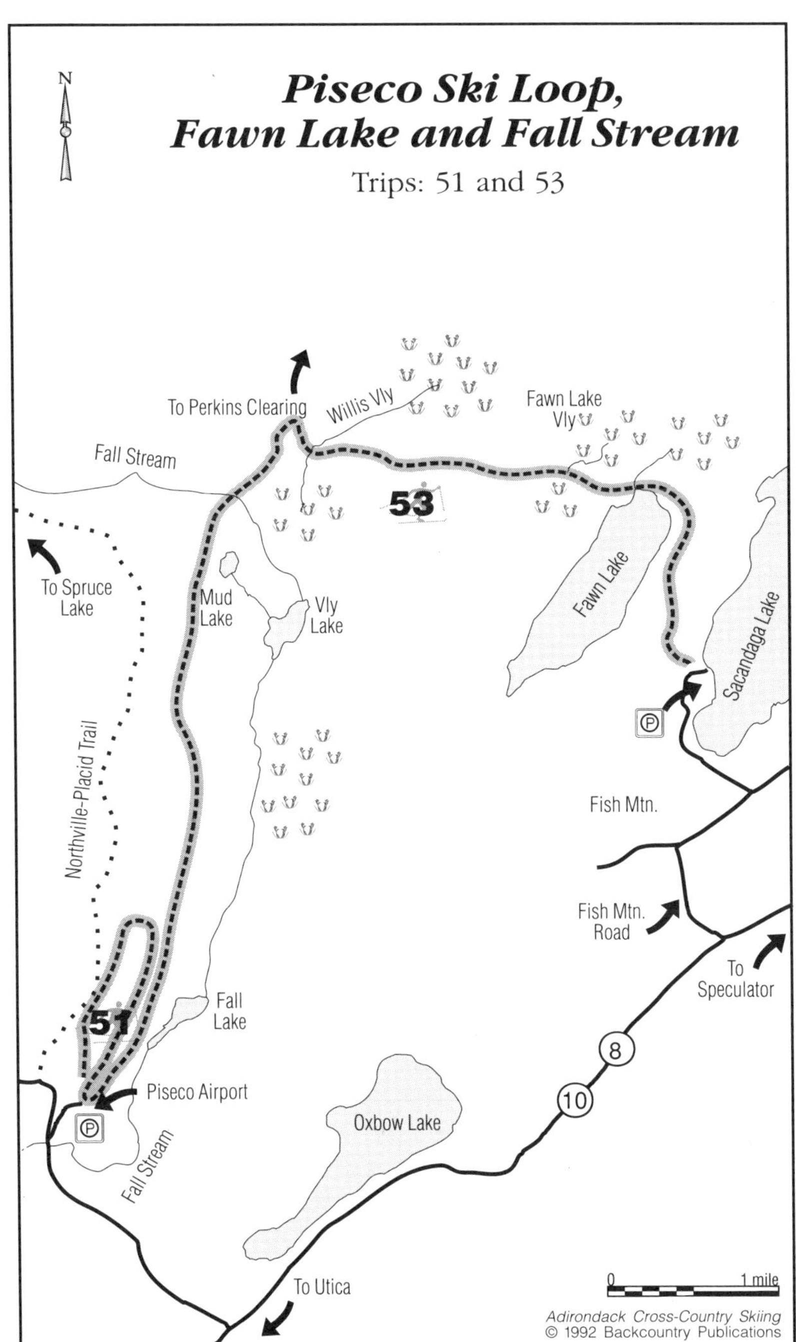
N
Piseco Ski Loop,
Fawn Lake and Fall Stream
Trips: 51 and 53
To Perkins Clearing
Willis Vly
Fawn Lake
Vly
Fall Stream
53
To Spruce
Lake
Mud
Lake
Vly
Lake
Fawn Lake
Sacandaga Lake
Northville-Placid Trail
Fish Mtn.
Fish Mtn.
Road
To
Speculator
Fall
Lake
51
Piseco Airport
Fall Stream
Oxbow Lake
8
10
To Utica
0
1 mile
Adirondack Cross-Country Skiing
© 1992 Backcountry Publications

The trail now starts up a slight grade through snow-covered, picturesque conifers. Soon it breaks out into handsome, second-growth hardwoods with a fairly dense balsam fir understory. It climbs gradually; a few short rises demand a herringbone step, but there is plenty of room on the six-foot-wide trail to spread the tips of your skis. After 40 minutes a cutoff to the right leads over to the Lower Trail and a loop back to the car. Real beginners—shufflers—could take this turn for a 2-mile round-trip.

Continuing, you climb a little less gradually and pass a second, more difficult, cutoff that has a small hill at the end. After this, on the Upper Trail, there is a nice run down to a right turn. You are near a major snowmobile trail that goes north to Elm Lake. As you swing right you pass a dense red pine plantation on the left. Beyond it look for an unmarked road to the left; you can ski down it and cross a gravel pit. On the far side a bank bars the way to the marshy floodplain of the Kunjamuk River, so swing around the level pit and back out to the trail. Continue south, parallel to but away from the river, and you will see another road to the left. This route reaches the Kunjamuk River in 200 yards. The footbridge has washed out, but you can ski across the frozen stream that is only 15 feet wide at this point. This dead-end trail leads up a slight rise to an opening and then continues left on an uphill angle. Fifteen minutes after leaving the loop trail you reach the Kunjamuk Cave, a small round opening in a vertical fractured wall. It appears shallow and could have been manmade in a search for gold or silver. Moisture, oozing from the cliff to the right, has frozen into thick multihued icicles that are worth skiing over to see. When you get back to the main trail, it will have been almost two hours since you left the car.

The Lower Trail, which you are now on, follows along the river. Some say you can ski down the Kunjamuk on the ice, but there are thin spots over fast water. The trail is pleasant and much safer. It is mostly level, with a few small hills for variety. You pass both cutoffs and are soon out on the marsh of the Sacandaga River again. After 15 minutes gliding in the open through shrubs and grasses, a large unusual rock and a lone white pine break the sweep of the frozen slough.

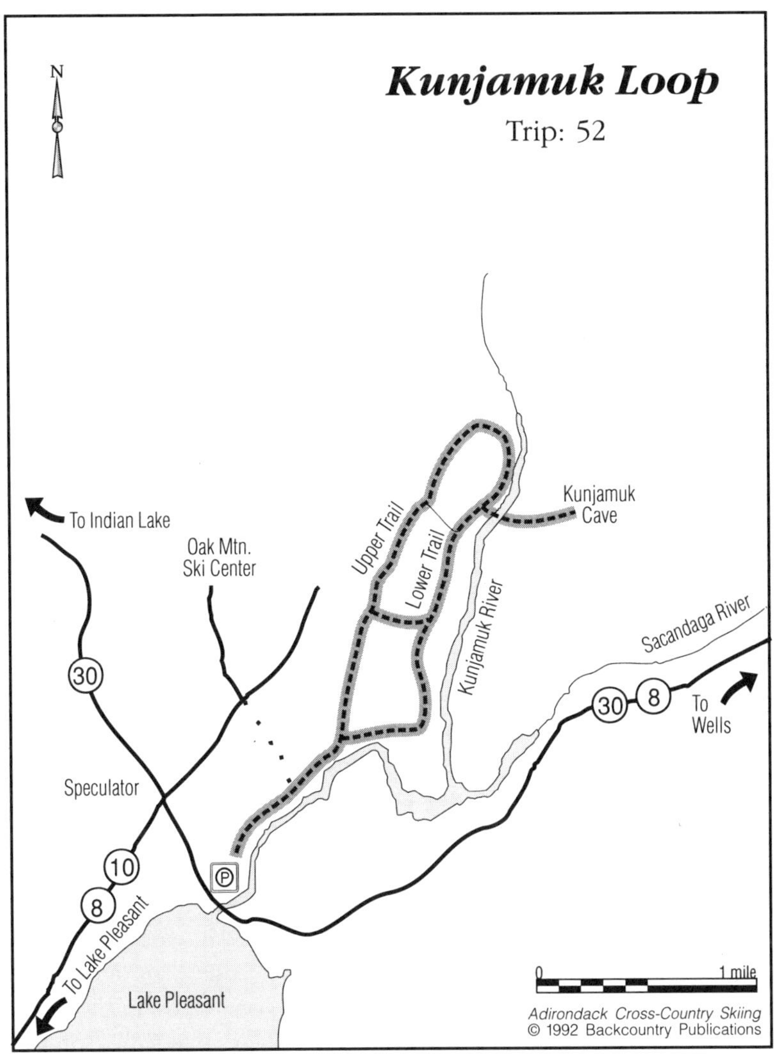

Now you duck back into the woods and meet the original trail. Turning left, every intersection is clearly marked, you reach your car in less than three hours for the round-trip.

53. Fawn Lake and Fall Stream Roundabout

■

9.4 miles one way
Skiing time: 3 hours and 15 minutes
Competent Beginner
USGS Piseco Lake, Indian Lake, & Lake Pleasant 15'
Map—page 201

If you absolutely refuse to ski on a trail where you might meet a snowmobile, skip this one. But if you can ski on weekdays or in early spring, you are not likely to meet more than one or two snow machines, if that; the beauty of these diverse woods is worth smelling the exhaust fumes once or twice. Start early, as it is a long trip that requires a shuttle car. An alternative is to use one car, ski part way in and turn back when you feel like it. The entire route is relatively level, although an absolute beginner will find several short steep drops hard to handle.

Leave a shuttle car at the Piseco Airport, following the directions in Trip 51. A large DEC sign at the airport turn gives mileage to Oxbow Inn 3.1 miles, Big Brook 9.2 miles, Sacandaga Lake 9.4 miles, and Speculator 11.6 miles. Turn right for a few hundred yards and leave a car in the plowed parking area. Drive your other car back to NY 8, head east for 4.1 miles, and turn left on Fish Mountain Road. Take this road for 0.7 mile, turn right for 0.6 mile then left (north) again. Keep going northerly, as the road winds and turns, until you see a DEC sign marking the beginning of the snowmobile trail. The sign indicates Fawn Lake Outlet is 1.0 mile, Valley Lake is 4.2 miles, and Piseco Airport is 9.8 miles (0.4 mile farther from this direction!). Park your car beside the road.

This trailhead is not far from the west shore of Sacandaga Lake, at an altitude of 1,825 feet. You will drop about 100 feet in the first mile to Fawn Lake; from there it is fairly level. In spite of the even terrain there are extensive moisture changes in the snow on this trip, so carry a good range of waxes or use waxless skis. The trip can be skied in late spring because snowmobiles have packed the snow, and it stays longer. An odd phenomenon develops with waxable skis, however. Petroleum residue from gas and oil is concentrated on the track and sticks to the wax on the skis, forming a gooey crud. If you are waxing, be sure to carry a scraper.

Ski north toward Fawn Lake. Within 50 feet there is a barrier that blocks all vehicles except snowmobiles. Very large white pines, interspersed with some birch and balsam, provide a thick, dark canopy. Local people feed the deer in these woods, so you will see many tracks and have a good chance of seeing these gentle, graceful animals. Within 100 yards the path forks; your route goes to the right along the marked snowmobile trail. If you are just out for a short time you can take the left fork, which is the shortest way to Fawn Lake.

Going right, you can fall into an easy stride-and-glide along the wide trail. New York State has owned this land for some time, and thus it has not been lumbered recently, so the white pines are large and beautiful. Within 20 minutes you move into a hemlock grove and you can see the lake through the trees to your left. In 25 minutes you are looking down the frozen sweep of ice from a popular fishermen's campsite; Fish Mountain is on the near horizon. Skirting the northern end of the lake you cross a bridge. Soon, with an open marsh on your left, another bridge crosses the outlet that flows northwest into Fawn Lake Vly. You would not be able to pass here without the bridges that were built for snowmobiles, so there are some advantages to the machines.

You climb again as you move away from the marsh and enter an open maple, birch, and ash forest. The height of land is about 1,800 feet, but the climb is gradual and you hardly notice it. After skiing 1 hour and 15 minutes you reach a bridge over a wide open stream called Willis Vly on your map. One-third of the way into the trip, the plank bridge makes a nice place for lunch because the sun often melts a dry place to sit. The vly is open; grass borders the stream, then alders and, near higher ground, tamarack and black spruce.

About 200 yards from Willis Vly you come to a snowmobile trail intersection. Go straight ahead; the right fork goes to Big Brook Trail and eventually to Perkins Clearing. Large erratics, covered with polypody ferns, border the route through this open, maturing forest. This section has a short but steep hill that takes a herringbone step to climb.

After skiing just under two hours, you reach a fast-moving stream flowing from the right. It is Fall Stream, with a sturdy bridge across it. You are skiing in a southwesterly direction, about 210 degrees magnetic, and will keep more or less on this tack, along an old wagon road, until you reach the airport. In a little way you will see an opening on your left; this is Mud Lake. It is a small pond and you can take a short detour and explore it if you have the time. In another 10 minutes you reach another small stream; it is iced over in midwinter but can be crossed on a small bridge in late spring. You have skied over two-thirds of the way at this point.

Continuing through maples interspersed with ridges of spruce, the road follows the contour just up from the Fall Stream valley on your left. Soon you reach an area that is repeatedly flooded by beavers. There is a bridge over the stream, but in late spring this area can be quite wet. Going on, you cross another bridge and then, about 0.8 mile from the airport, a marked snowmobile trail goes left (west) to Fall Lake and Oxbow Lake. You can ski it and make a loop back to the airport if the lakes are frozen. Proceeding on the wide woods road, you may see ski tracks cutting off to the right on informal paths; they go over to the nearby airport runway, although you can't see it through the trees. In just over three hours you will suddenly emerge from this beautiful forest. It is a surprise, after feeling so isolated, to see your car, buildings, and a plowed road.

54. Perkins Clearing to Pillsbury Lake

▪

14.6 miles round-trip
Skiing time: 5 hours plus
Competent Beginner
USGS Indian Lake & West Canada Lake 15'
Map—page 208

This is a long trip on a wide, old roadway. Snowmobiles use it sometimes, although they are not supposed to go beyond the wilderness line. There are two or three fairly fast hills so it is not for "shufflers," but competent beginners who can keep their balance on fast, straight hills can handle it. Early on in the trip some of the forest has been logged but as you climb, logging becomes less obvious and, as you near Pillsbury Lake, there is a dense, spruce-fir forest that is very attractive. It is possible to ski another two miles to Whitney Lake, but the trip is long enough as it is. Of course, you can go equipped to stay overnight in the Pillsbury Lake lean-to and have time to explore farther.

To reach the trailhead, drive south from Indian Lake on NY 30 for 15.9 miles. Turn right (southwest) on a plowed dirt road that is unmarked. Pass Mason Lake close on the left; 3.3 miles from NY 30 a DEC trail sign says: Miami River Lean-to 1.0 mile, Pillsbury Lake Lean-to 7.3 miles. This road to the right (west) to the Miami River is passable in the summer and is no longer restricted or gated as indicated on the topographic map. It is not plowed in the winter unless International Paper Company happens to be logging up that road. This area is called Perkins Clearing. Park your car at the signpost and start out on the wide, well-packed snowmobile tracks. The first mile crosses a flat, marshy area, with a nice view ahead of a portion of the Blue Ridge, probably a shoulder of Pillsbury Mountain. It takes 23 minutes to glide along the first mile to the sturdy bridge over the small Miami River.

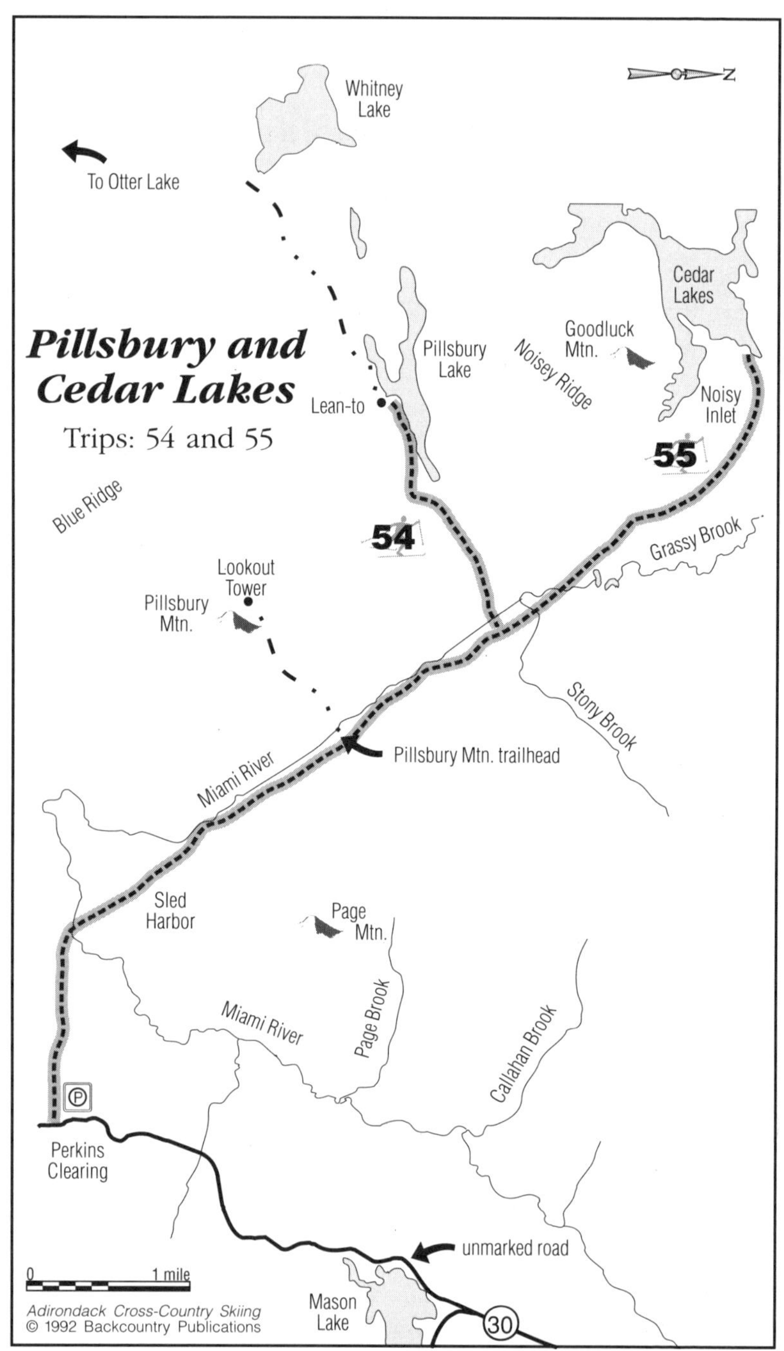
Whitney Lake
To Otter Lake
Cedar Lakes
Goodluck Mtn.
Noisey Ridge
Pillsbury Lake
Pillsbury and Cedar Lakes
Trips: 54 and 55
Lean-to
Noisy Inlet
55
Blue Ridge
54
Grassy Brook
Lookout Tower
Pillsbury Mtn.
Stony Brook
Pillsbury Mtn. trailhead
Miami River
Sled Harbor
Page Mtn.
Miami River
Page Brook
Callahan Brook
Perkins Clearing
unmarked road
0
1 mile
Mason Lake
30
Adirondack Cross-Country Skiing
© 1992 Backcountry Publications

You will not find a lean-to here. Until the mid-1980s the entire area bisected by this ski trip was a checkerboard of state land and the private holdings of the International Paper Company. A land swap was made; International Paper gained all the uncut public land east of Sled Harbor in exchange for their holdings in the rectangular area to the west of Sled Harbor. The Miami River lean-to was on public land and was removed because the company does not permit camping or fires.

After crossing the quiet stream, the road angles to the northeast and begins a gradual climb. In a few minutes the road forks, with an arrow and a red disk routing you left. Thirty-six minutes from the start there is a large, summer parking area; beyond that, a trail sign at a fork sends you right. The road narrows and winds around a small knoll as you climb more steeply. After the sweeping, uphill turn, a small opening marks Sled Harbor. The name comes from the days when loggers used horses instead of skidders. In the winter, loaded sleds were pulled out of the woods to staging areas. The bark and logs were then sent to nearby tanneries and sawmills. Standing here it is hard to picture this piece of history, as no traces remain. There are no sounds, but you can imagine the din of log-laden sleds pulled by huge work horses scraping into this staging yard, their breath steaming and harnesses creaking.

Beyond the opening a metal gate bars the roadway to vehicles. The West Canada Lakes Wilderness Area begins here. Signs on trees say: No Motorized Vehicles. This has not stopped all the snowmobiles, however, as a few tracks may go around the gate and up the road. You have climbed about 200 feet in the 54 minutes it has taken to ski in from Perkins Clearing. The road continues to climb. On the left side a sharp drop into a valley marks the upper reaches of the Miami River. The route is called the Old Military Road and, at one time, it went through to the Moose River Plains and beyond. Now it takes skiers and hikers into the heart of the backcountry made famous by French Louie and other historic backwoods stalwarts. One hour and twenty minutes from the car you reach the spur trail to Pillsbury Mountain, a high rocky mass on the left. There is a fire tower on the summit, but it is very hard to reach in winter; you must descend to the stream and then climb a slope, too steep for snowshoes. A sign says Pillsbury Lake Lean-to is 3.5 miles, Cedar Lakes 4.3 miles, and West Canada Lakes 9.7 miles from this junction.

The roadway steepens and becomes more interesting. Large erratics provide variety and beauty; scooped out of some faraway summit by a moving glacier, they were dropped here as the ice mass melted 10 thousand or so years ago. Pillsbury Mountain commands the view to the left. The route continues north-west, climbing, with the exception of one sharp, washed-out gully. You reach 2,550 feet before enjoying a short glide down to a major fork. It takes 1½ hours, counting a short stop for lunch, to reach here.

This stretch is a relatively flat, high plateau. The intersection sign shows the Pillsbury Lake Lean-to is 2.0 miles to the left and Cedar Lakes is 2.7 miles straight ahead. The sign points back to Miami River 3.7 miles and Perkins Clearing 6.25 miles (this last figure must be wrong; it is not unusual for DEC signs to be inaccurate). Note that if you add the distances from the car to Pillsbury Lake Lean-to you get 6.7 miles, instead of the 7.3 miles on the original sign.

Going left (west), there is a short grade down an easy hill. After a brief climb, there is a delightful, long downhill until you enter the spruce-fir flats surrounding Pillsbury Lake. The forest is dense and crowds the narrow but clear road, which keeps away from the shore. In the first open clearing, you come to where there used to be an impressive log building, but this has been removed. Next comes a large beaver meadow, a short rise, then a drop to another small beaver pond on the left. There is a stunning view of Pillsbury Mountain cliffs in profile. After another climb a track goes right down to the lean-to, which you reach in just over three hours skiing from the car. The lake is at 2,493 feet, about a 60-foot drop from the last fork. The lean-to is traditionally Adirondack, a three-sided log building on a small knoll, with a view of the long, narrow lake through the trees. The site is clean, the lean-to in good repair, and there is a privy. The red-disked trail goes on to Whitney Lake. It is about two miles one way, at least 1½ hours round-trip skiing fast, from Pillsbury Lake. It is easy to explore that far if you spend the night in the lean-to. The jeep trail that shows on the topographic map going south to Otter Lake has not been kept open.

The trip out is a lot faster than coming in, unless there is deep snow. There is a sharp drop just before you reach the fork to Cedar Lakes. As you head southeast from the fork, the first hill is very fast and long. In 1 hour and 23 minutes you are at the gate near Sled Harbor, leaving the wilderness. Two hours after leaving Pillsbury Lake, you are back to your car. That's a very fast time to ski 7.3 miles, so maybe the newer DEC signposts are correct, and it is only 6.7 miles one way. In any case, it is a long trip, and you shouldn't try to go the whole way unless all in your group are robust skiers. Of course new beginners can ski only as far as Sled Harbor or the Pillsbury Mountain trailhead and turn back, but that is not the most scenic or interesting part of the trip.

55. Spur to Cedar Lakes

▪

14.4 miles round-trip
Skiing time: 6 hours plus
Competent Beginner
USGS Indian Lake & West Canada Lakes 15'
Map—page 208

An alternative to the Pillsbury Lake destination is a somewhat longer one to Cedar Lakes. The first 4.7 miles of the trip is the same as for Trip 54. It takes about 2½ hours to reach the fork in the trail, where the sign reads: Cedar Lakes 2.7 miles.

The Cedar Lakes Trail is an old tote road. From the intersection it drops gradually until it crosses Stony Brook on a bridge. Coming out of the valley you glide into a small meadow area and then through a beautiful stand of snow-covered evergreens. In less than 1 mile you enter the upper marshy areas of Grassy Brook, which is crossed by another bridge.

After rising slightly you follow the contour around Noisey Ridge, a crescent-shaped land mass that separates you from the lakes to your west. The terrain is pleasant and easy skiing, with some mounds and short glides; it is easy to follow the trail. You drop gradually to the dam at the beginning of the Cedar River in about 1 hour and 15 minutes from the fork, 3 hours and 45 minutes from your car. On the other side of the bridge that crosses the outlet, you turn left (southwest) to the main lake. This is the site of the former Cedar Lake Headquarters of the Conservation Department. The buildings were demolished after the wilderness area was established. The telephone line to the cabin was mounted on stout creosote-coated poles that stood along the trail you have just skied. Black bears are attracted to creosote and every pole was a mass of splinters where bears had clawed them. Most of these poles were taken out, but if you see a splintered pole, that is the reason.

The lakes are attractive and, if you explore, there are nice views of Noisey Ridge and Pillsbury Mountain to the southeast. If you are not camping, however, not much time can be spent here. You should count on three hours or more from the dam to reach your car at Perkins Clearing.

Garnet Lake Area

Views of Crane and Blue

■

Rising south of Johnsburg, Crane Mountain is one of the most magnificent and impressive mountains in the southern Adirondacks. A mammoth upthrust of anorthosite rock, the mountain outcrops in abrupt cliffs and a distinctive summit. You will recognize Crane by its twin hummocks and its large mass. In the depression between the two peaks lies a large pond, frequented in the past by great blue herons. In the old days, locally, these birds were called cranes, and this is one version of how the mountain got its name. Until a few years ago there was a fire tower on its southern summit, but this has been removed. The paths to the top are too steep to ski, but the presence of the mountain adds to the enjoyment of ski touring for miles around.

Trip 56 follows the upper reaches of Putnam Brook, passes land known as the Putnam Farm, and skirts the side of the mountain. The rich history of the farm and the people connected with it has been recorded in poetry by Jeanne Robert Foster in a delightful book, *Adirondack Portraits*. The poems are beautifully illustrated with photographs by O. D. Putnam, who was born nearby.

To the west of Crane Mountain a stream meanders through a wide valley. Fed by Crane Pond and Garnet Lake, Mill Creek flows north, then east, to the Hudson River. Near Johnsburg and Wevertown there are steep drops which, in the late 1800s, provided water power for small industries: a sawmill, a gristmill, and small factories. A tannery came later. As you drive south from Johnsburg on the way to these trailheads, however, you will now find a rural area with only occasional houses near the frozen placid headwaters.

Trip 57 for intermediate skiers starts from Garnet Lake, which in the 1876 County Atlas of Warren, New York, is more appropriately called Mill Creek Pond. From the shore of the lake the cone of Mount Blue, a lower but majestic peak, rises to the southwest. The mountain scenery makes these outings a special treat on a clear, sunny day. A more strenuous Trip 59 goes east to Round Pond from the same parking area. The trailhead for easier Trip 58 to Mud Pond starts farther south on Garnet Lake Road.

To the north, separated from Crane Mountain by a deep valley, rises Huckleberry Mountain, equally impassable on skis. There is a skiable trail, reached from Hudson Street, up the Paintbed Brook valley between these two mountains. It leads to an outcrop of a special red soil. When mixed with oil (some say they also added buttermilk), the pigment was reddish but was called York Brown. It was used for house and barn paint in the 1870s.

There are no groomed trails in this area; some routes are occasionally packed by nearby resident snowmobilers.

56. Putnam Farm Road Beside Crane Mountain

▪

4.5 miles round-trip
Skiing time: 1 hour and 45 minutes
Intermediate
USGS North Creek 15'
Map—page 216

This wonderful excursion along the southwestern flank of Crane Mountain is an easy half-day trip on your skis. It can be a one-way trip, if you leave a shuttle car at the south end, but it is short enough, and so delightful, that it is described as a round-trip. Most of the way the route climbs gradually along the valley of Putnam Brook. It doesn't seem onerous, except for one or two steep pitches, but on the way in you actually rise from an altitude of 1,550 feet to almost 2,100 feet; imagine the thrill skiing out!

You reach the trailhead by driving west from Wevertown on NY 8 for 1.75 miles, then south from Johnsburg on the Garnet Lake Road. Turn left 4.8 miles after leaving NY 8 onto small Crane Mountain Road, just past a group of mailboxes. It is 1.55 miles north of the turn to Garnet Lake if you drive in from the south. Drive up the road (east) 0.75 mile until you come to the snowplow turnaround. Park off the road as far as possible, so as not to block the turnaround for the plow. Continue up the road on skis 0.1 mile, past a rustic cabin on the right. The trailhead is the seasonal road that angles right downhill into a dip just past the cabin.

The road winds around to the right and starts uphill. There is a pond on your left. During the gradual climb the source of the pond, Putnam Brook, appears on the left. The road rises between the brook and a steep ridge on the right, bordered by a deep, mixed forest. During the first mile you climb 150 feet up the valley to where the road crosses the brook. Now the road swings east, crosses the brook

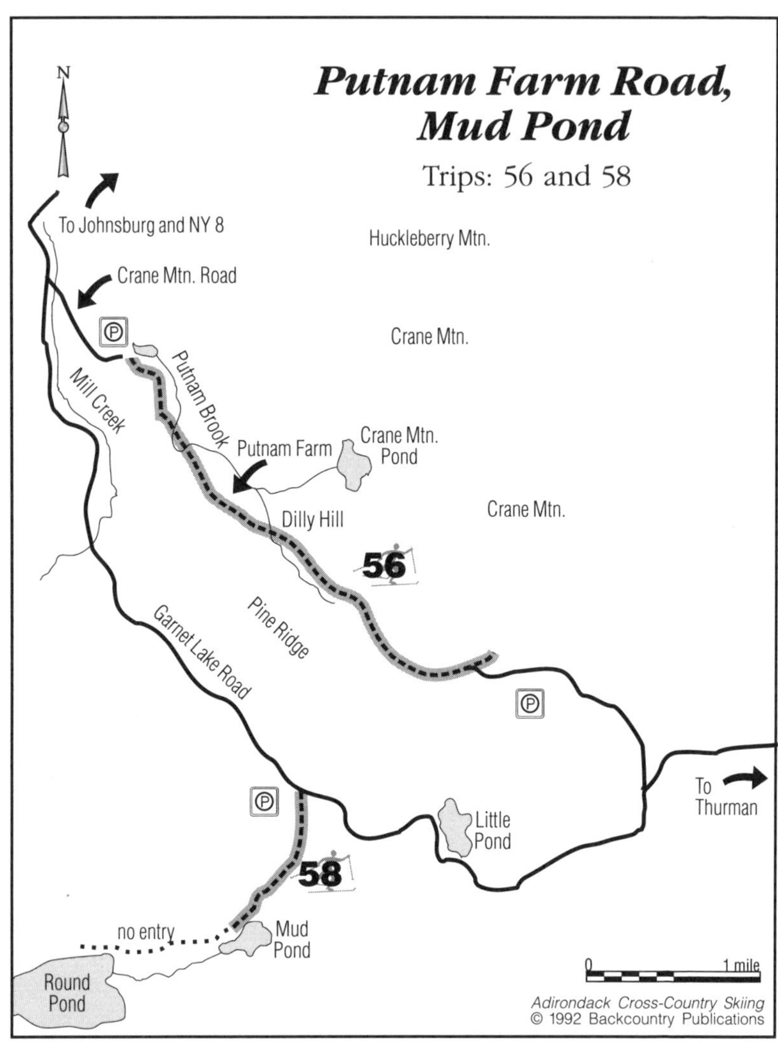

again, and you emerge into a large clearing. The barn of the Putnam farm stands alone, framed by the towering ledges of the west ridge of Crane. It takes 25 minutes to ski to this beautiful clearing.

The old road, which now becomes more of a trail, goes through the clearing to the southeast, bearing right up a hill. It is somewhat overgrown but recognizable when you are on it. There is a steep hill to climb, called Dilly Hill. Mark it well, because you will want to remember the corkscrew and the brook crossing as you careen down it on the way back; it's a dilly, alright. About 20 minutes from the Putnam farm the road traverses a level area through a magnificent beech grove. The rocky cliffs of Crane Mountain rise steeply on your left, seemingly impassable to even the animals of the forest. On your right lie the marshy beginnings of one source of Putnam Brook; the other feeder flows from Crane Mountain Pond high on the mountain.

After the long level section the trail bears right, slightly uphill, and then left, still climbing. About one hour after starting you are at the trailhead for the other hiking entrance to Crane Mountain. There is a register and a signpost that indicates that Putnam Farm Junction is back 1.0 mile (it is actually more like 1.75 miles). To the left, uphill, is a parking lot (unplowed) for summer climbers. Nearby, at the base of the mountain, is the fire warden's cabin. It has not been occupied since wardens began using airplanes to do the job of fire spotting. This area is reached by an unplowed road; ski down it to reach the plowed road that comes in from Thurman (and the parking area for your shuttle car).

The trip back is sporty. It is only 20 minutes until you are careening down Dilly Hill and 25 minutes to the Putnam farm clearing. In about 45 minutes, on a fast day, you are back at your car. Panoramic views of Crane Mountain are missing on this trip; in some ways, though, you sense it more intently, for you stride along its massive base.

57. Lizard Pond

▪

4.0 miles round-trip
Skiing time: 2 hours
Intermediate
USGS Thirteenth Lake 15' or
Bakers Mills 7.5' x 15' metric
Map—page 219

This trip begins by crossing Garnet Lake on skis, so don't attempt it unless there has been a lot of cold weather. One sure way of knowing if the ice is safe is to look for recent snowmobile tracks; if you don't see tracks, keep off the ice.

Garnet Lake is south of the village of North Creek, west of NY 28. One way to reach the lake is to start at the intersection of NY 28 and NY 8 in Wevertown. Go west on NY 8 for 1.75 miles and turn left (south) on Garnet Lake Road. Drive south 8.1 miles, and you will see a sign on the right to Garnet Lake. In 0.75 mile you will reach the small community along the shoreline; go left, along the eastern shore, in front of the houses and camps as far as you can drive. There is a small public place to park in a turnaround near the lake.

If there are recent snowmobile tracks or ice-fishing flags on the lake, ski left along the shoreline south-southwest, about 200 degrees magnetic. You will enjoy the view of cone-shaped Mount Blue, with open snow patches on rocky outcrops, ahead to the right. It is a majestic, trailless peak, and steep even for snowshoeing. In 20 minutes you will reach the narrowest part of the lake. Ski right, across the ice at the narrows (a heading of 250 degrees magnetic), to the valley at the foot of the slope of Mount Blue. You may be following snowmobile tracks because the trip to Lizard Pond is popular with local residents.

On the other side of the lake, look for an opening in the woods where pines and hemlocks shelter a summer camping area with a picnic table. Ski into the opening and bear right for a marked trail that runs up the small valley, still on the 250-degree heading. In about 150

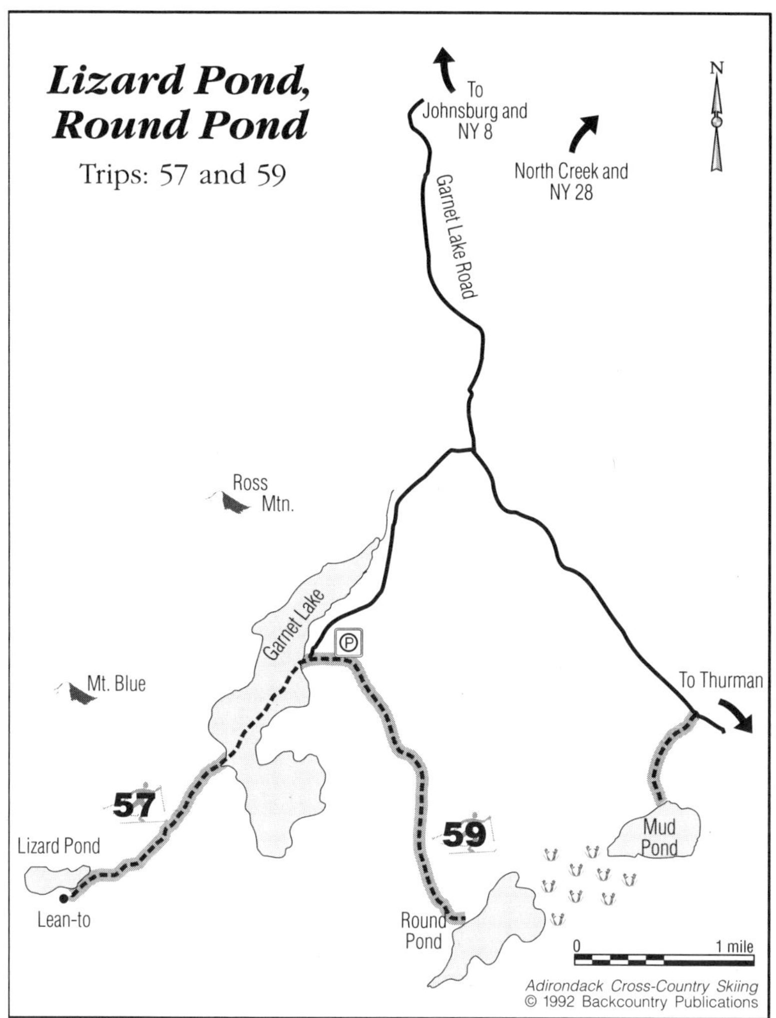

to 200 yards an unmarked path goes left, in a southerly direction, parallel to the lakeshore; this branch route ends shortly in blowdowns. Continue up the narrow, blazed trail in a slight draw, climbing steadily. At times you may wish to zigzag through the open hardwoods to make the going easier, particularly if there are narrow snowmobile tracks.

After a vertical rise of 200 feet, the trail levels off in the alder-choked eastern bay of Lizard Pond. Follow along the left (south) side to an opening that leads onto the ice. You can continue in the woods on the hiking trail or go out onto the frozen pond.

The 0.5-mile route down the center of the pond is best. It is flanked by evergreens, and there are islands to explore. You feel dominated and awed by towering Mount Blue. Looking back through the notch there are picturesque views of distant high peaks. Two-thirds of the way up the pond, on the left (south) shore, look for an Adirondack lean-to with a table and fireplace. Protected from the wind by a grove of red spruce, it is an ideal place for winter camping. There are many signs of deer and winter birds in this especially attractive basin.

The trip back is fast and tricky. The path is narrow and too steep to ski easily, especially if the snowmobile grooves make it hard to push the heels of your skis out in a snowplow. It is better to zigzag back and forth through the hardwoods, but you must be able to handle sharp drops and turns in deep snow. Backcountry skis are needed to maneuver easily. (If you are using wooden or inexpensive light touring skis, a spare tip in your pack is a necessity on this trip.)

Thirty minutes after leaving the lean-to you are down and across Garnet Lake. Twenty minutes more and you are back at your car. This is a nice trip following a heavy snow as it makes the return trip easier. Try it for an overnight winter camping experience in the rustic lean-to.

58. Mud Pond Jaunt

▪

2.0 miles
Skiing time: 1 hour and 15 minutes
Competent Beginner
USGS North Creek 15'
Map—page 216

If you want a short workout, and a chance to see an otter, this is an interesting trip on a fairly wide trail. The trailhead is on Garnet Lake Road. Follow directions from Wevertown in Trip 57 to the Garnet Lake turn. When you reach the right turn to Garnet Lake do not take it, but continue straight (south) for 1.85 miles from the turn. An old wooden sign on the right, at the opening of a side road, says: Mud Pond 0.8 mile, Round Pond 1.6 miles. Park beside the road.

Ski up the road, which has probably been packed by a snowmobile, through pretty, snow-covered woods; tracks of unseen snowshoe hares, red squirrels, red foxes, and coyotes dot the trail. After a 30-minute climb, during which you gain 250 feet in altitude, you arrive at an opening on the left large enough to park in the summer. Go left there, and find a small path that drops 60 feet to the pond. If you miss the turn the road continues downhill for 100 yards to a gate and Posted sign; this prevents you from skiing through to Round Pond without permission.

As you glide onto the ice at the pond you come to a large beaver lodge. It is active if there is an ice-rimmed air vent at the top; the moisture that rises from the beavers' bodies freezes as it meets the cold. Be cautious on the ice as there are thin spots caused by springs. It is best to ski right, up and over the luxurious growth of leatherleaf poking through the snow. The water level of Mud Pond is maintained by a low beaver dam that extends 100 feet along the southern shore. The pond drains through several leaks in the dam, and the ice at those places is thin, so ski on the dam or in the frozen marsh behind it. One thin spot, where water may be visible, is at the base of the first sizable tree along the dam. Otter keep this spot open as they dive and swim for fish, frogs, crayfish, and turtles. You may also see an otter hole in the ice 20 feet out from the shore. Look for otter slides—smooth, six-foot-long troughs with occasional paw prints in the snow; the otter pushes off and slides as it travels. Otters range many miles to fish, so they may be over in Round Pond or in the next valley, but you might try watching the holes quietly for several minutes. If otter are there they will come out onto the ice to eat their catch.

After you leave the pond and climb back to the road, it takes only eight minutes for a fast run back to your car.

59. Round Pond

▪

4.6 miles round-trip
Skiing time: 3 hours plus
Advanced & Snowshoeing
USGS Thirteenth Lake 15' or
Bakers Mills 7.5' x 15' metric
Map—page 219

If there is deep snow and skiing conditions are good, it is possible to reach this attractive pond. It is not easy going, however, and unless you are up for a strenuous workout, you may want to do it on snowshoes.

Follow the directions to Garnet Lake described for Lizard Pond (Trip 57), and leave the car at the same spot. The trailhead begins at the parking place, with a DEC sign indicating that Round Pond is 2.3 miles.

The first small climb from the car is steep and too narrow to herringbone; it is easy on snowshoes. You can walk it easily if snowmobiles have broken the trail, although it is unlikely since this is not a popular route. Once you have topped the first rise the trail swings around to the southeast and crosses a fairly level area. You traverse a young hardwood stand of maple and birch and, as you head farther south, attractive rock ledges appear on your left. After 10 or 15 minutes, you drop sharply into a gully running south. Trees crowd the runout; skiers have been known to walk down this short hill.

The trail climbs gradually along the gully through a pleasant deciduous and evergreen forest. You cross a small log bridge, angle around a hill going southeast, and work your way up a small ridge. It has taken 1½ hours to ski this far. Before you lies a sharp plunge, then a very steep climb to a saddle between two small hills. From this saddle the trail drops 200 feet to the pond. This stretch is for advanced skiers.

Assuming the pond is frozen, you can explore the circular shoreline. There is private land with a cabin on the west shore, and it is posted to cross-country skiers. This is too bad, because otherwise you could ski down the dirt road to Garnet Lake Road (see Trip 58). It is possible, if there is lots of snow and cold weather, to find a way through the alders and over the beaver dams between Round Pond and Mud Pond. The 0.5 mile is tortuous, and the connecting streams are rarely frozen, so it is not recommended.

The 4.6-mile round-trip into Round Pond on snowshoes makes a fine trip, although the woods block distant views. Before you try the Round Pond trip on skis, however, make sure there is plenty of snow and that it has been cold enough to freeze the pond. A good indication of the safety of the ice is whether snowmobiles have recently been out on Garnet Lake.

■

Winter friend

The Glen and Pharaoh Lake Areas

Places South and East

■

West of the Glen (south of Wevertown where NY 28 crosses the Hudson River) lies Dippikill Mountain and pine-rimmed Dippikill Pond. Much of the area is owned by the State University of New York in Albany and is frequented by students, especially on weekends. The university graciously allows the public to ski the trails, providing you check in at the office on the site. (They supply a map). Trip 60 will delight competent beginners and Trip 61 is a great schuss.

East of the Glen, at Friends Lake, a Nordic center has been developed by the owners of Friends Lake Inn. Further east, the other side of I-87, the Pharaoh Lake Wilderness Area lies north of NY 8 and the town of Brant Lake. A popular competent beginner's trail is described in Trip 62.

Friends Lake Inn Nordic Ski Center

A new 25 kilometer groomed trail system has tracks that range in difficulty from beginner to *Black Diamond;* lessons are available to improve your ability. You can either stay at the inn and enjoy the fine food and informal camaraderie or pay a reasonable rate for a daily pass. A couple of full-moon jaunts are planned. Rentals are available. The center can be reached from NY 8, NY 28 or exits 23 or 25 off the Northway (I-87). Write Friends Lake Inn, Friends Lake Road, Chestertown, NY 12817; telephone: 518-494-4751.

Warren County Trails

South of The Glen, Warren County has a free cross-country ski trail system between Golf Course Road and the Hudson River. There are 10 miles of beginner trails in a wooded area and on Cronin's golf course.

You reach the parking area by driving northwest on Hudson Street (also called Golf Course Road) in Warrensburg for 2.55 miles. Coming from the north on NY 28, turn right 3.35 miles south of The Glen bridge over the Hudson River; the trailhead parking sign is 2.25 miles south of the NY 28 turn. For further information write: Warren County Tourism Department, Municipal Building, Lake George, NY 12845; telephone: 518-792-9951 Ext. 245.

Pack Forest

In the same general area is the Charles Lathrop Pack Demonstration Forest, an extensive acreage managed by the State University College of Environmental Science and Forestry. You enter the area from NY 9, 0.7 mile north of the fork with NY 28 north of Warrensburg. Turn left (west) and drive in 0.5 mile to a parking lot. There are numerous trails. One route goes to Ben Wood Mountain with a sweeping view south of outlying hills and ponds. Beginners and more experienced skiers will find much to explore and enjoy in this free, accessible area.

Crandall Park

Lighted cross-country ski trails are found in the city of Glens Falls, off Upper Glen Street. Crandall Park has exceptionally fine trails that have been used for sanctioned, international cross-country ski competition. The trails were built in 1968/69—the first lighted trails in North America. Later they were expanded and widened to permit skating, a style of cross-country skiing developed by Bill Koch and others. The 7 kilometers of international quality, lighted trails are available free and are open from 7:00 A.M. to 10:00 P.M.

Pharaoh Lake Wilderness

In addition to Trip 62 described below, there are miles of other trails to explore in this wilderness. The advanced Sucker Brook trail can be reached from the vicinity of Ticonderoga. Part of the northern part of the wilderness can be reached by skiing Crane Pond Road. Trailhead descriptions can be found in Barbara McMartin's *Discover the Eastern Adirondacks.*

60. Dippikill Camp Loops

▪

3.0 miles (two loops)
Skiing time: 1 hour and 20 minutes
Beginner
USGS North Creek 15'
Map—page 229

Marked trails begin at the parking lot of the SUNY Albany cabins. In 20 minutes you can ski around the cabin area. There is one short hill, but it can be handled by beginners who don't mind falling. Other loops begin across the road.

You reach the parking lot by driving south on NY 28 from the Wevertown crossroads for 2.25 miles. After crossing a small cement bridge turn right (west) on a narrow dirt road called Glen Creek Road (but labeled Glen Brook Road on the topographic map). Drive uphill on the scenic road for 2.4 miles then turn left (south) over a bridge on unmarked Dippikill Pond Road. Continue uphill for 0.65 mile on a narrow road until you see a small building and a large gray house with white trim, on the left. This is the camp office; you must check in for a map and to let the caretakers know you are skiing on SUNY property. From the office, continue 0.2 mile to a parking lot on the right.

One trail begins at the west end of the parking lot and is marked in yellow. You go gently through some dense woods and enter a meadow. Here one trail swings right, downhill, and crosses a bridge. Climbing, you will see a log cabin called Collins Lodge on the right. The trail goes uphill in front of it, then loops left on an unplowed road to return to the parking lot. On the way back you pass other cabins that have been built by SUNY students. The log cabins are trimmed in the rustic style. During the weekend the cabins are generally filled with students who are having a good time, and seem to enjoy sharing the snow with you.

The first loop is a nice warm-up before starting for Dippikill Pond, reached by another loop that begins on the other side of the road. From the parking area walk down the road for about 100 yards until you come to the first sign on the left. This trail takes you down to the pond, about a mile away; it is also a return route if you take the next trail and want to return from the pond. The Dippikill map shows several other trails that loop back to the road.

61. Dippikill to The Glen

▪

2.0 miles one way
Skiing time: 45 minutes
Intermediate
USGS North Creek 15'
Map—page 229

You need two cars for this short, fast trip if you want a quick downhill dash without a climb. The entire trip follows an old, wide tote road,

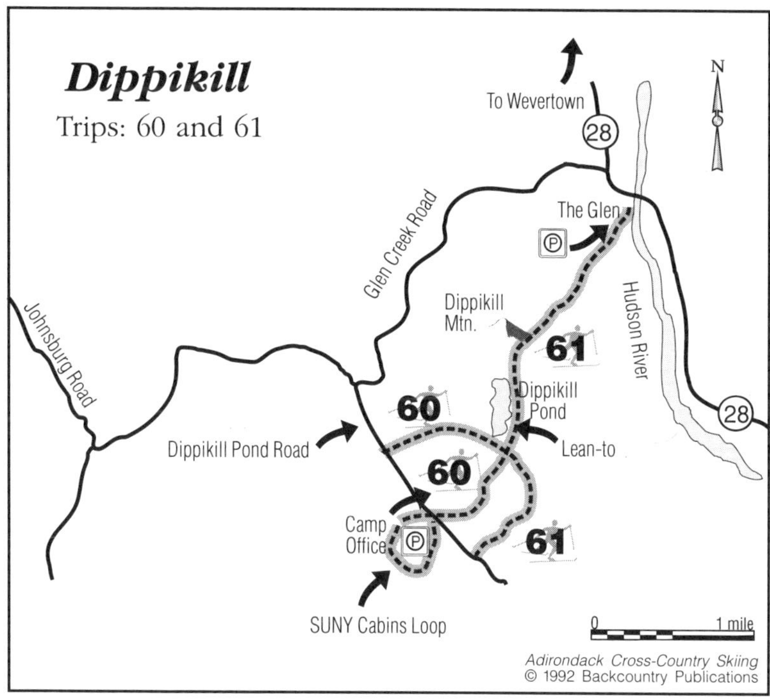

so there is room for telemark turns. The first part of the trail to Dippikill Pond is especially attractive. There are various routes to the pond and back shown on the map available at the caretaker's office; they can be skied by an experienced beginner. The run to The Glen begins at the pond lean-to and drops too steeply for beginners.

Leave one car along the dirt road off NY 28 downriver and west of The Glen bridge. Park the other car at the lot as described in Trip 60. Walk down the road 200 yards until you come to the second trailhead. This second trail is the best one to take if you are going to ski through to The Glen.

The gradual run down to Dippikill Pond follows a cleared logging road and in no time you are at the pond. Skirt the south side of the pond to a lean-to used by students in the summer. Ski past it on an obvious, wide logging road. The trail then begins to drop steeply downhill. If the conditions are icy, or the snow is packed, it can be a very fast trip.

The fairly straight schuss, through an open hardwood forest, is a good place to practice stem christie and telemark turns. You are at The Glen near the Hudson River almost before you know it. When you reach the level, ski straight out, across the railroad tracks, to the road. You will be within sight of The Glen bridge and your car. The entire trip should take considerably less than an hour to drop from 1,390 feet to 550 feet.

62. Pharaoh Lake

■

7.0 miles round trip
Skiing time: 3 hours and 20 minutes
Competent Beginner
USGS Bolton Landing 15'
Map—page 231

This trip is east of I-87 and easily accessible. A handsome forest, views of nearby mountains, and a large destination lake make this an especially memorable journey. There is less snowfall at this 1,000-foot elevation, so wait for midwinter to enjoy it.

The trailhead is reached by driving east on NY 8 from I-87 Exit 25 through the community of Brant Lake. Go past the first Palisades Road, on the left, and on to the head of the lake, about 8.0 miles from I-87. Turn left on this east end of Palisades Road, go 1.4 miles then right (north) on Beaver Pond Road. After 1.0 mile on this road, turn right (north) on Pharaoh Road. There may be a trailhead sign at the turn. Drive 0.35 mile on Pharaoh Road to a parking area near the wilderness line, past the blue house on the left. A barrier may be erected in the future to prevent vehicles, including snowmobiles, from entering the wilderness.

The trail begins along a wide, level road through a mixed forest, with a marshy area and hemlocks off to the right. Occasionally, old logging roads branch off but the main track is easy to follow. In 20 to 30 minutes, depending on how long it takes you to ski a mile, you reach a large clearing. Before coming to it, notice how the forest has changed. Straight,

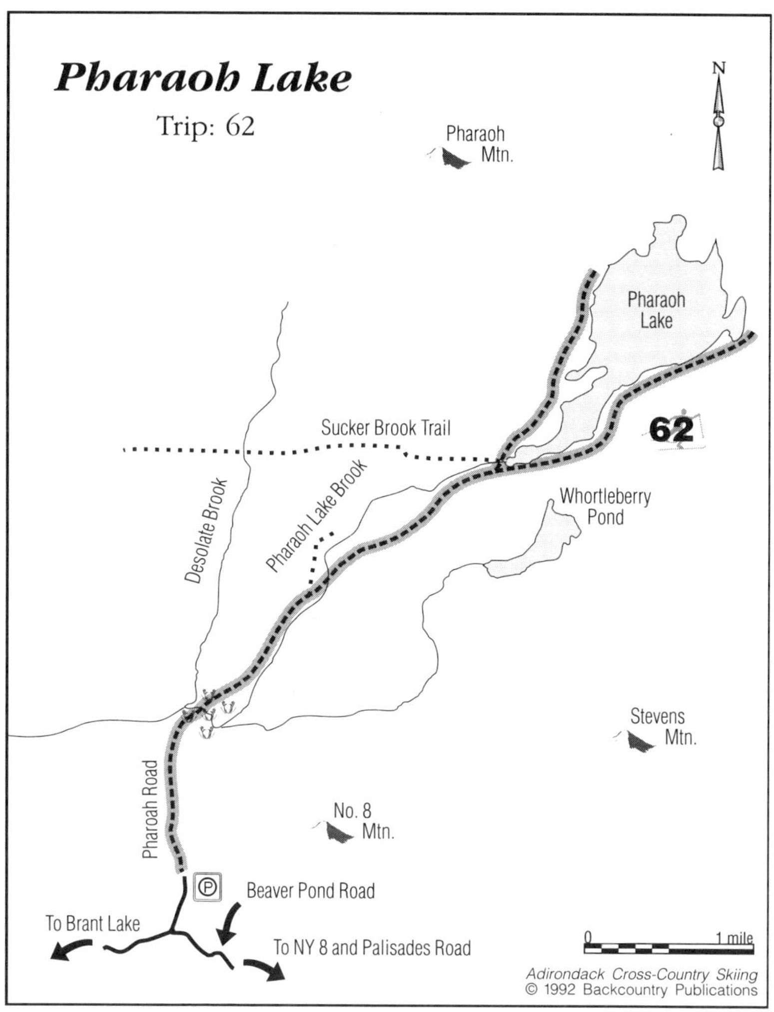

40- to 50-foot-tall red pines form a handsome, majestic grove. The route continues straight beyond the clearing, with vehicles barred by large rocks. One hundred feet from the clearing the trail crosses Pharaoh Lake Brook/Mill Brook on a wide plank bridge. The brook is 10 feet wide and deep, with a substantial marsh on each side.

Beyond this flow the trail climbs gently through white pines, with occasional side paths that you can explore in the pretty woods. Soon you are again in red pines; this extensive grove was planted by the Civilian Conservation Corps in the 1930s on the open fields of a farm, and the red pines contrast with the usual Adirondack forest species. Continuing straight on the obvious, but unmarked, trail you reach a steeper section that goes up a five-foot-wide draw. You climb 150 feet in a brief time but it is easy to negotiate, and it is a pleasant run coming out.

After gliding along a level stretch, you reach a bridge across Pharaoh Lake Brook. Here there is an alternate route to the left. It takes you to a huge beaver pond with an overlook of the valley formed by the outlet of Pharaoh Lake. Relish your first look of Pharaoh Mountain, with its controversial abandoned fire tower. If it has been cold you can ski up the shallow pond but the brook crossing is questionable; try it only if you can follow the recent tracks of others. Toward springtime you may see beavers on the ice near their lodges.

The main trail continues northeast. As you cross the bridge look upstream at the gigantic beaver dam. A rotten-egg odor comes from decaying matter in the beaver pond. The stream is beautiful but don't drink from it as it may be loaded with the protozoa that cause g iardiasis.

Close to Pharaoh Lake there is an intersection with the Sucker Brook-Desolate Brook Trail that comes in from the left. The outlet of the lake is just beyond. You reach the lake in about two hours after leaving your car, a climb of about 200 feet.

You can turn left at the outlet and follow the red-disked route along the west side of the shore for a ways. Crossing over, you can ski up the east side of the lake on a yellow-disk-marked trail. The views of Pharaoh Mountain as you ski beside this large lake are outstanding, considering the relatively low elevation. There are also lean-tos where you can enjoy lunch. Explore as much as you have time for; the downhill run back will take only about 1 hour and 20 minutes from the lake.

Northeast and Lake Champlain Areas

Low Hills and Palisades

■

The northeastern portion of Adirondack Park is lower in altitude, but some years it gets a hefty amount of lake-effect snow from Lake Champlain. The ski-touring trails in the Hammond Pond Wild Forest Area and the small public land area along the Champlain Palisades have been described rather thoroughly in *Discover the Northeastern Adirondacks* and are not included in this volume.

North of Mineville you can explore the Black River Road (2.3 miles one way) and the Fletcherville trail. West of Westport there are the delightful trails around the Pinnacle: the steep and long nine-mile round-trip up to Nichols Pond that is packed by snowmobiles, and the challenging Phunyea Hollow telemarking tour. You can reach the shore of Lake Champlain north of Westport on a trip to Barn Rock via Split Rock Mountain. There are others, but these are some of the favorites, ranging from beginner to advanced.

Lake Placid/Keene/ Keene Valley Area

High Peak Treats

■

This chapter covers impressive ski routes near Wilmington, Lake Placid, Keene, and Keene Valley. You reach several trailheads from the Adirondack Lodge Road a short way from Lake Placid. The truck road to Marcy Dam (Trip 63) enables beginners to reach one of the most famous places in the Adirondack high peaks. The Mr. Van Ski Trail for competent beginners (and intermediates if you ski past South Meadow Brook) is described in Trip 65. The intermediate to advanced Whale's Tail Notch Trip 64 is a very exciting route to Marcy Dam.

Backcountry experts regularly ski many other trails in the high peaks, but these more difficult routes, with their potentially severe winter conditions, take special competence, equipment, and training. If you have the urge to try extreme backcountry skiing, get special instruction. Also ski with people who know the area and are trained to handle the rigors and dangers of the peaks in winter.

Northeast of Lake Placid and visible for miles is the steep cone of the Adirondacks' fifth highest peak, 4,867-foot-high Whiteface Mountain. Trip 66 tells you how you can climb it on skis!

Keene Valley lies along the East Branch of the Ausable River. East of the valley a favorite trip of many intermediate skiers leads to Owl Head and into the Giant Mountain Wilderness Area as described in Trip 67. Nearby, outside of Keene at Crows Clearing off East Hill Road, is a short, 2.2-mile round-trip for beginners to the Gulf Brook Lean-to.

An easy and popular trip starts at the Ausable Club in St. Huberts and goes 3 gradual miles up an unused road along a scenic brook to Lower Ausable Lake. Snowfall in the valley is less plentiful so check local conditions before driving far. For information on other local trails call the town of Keene Valley; telephone: 518-576-4444.

Adirondack Loj

One feature of this region of the Park is the Adirondack Loj, owned and operated by the nonprofit Adirondack Mountain Club (ADK). One of the premier Nordic skiing and wilderness snowshoeing centers in the northeastern United States, it is located on the edge of the High Peaks Wilderness Area, eight miles south of Lake Placid. The Loj and its facilities are open to the public; members receive a discount. The ADK has over 20 kilometers of trails and two ski slopes on their property. The recreational loops vary from easy to most difficult and are described in a trail map. The High Peaks Information Center near the entrance to the parking area is open from 8:00 A.M.to 5:00 P.M. Saturday and Sunday for ski and snowshoe rentals. (Monday through Friday rentals are from 8:30 to 9:30 A.M.) There is a daily parking charge for nonmembers.

In order to promote safe and environmentally sound recreational use, the ADK offers a wide variety of programs and outdoor activities that are open to the public free of charge. An impressive variety of backcountry skiing, telemarking, snowshoeing, ski mountaineering, first aid, and winter photography workshops are offered from December through March at low cost. A calendar of programs is available by writing to: Adirondack Mountain Club Programs, Box 867, Lake Placid, NY 12946; telephone: 518-523-3441 between the hours of 9 A.M. and 7 P.M.

The Jackrabbit Trail

This imaginative route links the communities of Keene, Lake Placid, and Saranac Lake by connecting a number of existing trails and ski centers. It is constructed and maintained by the Adirondack Ski Touring Council (ASTC), a not-for-profit corporation formed to improve and promote cross-country skiing in the Tri-Lakes area. The trail was named in memory of Herman "Jack Rabbit" Johannsen, a pioneer of Lake Placid skiing. ASTC's goal is to extend the Jackrabbit Trail system from Keene to Tupper Lake and to have links to Keene Valley, Wilmington, and the Adirondack Park Visitor Interpretive Center at Paul Smiths.

The active efforts of Tony Goodwin and other local skiers have forged a partnership with businesses, landowners, and skiers to create this unusual recreational resource. Much of the route is on New York State Forest Preserve land and has no trail fee. There is a charge for those sections of the trail within the boundaries of commercial ski centers. A brochure and map describing the Jackrabbit Trail is available free in the Tri-Lakes area or by writing: Adirondack Ski Touring Council, P.O. Box 843, Lake Placid, NY 12946. Better yet, join ASTC by sending a check for $20 for an individual membership, or $30 for a family.

Mt. Van Hoevenberg Cross-Country Center

The cross-country center at the Olympic Sports Complex in Lake Placid has 50 kilometers of groomed trails constructed for the 1980 Winter Olympics. There are ten marked loops offering three novice, six intermediate, and one expert track. There is snowmaking on 5 kilometers of the trails. Contact ORDA, Lake Placid, NY 12946; telephone: 518-523-2811.

Cunningham's Ski Barn X-C Center

Cunningham's Ski Barn has 30 kilometers of track-set trails with a skating lane at their Lake Placid Club headquarters (Main Street, Lake Placid, NY 12946; telephone: 518-523-3706). You can walk or ski to the trails from the village, and the trails join the Jackrabbit Trail. Equipment can be rented or purchased at the Ski Barn.

Cascade Ski Touring Center

This center is located on Route 73 and on the Jackrabbit Trail. Its 15 kilometers of groomed trails connect with the Mt. Van Hoevenberg Cross-Country Ski Center. For information write: Box 190, Lake Placid, NY 12946; telephone: 518-523-9605.

Barkeater Inn and X-C Ski Center

The Barkeater is located north of Keene, 0.5 mile off NY 73 on Alstead Hill Road. A delightful country inn with a complete cross-country ski center, it was established by Joe-Pete Wilson, author and Olympic coach. It has easy-to-ski trails and excellent instruction. It is near the Keene end of the Jackrabbit Trail. Write: Box 139, Keene, NY 12942; telephone: 518-576-2221.

High Peaks Base Camp

This bunkroom style facility with affordable home cooking has rentals, instruction, and 2 miles of free trails. Other trails are nearby. The camp is 4 miles from Whiteface on Springfield Road. Write: Box 91, Upper Jay, NY 12987; telephone: 518-946-2133.

Whiteface Inn Resort & Club

There are 20 kilometers of groomed trails on the premises, and the resort connects with Jackrabbit Trail. Write: Box 231, Lake Placid, NY 12946; telephone: 518-523-2551.

63. Truck Road to Marcy Dam

■

5.8 miles round-trip
Skiing time: 2 hours and 15 minutes
Beginner
USGS Keene Valley 7.5' x 15' metric
Map—page 239

Perhaps the most popular trip in the high peaks area is the one that begins at South Meadow and heads up a truck emergency access road to Marcy Dam. This road is marked "restricted" on the 1979 metric topographic map, but it is open to skiers.

South Meadow is reached by driving up the Adirondak Lodge Road from NY 73 east of Lake Placid. Turn left on South Meadow Road 3.8 miles from NY 73, at a signpost on the right; drive up 0.9 mile, then right at the fork to the end, 4.8 miles from NY 73. The one-mile South Meadow Road spur from Adirondak Lodge Road is unplowed and may be closed to vehicles in the future, making the ski trip that much longer. If South Meadow Road is impassable, park on the side of Adirondack Lodge Road.

The trail starts at a barred gate and a sign-in register. After going around the gate you cross the stream from South Meadow, the begin-

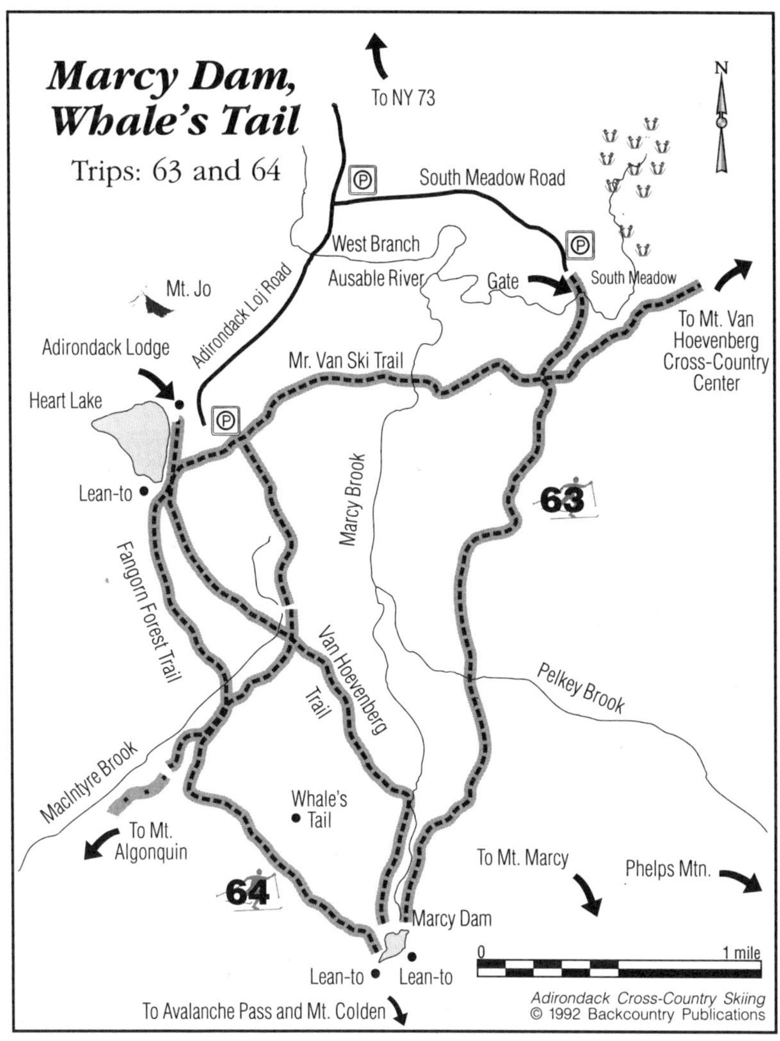

ning of the West Branch of the Ausable River. The road is almost level for 0.5 mile; there it crosses the Mr. Van Ski Trail that goes right to the Loj and left to the Mt. Van Hoevenberg Cross-Country Center. After passing this intersection, you climb 312 feet (95 meters) on a

■

Mt. Colden from Marcy Dam: Trip 63

wide road. Skiers generally make tracks when skiing on a well-traveled route, and you can ski in them or in the center of the road. The wide center surface is a good place to practice skating. You pass through a hardwood forest and cross three bridges. There are some switchbacks, but generally the trail is uneventful and all the slopes are gentle. Views of distant mountain peaks catch your eye as you climb to Marcy Dam, hub of many difficult backcountry trips, including the ascent of Mount Marcy. Seven lean-tos are available at the dam for overnight use. It takes about 1 hour and 15 minutes to reach the dam, unless you are sprinting or skating.

When you have finished exploring the area, there are three ways to descend. Returning by the same route will take you to South Meadow in less than one hour, if the snow is fast. The second route takes you across the dam and down the Van Hoevenberg blue-disked trail almost to the Adirondak Loj (2.1 miles), then right on the Mr. Van Ski Trail to the truck road, following yellow disks (1.3 miles), then left on the truck road to South Meadow (0.5 mile). This descent to Adirondak Loj is a popular snowshoe, and the trail is apt to be uneven, steep, and icy except for two skiing bypasses; it requires a lot of snow and *intermediate* ability.

A third alternative is to ski to the Adirondak Loj by the Whale's Tail Notch Ski Trail (see Trip 64), which is intermediate to advanced, depending on conditions, and is *not* recommended for beginners.

64. Whale's Tail Notch Ski Trail

▪

6.0 miles round-trip
Skiing time: 1 hour and 55 minutes
Advanced
USGS Keene Valley 7.5' x 15' metric
Map—page 239

If you stand on the east side of Marcy Dam and look west, you can visualize the northeast shoulder of massive Wright Peak as the body of a whale, and see the whale's tail in the lower peak northwest of the dam. The 2,936-foot (895-meter) peak is written Whales (sic) Tail Mountain on the topographic map (no copyeditor). A DEC ski trail has been cut through the col between the tail and the body. It is steep, but if you have the ability, it is one of the best short ski trails described in this book.

The beginning of the trail is from one of the several paths that you can take to reach the main yellow-disked trail to Algonquin Peak. Starting from Adirondak Loj, the easiest way is to start at the lean-to area on the southeast shore of Heart Lake. Ski along a trail past lean-tos 1, 2, and 3 to the edge of Loj property where a sign reads Old Marcy Trail straight ahead and Fangorn Forest Trail to the left. Just after this intersection take an unmarked path right uphill. In 25 minutes you will come to a junction. On the left, with yellow markers, is the main Algonquin Trail back to the Loj. Go right uphill (southwest) and in 100 yards a new sign shows Whale's Tail Ski Trail to the left.

The wide, cleared trail climbs steeply; 35 minutes after leaving the Algonquin Trail you gain 394 feet (120 meters) to the height of land in a col. It is a pretty route with pinkish-tinted white birch, red spruce, and balsam. You climb steadily but the turns are wide, with room enough for stem christie and telemark turns by a returning skier.

As you start down the back side, it is steeper. Wide turns drop gloriously into short runs and more turns in this well-designed trail. At one point a beautiful view of the slides on Mount Colden above Avalanche Lake are seen clearly through the trees. In no time you are at the trail rimming the pond at Marcy Dam. A left turn (north) takes you in front of a lean-to on the bluff, past the Van Hoevenberg blue-disked trail which goes back to the Loj, then over the dam.

It is pleasant to ski around the dam area and share your lunch with the gregarious chickadees that will eat out of your hand. (This is a hub for many trails to the high peaks including Phelps, Marcy, Avalanche Pass, and the Flowed Lands. Many of these trails are skiable but are beyond the scope of this book.)

There are three choices for the descent. The truck road to South Meadow goes left (north) from the ranger headquarters on the east side of the dam. This is the easiest way (see Trip 63); it is 2.5 miles down to the Mr. Van Ski Trail, then left 1.3 miles to the Loj. It should take 1½ hours. The Van Hoevenberg Trail (blue disks) goes north from the west side of the dam. It is heavily used by snowshoers and quite steep and icy in spots; two sections have skier bypasses, but it is still a demanding and awkward ski route. It is 2.15 miles long and takes 45 minutes; you may have to walk some steep, icy sections. The third alternative is to return via Whale's Tail Notch Trail. This requires an initial 390-foot (120-meter) climb for 0.8 mile, but it is a very nice run from the col back to the Loj and also takes about 45 minutes. Each of these routes is heavily traveled, particularly on weekends, so it is preferable to ski them after a good snowstorm to get the best conditions.

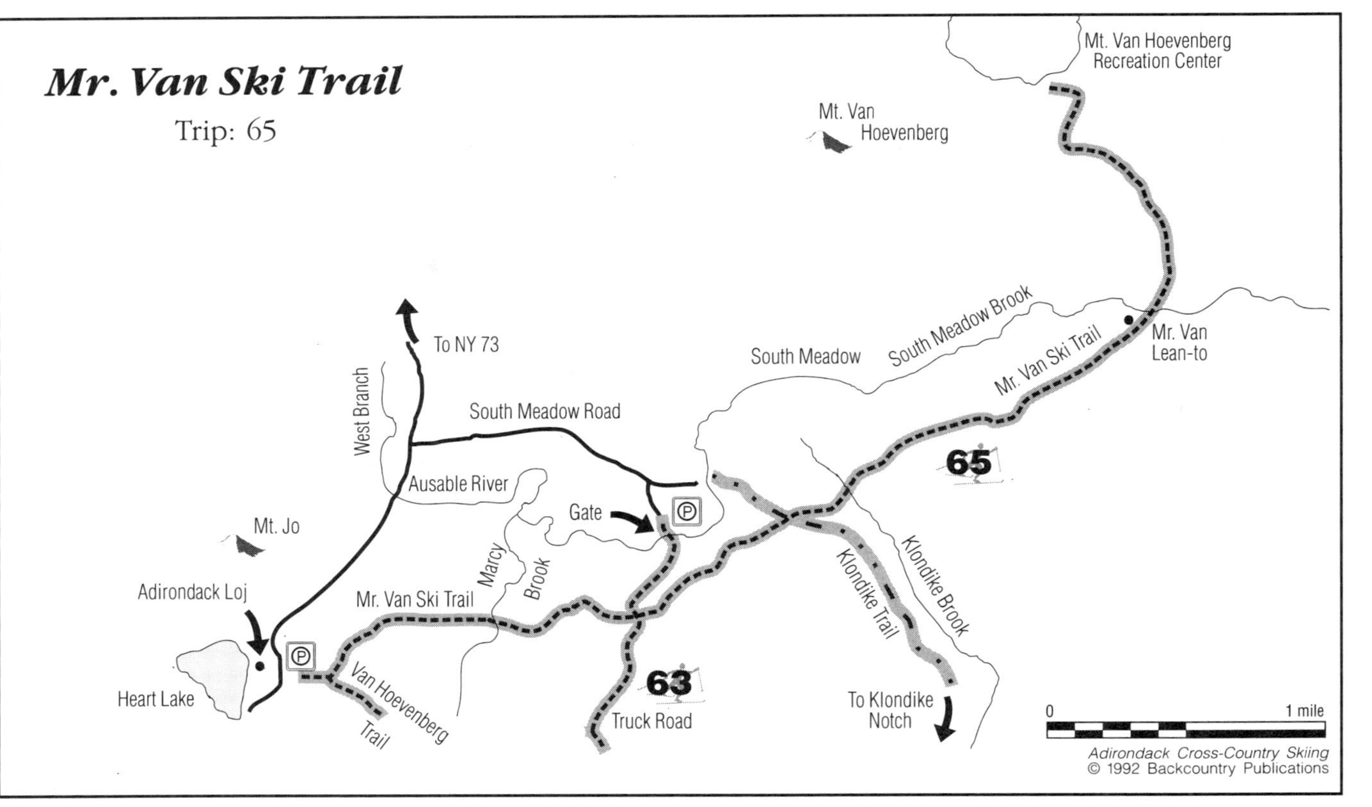

Mr. Van Ski Trail
Trip: 65
Mt. Van Hoevenberg Recreation Center
Mt. Van Hoevenberg
To NY 73
West Branch
South Meadow Road
South Meadow
South Meadow Brook
Mr. Van Ski Trail
Mr. Van Lean-to
65
Ausable River
Gate
Mt. Jo
Marcy Brook
Adirondack Loj
Mr. Van Ski Trail
Klondike Trail
Klondike Brook
Heart Lake
Van Hoevenberg Trail
63
Truck Road
To Klondike Notch
0
1 mile
Adirondack Cross-Country Skiing
© 1992 Backcountry Publications

65. Mr. Van Ski Trail

▪

9.4 miles round-trip
Skiing time: 4 hours and 55 minutes
Intermediate
USGS Keene Valley 7.5' x 15' metric
Map—page 243

This trail has been cut by DEC to link Adirondak Loj and the Mt. Van Hoevenberg Cross-Country Ski Center off NY 73. The mileage given is from the Loj to the top of the Mt. Van Hoevenberg trail system and back. It can be shortened by parking at South Meadow and skiing 0.5 mile up the Marcy Dam truck road, where this trail crosses (as described in Trip 63). You can also leave a shuttle car in the Mt. Van Hoevenberg Cross-Country Center parking lot, pay the fee for skiing those trails, and make it a 5.7-mile one-way trip from Adirondak Loj. Or, you can leave a second car at the Loj and reverse the direction, starting on the Mt. Van Hoevenberg commercial trails. It's good enough to try it each way.

Assuming you are skiing a round-trip from the Loj, park in the High Peaks Information Center lot to the left of the entrance booth and go to the end of the lot. A sign will direct you left to the Marcy Dam lean-to, following blue disks. Ski left through the woods for 200 yards to a crossroads in a conifer grove and a sign indicating Mr. Van Ski Trail to the left with yellow disks. Ski left, cross one of the Loj trails, and then descend into a swampy area cut through alders. In 20 minutes you cross Marcy Brook and in another 15 minutes you reach the truck road that goes right to Marcy Dam. (South Meadow, another possible starting point to reach the Mr. Van Ski Trail is to the left 0.5 mile.) Continue straight across the truck road following the signs to the Mr. Van lean-to 2.1 miles, and Mt. Van Hoevenberg parking lot 4.4 miles.

The trail goes northeast through a meager forest of cherry, balsam, poplar, and large, dead yellow birch. A small peak on the right shows the gash of a slide. About 10 minutes after leaving the truck road you

▪
Mr. Van's lean-to: Trip 65

turn right on the Klondike Trail following red disks. (A left turn downhill on the Klondike Trail also takes you to South Meadow.) Skiing up the Klondike Trail less than 0.2 mile, you come to a signpost directing you left to the Mr. Van lean-to. This is a nice stretch of the trail—wide, skiable, with gentle ups and downs. You reach the clean, attractive lean-to in a brook setting about 1 hour from the truck road, just over 1½ hours from Adirondak Loj.

Continuing north, you cross South Meadow Brook immediately after leaving the lean-to. The crossing is on a collapsed bridge and beaver dam but is iced in and feasible. You climb into a beautiful red spruce grove with towering trees and a dense understory. After this sylvan splendor, the trail climbs more steeply through open hardwood. There is an especially steep section before it swings westerly, climbing along the south face of a ridge. The trail turns north over the ridge at Hi-Notch, about 50 minutes from the lean-to, and joins the Mt. Van Hoevenberg cross-country ski trail complex. From here, if you have paid the fee, you can ski down to the ski center parking lot, following their trail map and the signs for the stadium.

If you turn around at Hi-Notch, it is a sporty 35-minute run back to the Mr. Van lean-to, 1 hour of delightful glides to the junction with the Klondike Trail, and another easy hour back to Adirondak Loj. The trail is well designed, with variable grades. It is rated intermediate because of the steep section from the Mount Van Hoevenberg ridge down to the lean-to. A competent beginner can handle all of it as far as the lean-to, and this alone is an enjoyable trip. The frequent signs along the trails will keep you on the right track.

66. Whiteface Mountain Access Road

■

10.0 miles round-trip
Skiing time: 4 hours plus
Competent Beginner
USGS Wilmington & Lake Placid 7.5' x 15' metric
Map—page 247

Do you want to get high enough to see rime ice on trees and take fabulous photos of panoramic views? You can do it by skiing up the paved road that goes almost to the summit of Whiteface Mountain. Bordered by squared-off rocks this route lacks the beauty of a natural trail, but it is a different and memorable experience. You should not be overconfident about the ease of skiing up this road. The mountain

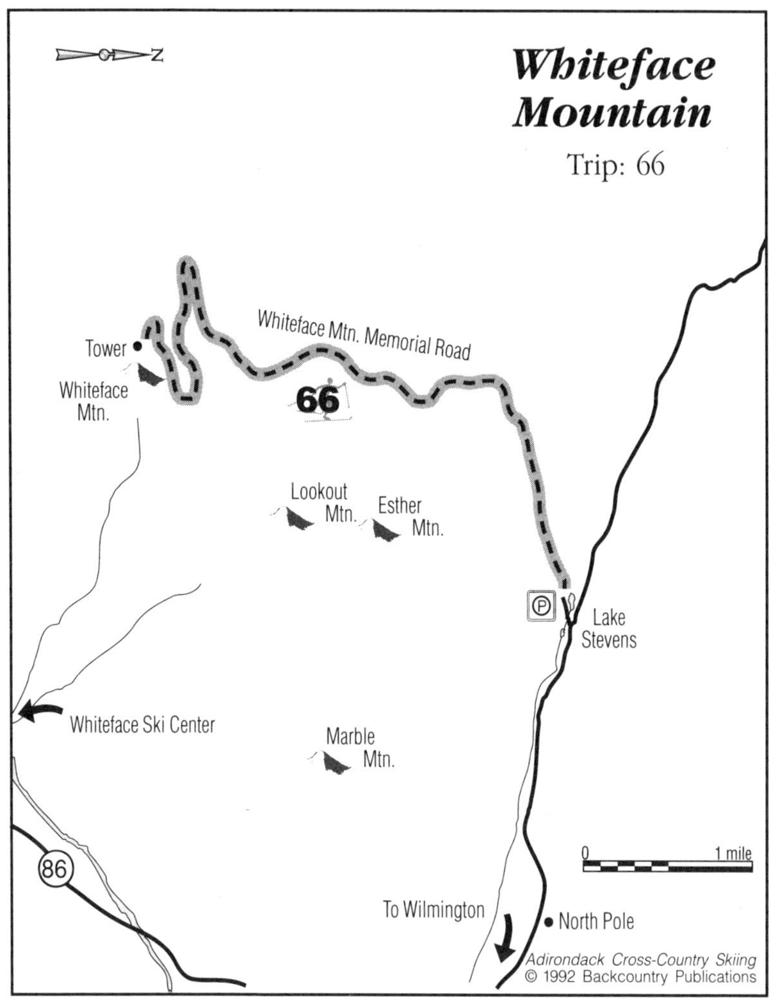

is high, the wind can be fierce, and you will usually face severe winter conditions. By all means put a down jacket and a face mask—or wool scarf—in your pack; you will need them when you get near the top.

Drive to Wilmington on NY 86 out of Lake Placid. The pretty, winding drive takes you beside the West Branch of the Ausable River.

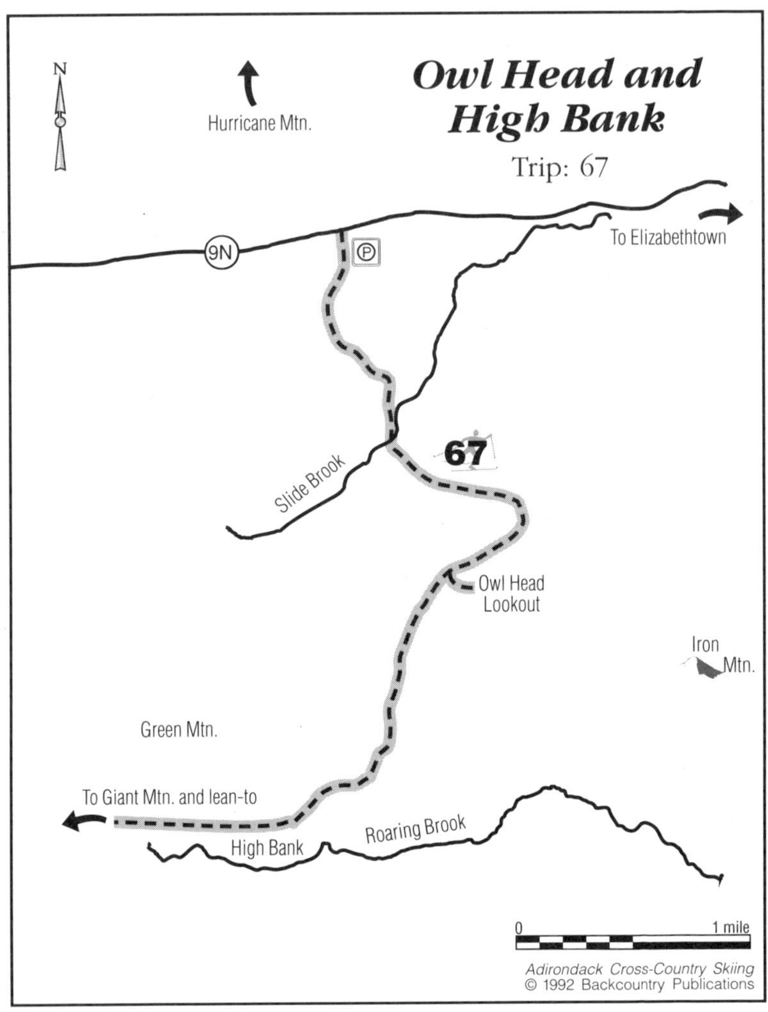

At the T in Wilmington, turn left (west) and drive up the mountain as far as the road is plowed. There is ample parking at the turnaround before the gate.

The trip is a 5-mile gradual climb up the wide paved road. Waxable skis with the correct wax, or waxless skis, will make the hill without slipping back; it is not steep enough to require skins. There are magnificent vistas almost from the beginning. Depending on the weather conditions, you will reach the lower edge of the rime ice fairly quickly. Look over the conditions of the road surface as you go up; if the roadway is icy, then it is better to cancel the trip that day and ski somewhere else. (The Jackrabbit Trail and Adirondak Loj are nearby and may have better conditions.) It will take about three hours to climb to the top.

It is important to dress correctly, and layer your clothing, on this trip. As you climb and warm up, take off the sweater or wool shirt that is under your windbreaker. If you pause for very long, put the sweater or shirt back on to avoid windchill. When you stop for lunch, put on a face mask and the extra down jacket: avoid hypothermia.

Weather conditions can change rapidly at this altitude. You can start in bright sun and, an hour later, it can be very cloudy, cold, and unpleasant. Trip leaders should not strive for the top if the sensible thing is to turn around. The icy top is a cold and hostile environment with only a windbreak to huddle behind for lunch.

The trip down will take only an hour. With good snow it can be skied by a competent beginner. Intermediate skiers will find it is a great place to practice stem christie and telemark turns. Even if it is a warm, sunny day—and it should be if you take this trip—you will become chilled as you ski down. If it is windy, you will be *cold.* You will learn a lot about the elements, and how to dress for them, on this excursion to the highest point described in this book.

67. Owl Head and High Bank

■

8.4 miles round-trip
Skiing time: 3 hours and 30 minutes
Intermediate
USGS Elizabethtown 7.5' x 15' metric
Map—page 248

This trail will introduce backcountry skiers to the stupendous Giant Mountain Wilderness Area. The rocky, eroded sections require lots of snow cover, so wait until February to ski it. The tremendous views and open woods will guarantee that you return at least once each year. You can extend the trip 1.6 miles from High Bank to the Roaring Brook lean-to, nestled in the valley north of the peak of Giant Mountain. This makes a very long day trip, however, and it is best to camp overnight at the lean-to.

The DEC trailhead sign is on the south side of NY 9N, 4.4 miles west of NY 9 in Elizabethtown; 8.7 miles east of NY 73, if are you coming from Keene or Keene Valley. Park beside the road at the signpost that says: Slide Brook 1.2 miles, Owl Head 2.7 miles, High Bank 4.2 miles, Giant Mountain Lean-to 5.8 miles. Ski south down past the summer parking lot and sign the register. You are at 1,276 feet (389 meters), will climb to the 2,529-foot (771-meter) outlook at Owl Head, and then level out to 2,296 feet (700 meters) at High Bank.

At the start, you immediately cross a bridge over The Branch, a small stream that flows into the Bouquet River at Elizabethtown. Just beyond, the trail leaves the tote road and jogs left into the woods, marked by red disks. There is another bridge and then you climb gradually. This section winds through a hemlock grove and is icy without ample snow. After 10 minutes you pass a wilderness sign and soon afterward emerge into an open hardwood mixture of large maple, ash, beech, and white birch. There is a steep, rock-tumbled valley on your left before you reach a narrow, well-built bridge over Slide Brook, a major stream that joins The Branch. This sturdy and attractive bridge is built of wood and rock and is wide enough for skis or snowshoes.

The well-marked trail continues southeast after crossing Slide Brook. You angle upward along the contour, traverse a slight depression on snow-covered rocks, and gain altitude up a steep hogback. Correct waxing, or an effective herringbone step, is needed up the spine of this hill. The trail then continues up a dry watercourse, crossing it several times on either strategically placed rocks or two-log spans. These crossings are easy going up but require control and sharp, accurate turns to handle coming down. Look at this section carefully to remember it on your return. Climbing along, you will see pretty, multicolored icefalls covering the rock ledges.

The trail now swings to the southwest in a wide arc through sparse white birch. The way is steep but the forest is so open, with almost no understory, that you can zigzag through it on your return. In about 1 hour and 20 minutes a junction sign shows Owl Head Lookout to the left 0.2 mile and High Bank 1.7 miles ahead. Skiing left, you can go only 100 yards before you must remove your skis to climb the steep knoll. You will have worked up a good sweat by the time you reach the windy top, so put on a sweater or down jacket to keep from getting chilled.

A wide panorama greets you on the rocky outcrop. To the north you can see the fire tower on Hurricane Mountain. As you turn west there is Knob Lock Mountain and then massive Green Mountain. In the valley to the left of Green lies Roaring Brook, which you approach as you go on to High Bank. Left of the valley lies the distant peak of Giant Mountain, and nearer, Rocky Peak Ridge. Bald Peak is due south, a crest of open snow. The scene is remote and arctic and one of the best wintry vistas that you can easily reach on skinny skis.

Tumble through the deep snow back to your skis and the junction. The marked trail to High Bank goes left (west then south) around Owl Head. There is a steep drop and a right turn that calls for a snowplow and stem christie, but the slope is wide and negotiable. The trail continues gradually down toward the brook valley, dropping 328 feet (100 meters) in less than 1 mile. Swinging west, with the rock ledges of Green Mountain appearing ahead on the right, you can glide along

■

Polypody fern and snow crown a rock

the open course. In a seemingly short time—25 minutes from Owl Head—you reach an area of stunted white birch on the left. Go left onto this open bank created by a large deposit of gravel high up on this side of the valley. There is an impressive view of the eastern slides of Giant Mountain from this vantage point. Rocky Peak Ridge towers across the valley of Roaring Brook. Ski on a way for more views of Giant, which looms ever closer. The scene is reminiscent of the Rockies, where there are few trees on the jagged summits, unlike the forested, rounded peaks usually seen in the East.

Unless you are in very good condition, High Bank is a comfortable limit for a one-day round-trip. It is 1.6 miles farther to the Roaring Brook lean-to, but the trail climbs 886 feet (270 meters), becomes narrower, and is much harder to ski.

You can fall into a nice glide along the trail back to Owl Head because, although it climbs continuously, it skis very well. Before you know it, the impressive rock outcrop looms above and you are climbing the steep S-turn to the Owl Head junction. From here the trail down is steep and demanding. If you ski only on the trail, a strong snowplow is needed, together with a dependable stop turn. A better alternative is to make wide, sweeping arcs through the open woods. You can angle uphill to control speed or increase your velocity by dropping into gullies. If the snow is right, these wide sweeps can be a unique skiing experience.

When you reach the ice-covered rocks, ski cautiously as the trail has tight turns around trees. There are several places where you cross a small depression on rocks or narrow logs immediately after a turn; if you misjudge, you can take a bad fall. There is room, in almost every place, to run straight out, rather than take the crossing too fast.

The trip down from Owl Head will take only ½ hour if you push it. The entire trip, including lunch at High Bank, will take at least 3½ hours.

■

St. Regis Mountain from Paul Smiths Visitor Center

Lake Country

Northwestern Snow Belt

■

This region extends from Raquette Lake northerly alongside Long Lake and Tupper Lake and ends around St. Regis Ponds and Paul Smiths. Because of the lakes, winter storms often produce a lot of snow, and the trails here are relatively level—perfect for beginning skiers.

The Deer Pond Loop described in Trip 68 is first-rate. Beginners will enjoy the old Wawbeek Road that goes left from the parking area or the Bull Point spur that goes right. Those skiers with a little more competence can handle the loop to scenic, isolated Deer Pond. Just north of the Deer Pond trailhead (where NY 30 goes north and NY 3 forks right to Saranac Lake) is a marked DEC round-trip trail that runs 1.3 miles to Trombley Landing on the Raquette River. Look for the trailhead sign to the right (south) of the intersection, about 50 feet off the road.

Southwest of Long Lake, the North Point Road at Deerland goes to the trailheads of a somewhat more demanding 4.3-mile marked loop to Upper and Lower Sargent Ponds; it is a snowmobile route but seldom traveled. Branching from the North Point Road, along the road to the DEC Forked Lake Campsite, is a winter deer-feeding area. The Sargent Ponds and other cross-country trails are shown on a map available from the town of Long Lake; telephone: 518-624-3077.

The town of Tupper Lake has a three-mile ski loop that starts behind the L. P. Quinn Elementary School. Cross-country trails were available at the Big Tupper Ski Area several years ago and may be opened again. Information on the local trails is available from the Tupper Lake Chamber of Commerce; telephone: 518-359-3328.

As you continue north on NY 30 the St. Regis Canoe Area offers very popular skiing along the summer canoe routes and the 11-mile round-trip on the truck trail to Fish Pond.

Interpretive Center at Paul Smiths

An important feature of the area is the Adirondack Park Visitor Interpretive Center (in the town of Brighton) on land leased from Paul Smith's College. The rustic building is sited on a knoll overlooking a 60-acre marsh with St. Regis Mountain providing a distinctive backdrop. The purpose of the center is to inform visitors about the magnificence and ecological importance of the six-million-acre Adirondack Park. Exhibits and the interpretive signs help to explain the flora, fauna, geology, and natural resources of this unique region. The Interpretive Center is situated on 2,885 acres, including the marsh, five lakes, several brooks, tamarack and black spruce swamps, hardwood forests, and special glacial and geologic features. Open year-round. Skiers should register at the desk and get a winter trail map; telephone: 518-327-3000.

The diverse trail system at the center is appropriate for skiers of beginner to intermediate ability. You pass among dense evergreens, overlook a large marsh, travel through hardwoods, and glide along woods roads. A long loop takes you onto an esker.

If you don't have cross-country equipment, you should rent it in Saranac Lake or Lake Placid at one of the ski shops. Separate trails for snowshoers are also available.

Harrietstown Cross-Country Ski Trails

There are 11 kilometers of excellent, groomed trails for Nordic skiers (3.5 kilometers are for experts only) and separate paths for snowshoers

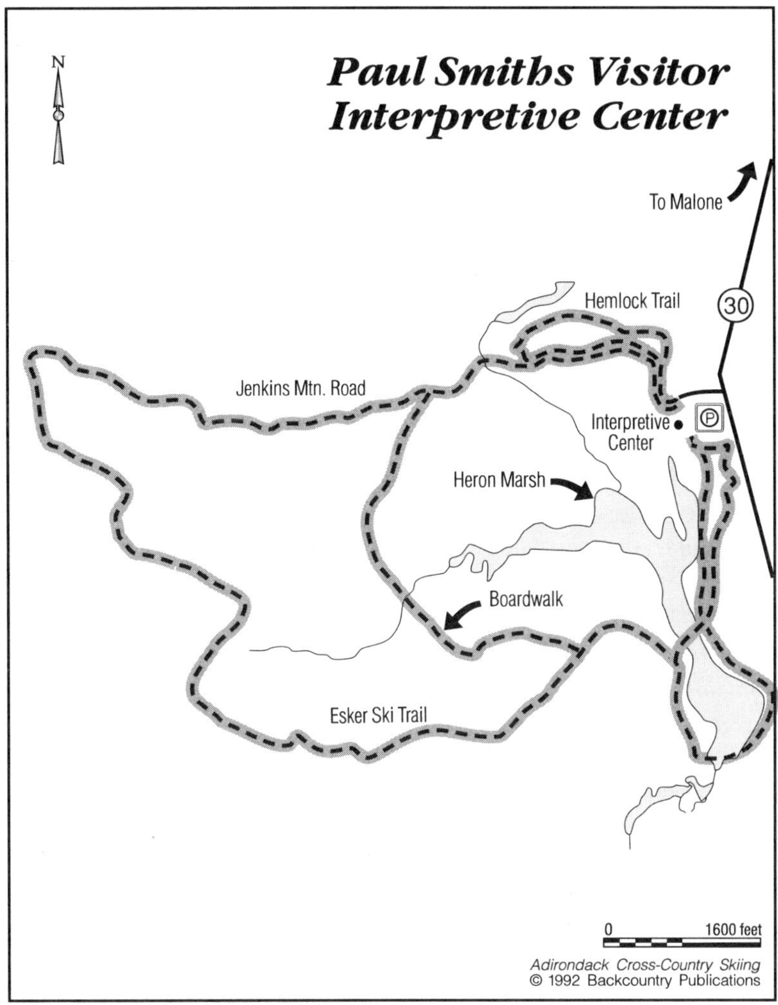

near Saranac Lake. The trails are laid out on Dewey Mountain and, although close to town, they are surprisingly rural and isolated. Some of the trails have lights for night skiing.

Skiing is open to the public with a moderate charge to cover costs. A cozy warming hut is located at the beginning of the trails. You reach the hut by driving west from Saranac Lake on NY 3 for 1.5 miles. Information is available from the town of Harrietstown; telephone: 518-891-2697.

68. Deer Pond Loop

■

7.1 miles
Skiing time: 2 hours and 45 minutes
Competent Beginner
USGS Long Lake & Saint Regis 15'
Map—page 259

The trailhead to Deer Pond is 0.6 mile west of the NY 3/NY 30 junction and 5.0 miles east of downtown Tupper Lake. A sign on the northwest side of the road reads: Deer Pond Loop 7.3 miles, NY 30 to Bull Point 2.1 miles. Parts of the trail follow old dirt roads, and there are several hilly areas. The first 1.2 miles and the last 2.1 miles of the Deer Pond Loop can be skied by beginners, but the hills in between require some degree of competence. Local snowmobilers use the trail, but it is unlikely you will meet one if you ski on a weekday.

Park in the plowed area off NY 3/NY 30. About 150 yards in, there is a yellow cross-country disk on a tree to the right (north). Ski in for about 100 feet and look for a pipe barrier; ski around it to begin the trail. You start on the old fire truck trail through a pine forest, on the level, for 1.2 miles. After 25 minutes the trail forks.

A sign indicates that NY 30 at Bull Point is right (east) in 0.7 mile. This route crosses a marshy area and a bridged stream. Skiing on the level you reach NY 30 near Upper Saranac Lake in 15 to 20 minutes from the fork. (You could leave a shuttle car at the signpost about 1.0 mile north of the junction of NY 3 and NY 30, but it is more fun to ski the 2 miles back to the car.)

The sign for the left (west) fork reads: Deer Pond 1.7 miles, Old Wawbeek Road 3.6 miles. It is marked with yellow cross-country

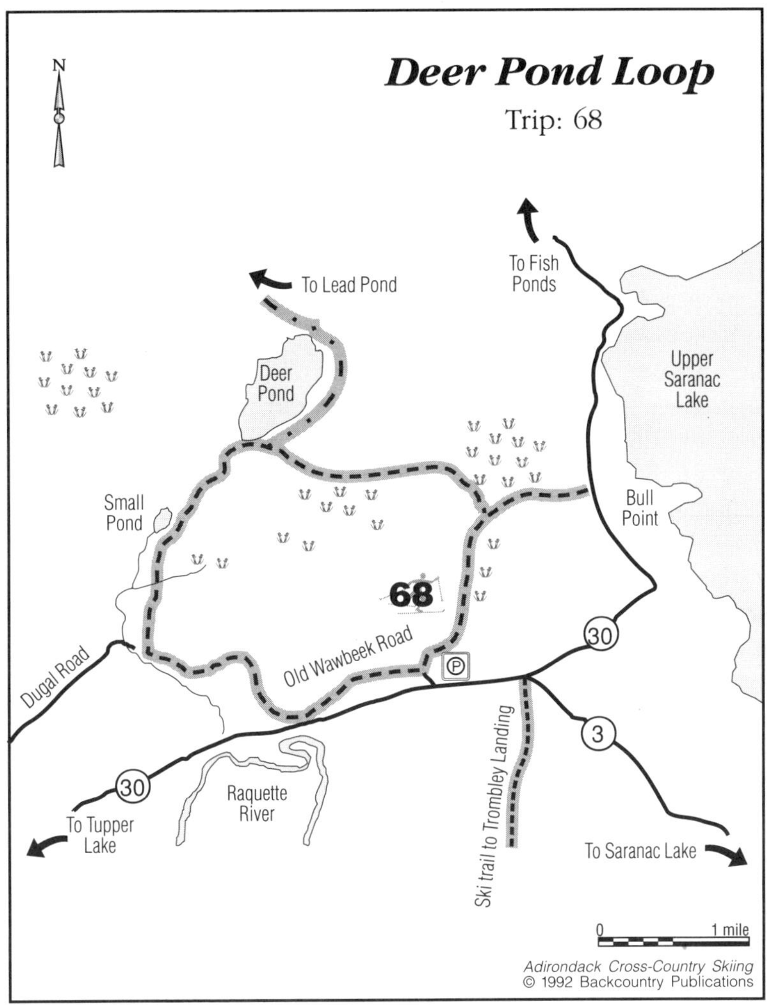

disks and is easy to follow. As you glide, the forest changes from pine to spruce. There is a level, marshy area with built-up bridging and, after crossing a flow with alders, you climb 100 feet through a young, open, deciduous forest. The trail enters an attractive draw, going left of magnetic north, and soon you can see the pond ahead. A magnificent rock outcropping with icicles invites your attention on the right of the trail. Another smaller draw takes you down to an intersection. The sign points left to Old Wawbeek Road 1.9 miles and NY 3 parking 3.0 miles; you have skied 3.0 miles. It is a short but steep drop from here down to the pond. (An unmarked trail goes right to Lead Pond but it may not be cleared.)

You reach Deer Pond in less than 1½ hours from your car. Look up the frozen surface to the north for a distant peak, framed on the right by lichen-covered rock, crowned with conifers.

Back at the signpost the main trail goes right (southwest) and skirts the southern edge of the pond. After 25 minutes of easy glides you descend to another smaller pond. The trail bears left; in 10 more minutes you reach a major beaver flow. The ice may be slushy, so cross on the dam. On the other side you enter a spruce plantation.

In 2 hours and 15 minutes you are at the outskirts of Tupper Lake, at the blocked end of Dugal Road. Another signpost shows how far you have come and indicates it is 2.3 miles to the NY 3/NY 30 parking area. This final section to the car is a wide dirt road, traveled by snowmobiles and four-wheelers. It is practically level and a good place for beginners to practice. It takes about 40 minutes to ski and seems less than 2.3 miles.

The entire trip takes less than three hours, including lunch and pauses for pictures. The distances on the signposts are inconsistent; a reasonable estimate for the entire loop is 7.1 miles.

Inlet/Old Forge Area

Easy Trips in the West

■

The Pigeon Lake Wilderness in the central western region of the Adirondack Park is a 51,000-acre expanse of low, rolling hills and ponds that extends from Raquette Lake west to the Stillwater Reservoir. The forest is a mix of near-mature and mature softwoods and hardwoods with some dense spruce-balsam fir thickets in the swampland. Most of the land is above 1,800 feet and usually receives a good deal of snow.

Big Moose Road leads past this wilderness to famous Big Moose Lake. As you drive from Eagle Bay to Big Moose you pass the trailhead for Trip 69 to Cascade Lake. The trip follows an old road to a former camp and continues to an impressive waterfall. Farther on Big Moose Road on the left is parking for Trip 70, another easy loop around a small pond.

If you drive farther on this road you reach famous Big Moose Lake. It was the setting for *An American Tragedy,* Theodore Dreiser's 1924 novel about how a young man's desire for riches can nullify a moral upbringing. It was also on this lake that Chester Gillette supposedly killed his pregnant sweetheart, Grace Brown, in order to marry the boss's daughter. Craig Brandon has carefully researched the events and his book, *Murder in the Adirondacks,* can be found in local stores.

Several miles west of Thendara near NY 28 lies another beautiful wilderness called Ha-de-ron-dah. It has low rolling hills and many beaver meadows and swamps. The southern half of the area has fire damage and the forest has not recovered. The northern portion has small stands of mixed hardwood trees. You can ski into the Ha-de-ron-dah Wilderness to Big Otter Lake on an old fire truck trail. Turn right off NY 28 just past the railroad underpass west of Thendara and drive 700 yards to the unmarked trailhead for this all-day, 16-mile round-trip. It is a level and clear route and, of course, you do not have to ski in all the way to enjoy it.

Inlet Cross-Country Ski Trails

The town of Inlet on NY 28 has 20 kilometers of groomed cross-country ski trails plus 2 kilometers of lighted trails. This free trail system for all ranges of competence begins at the Fern Park Recreation Area on South Shore Road; telephone: 315-357-5501. Equipment can be rented at the Inlet Ski Touring Center within walking distance; telephone: 315-357-6961. In addition to Trips 69 and 70 described below, the town of Inlet brochure lists a trail from Limekiln Lake to Third Lake (7 miles), a loop trail around Black Bear Mountain (6 miles), and the novice Golf Course trails off Limekiln Road.

McCauley Mountain Ski Area

Several miles west of Inlet, on the outskirts of Old Forge, there are 20 kilometers of private cross-country trails at McCauley Mountain; telephone: 315-369-3225.

Adirondack Woodcraft Ski Touring Center

This center has rustic lodging and lies on the shores of a pond in a beautiful area off Rondaxe Road between Inlet and Old Forge. There are 12 kilometers of some of the finest groomed trails. Skiing continues after dark on lighted trails around two secluded lakes. It is open weekends; telephone: 315-369-6031.

69. Cascade Lake

▪

5.4 miles round-trip
Skiing time: 2 hours and 30 minutes
Beginner
USGS Big Moose 15'
Map—page 264

This trip makes an enjoyable circuit of Cascade Lake, which gets its name from the wide waterfall on the inlet stream at the eastern end. The trailhead is on Big Moose Road 0.9 mile from NY 28 at Eagle Bay. Driving up a slight rise you will see an old road angle to the right, blocked by rocks. Just past it, on a turn, is a large dug-out open area to park. A very small sign on a tree at the south (Eagle Bay) end of the lot points east to the trail. About 100 feet in there is a register and a large map of the area. A sign here reads: Trail to Cascade Lake 1.5 miles.

The well-marked trail climbs gradually on an old road through open maple and beech. In 20 minutes you reach a signpost; you have skied 0.8 mile to here, Cascade Falls is 1.8 miles to the right, and the loop around Cascade Lake is 3.8 miles. Going left, in five minutes you cross a small bridge over the outlet. There are many rocks on the old road so this trip requires a good snow cover. Just beyond is a trail left to Windfall Pond; it is rocky, with many blowdowns, and not for skiers.

Continuing straight you glimpse the frozen lake to the right and soon reach a clearing on the shore. This is the site of a summer camp that shows up on the 1954 topographic map but is now gone. In 1 hour and 10 minutes you reach a beaver dam at the upper head of the lake. Ski along the dam and over a pretty ridge covered with red spruce. An easy glide drops to another marshy headwater of the lake. Here a small sign directs you to the 15- to 20-foot falls, a cascade of ice that, unfortunately, is in shadows and difficult to photograph in the afternoon. You can continue around the lake on a trail cut through open woods, away from the lakeshore, or return by the route you came.

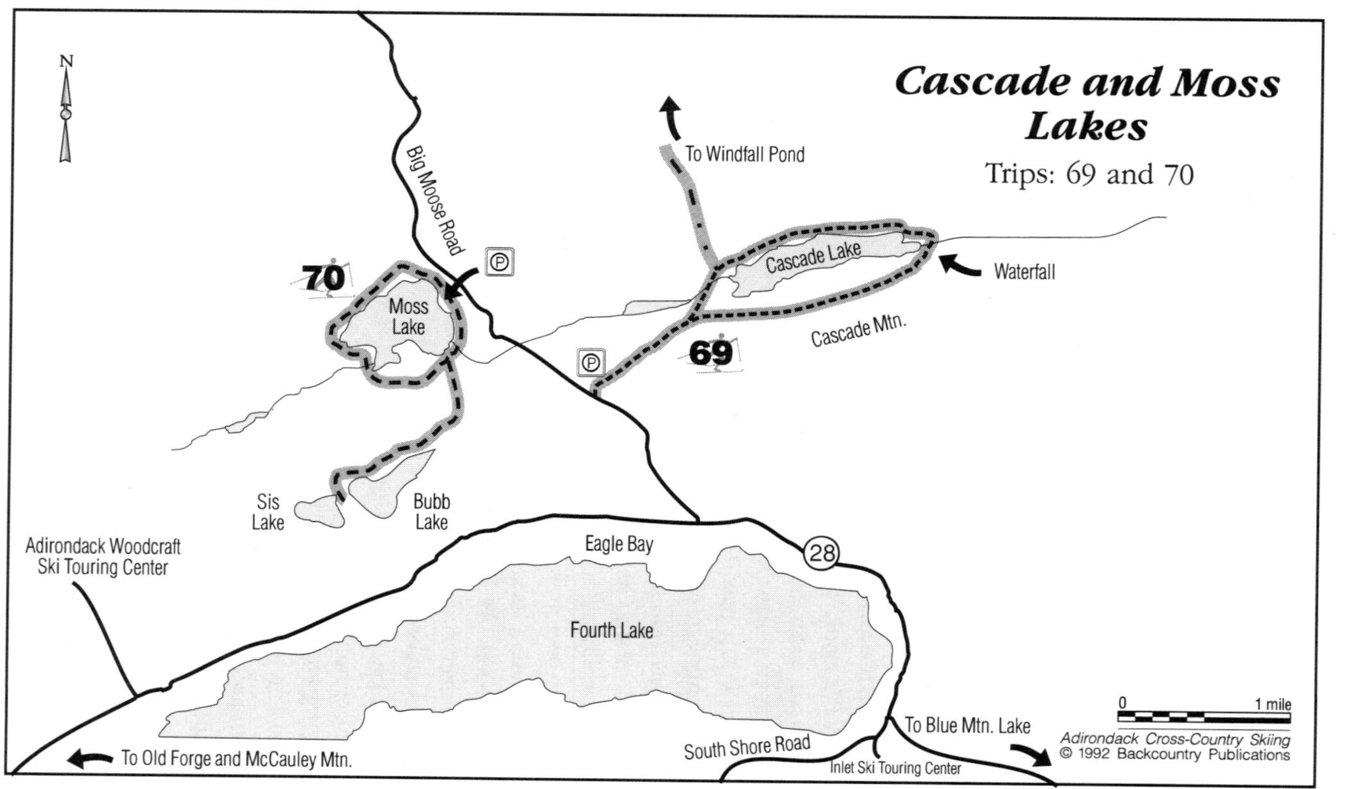

Cascade and Moss Lakes
Trips: 69 and 70
N
To Windfall Pond
Big Moose Road
70
P
Moss Lake
Cascade Lake
Waterfall
Cascade Mtn.
69
P
Sis Lake
Bubb Lake
Adirondack Woodcraft Ski Touring Center
Eagle Bay
28
Fourth Lake
To Old Forge and McCauley Mtn.
South Shore Road
Inlet Ski Touring Center
To Blue Mtn. Lake
0
1 mile
Adirondack Cross-Country Skiing
© 1992 Backcountry Publications

70. Moss Lake

▪

2.5 miles round-trip
Skiing time: 1 hour and 25 minutes
Beginner
USGS Big Moose 15'
Map—page 264

In the early 1970s there was a barricade on the Big Moose Road where this trail begins. The Mohawk Indians, claiming ancestral rights to the area, took over a girl's ca-mp on the lakeshore and set up a checkpoint through their claimed territory. After extensive negotiations with the then New York Secretary of State Mario Cuomo, the Mohawks moved to other lands. The numerous buildings which show on the 1954 topographic map are gone and the lakeshore is now a public campground and an easy skiing loop.

The trailhead is 2.2 miles from Eagle Bay on the left. There is a DEC sign and a plowed parking lot. Going left on the loop you pass through small hardwoods in an area that has been logged. The trail is almost level. As you circle around, the forest becomes richer with older hardwoods and some hemlock. Soon after you start there is a skiable marked trail left to Sis and Bubb lakes, which are over 1 mile away. About halfway around there is a strong bridge over the outlet, which flows into the north branch of the Moose River. This is a typical Adirondack high-country stream flowing through an extensive marsh area. Follow the clear open trail as it curves around the pond. Before you reach the parking lot there is an open area on the right where the camp was located.

This is a short trip. For a full day on skis it is easy to enjoy both Moss Lake and Cascade Lake (Trip 69) with time to spare.

Trips Listed by Difficulty

■

(Some trips start as beginner trips but become more difficult as they progress. Such trips are listed twice.)

Beginner

Trip No.

1. Thirteenth Lake
2. Old Farm Clearing
8. Prier Pond
13. Nate Davis Pond
14. River Road—from North Creek to Riparius
20. Vanderwhacker Mountain Road
24. Elk Lake
28. Bailey Pond
30. Hoffman Cemetery
31. Big Pond
35. Indian Lake Loops
40. Rock Lake
44. Round Pond
51. Piseco Airport Nordic Ski Loop
52. Kunjamuk Loop Trail
60. Dippikill Camp Loops

63. Truck Road to Marcy Dam
68. Deer Pond Loop
69. Cascade Lake
70. Moss Lake

Competent Beginner

Trip No.

2. Botheration Brook
9. Bell Mountain Brook
10. Bog Meadow and the Flow
15. Santanoni Great Camp (Newcomb Lake)
16. Moose Pond
18. Opalescent River and Twin Brook Lean-to
19. Blue Ridge Road to Lester Dam
22. Trout Pond to Round Pond
23. Up Crowfoot Brook to Crowfoot Pond
24. Elk Lake and the Dix Trail
26. Deer Creek
32. Stony Pond and Center Pond
36. Cedar River and McGinn Mountain Trail
37. Unknown Pond
38. Elm Island
42. John Pond
46. Northville-Placid Trail from Lake Durant
48. Cascade Pond Spur
53. Fawn Lake and Fall Stream Roundabout
54. Perkins Clearing to Pillsbury Lake
55. Spur to Cedar Lakes
56. Putnam Farm Road Beside Crane Mountain
58. Mud Pond Jaunt
62. Pharaoh Lake
66. Whiteface Mountain Access Road
68. Deer Pond Loop

Intermediate

Trip No.

3. Old Farm Clearing to Puffer Pond
4. Siamese Ponds Wilderness Trail
5. Spur to Siamese Ponds
6. Halfway Brook to Thirteenth Lake Road
11. Second Pond
21. Round Pond and Moriah Pond
22. Trout Pond to Sharp Bridge
25. Traversing Hoffman Notch from Blue Ridge Road
27. Huntley Pond to Hudson River Gorge
28. Bailey Pond and Beyond
29. Loch Muller to Big Marsh and Beyond
33. Stony Pond and Hewitt Pond Roundabout
34. Stony Pond and Sherman Pond to Irishtown
39. Rock River
43. Puffer Pond Loop
45. Kings Flow Loop
47. Stephens Pond and Lake Durant from Cedar River Road
48. Cascade Pond Spur
50. Tirrell Pond Roundabout
57. Lizard Pond
61. Dippikill to The Glen
65. Mr. Van Ski Trail
67. Owl Head and High Bank

Advanced

Trip No.

12. Highwinds to Second Pond
17. Goodnow Mountain
29. Loch Muller to Blue Ridge Road
49. Blue Mountain Access Road

59. Round Pond
64. Whale's Tail Notch Ski Trail

Snowshoeing

Trip No.

7. Peaked Mountain Pond
17. Goodnow Mountain
27. Huntley Pond to Hudson River Gorge
36. McGinn Mountain Trail
41. Sawyer Mountain
59. Round Pond

Sources and Suggested Reading

■

Barnett, Lincoln. *The Ancient Adirondacks.* New York: Time-Life Books, 1974.

Brady, Michael. *Cross-Country Ski Gear.* Seattle: The Mountaineers, 1987.

Brady, M. Michael. *The Complete Ski Cross-Country.* New York: The Dial Press, 1982.

Brandon, Craig. *Murder in the Adirondacks.* Utica, New York: North Country Books, 1986.

Carson, Russell M.L. *Peaks and People of the Adirondacks.* Glens Falls, New York: The Adirondack Mountain Club, 1986.

Cobb, Boughton. *A Field Guide to the Ferns.* Boston: Houghton Mifflin Company, 1963.

Conard, Henry S. *How to Know the Mosses and Liverworts.* Revised by Paul L. Redfearn, Jr. Dubuque, Iowa: Wm. C. Brown Company, 1979.

Conroy, Dennis, et al. *Discover the Northeastern Adirondacks.* Woodstock, Vermont: Backcountry Publications, 1987.

DiNunzio, Michael G. *Adirondack Wildguide.* Elizabethtown, New

York: The Adirondack Conservancy Committee and The Adirondack Council, 1984.

Dunham, Harvey L. *Adirondack French Louie.* Saranac Lake, New York: North Country Books, 1970.

Dunn, John M. *Winterwise: A Backpacker's Guide.* Lake George, New York: Adirondack Mountain Club, 1988.

Fennessy, Lana. *The History of Newcomb.* Newcomb, New York: published by the author, 1988.

Forgey, William W., M.D. *Wilderness Medicine.* Pittsboro, Indiana: Indiana Camp Supply, 1979.

Fosburgh, Hugh. *A Clearing in the Wilderness.* Garden City, New York: Doubleday & Company, 1969.

Foster, Jeanne Robert. *Adirondack Portraits.* Edited by Noel Riedinger-Johnson. Syracuse, New York: Syracuse University Press, 1986.

Goodwin, Tony. *Northern Adirondack Ski Tours.* Glens Falls, New York: Adirondack Mountain Club, 1981.

Hale, Mason E. *How to Know the Lichens.* Dubuque, Iowa: Wm. C. Brown Company, 1979.

Hochschild, Harold K. *Lumberjacks and Rivermen in the Central Adirondacks.* Blue Mountain Lake, New York: Adirondack Museum, 1962.

Kaiser, Harvey H. *Great Camps of the Adirondacks.* Boston: David R. Godine, 1982.

Kjellstrom, B. *Be Expert with Map and Compass.* New York: Scribners, 1967.

Krieger, Medora Hooper. *Geology of the Thirteenth Lake Quadrangle, New York.* Albany, New York: New York State Museum Bulletin published by the University of the State of New York, 1937.

Lederer, William J. and Joe Pete Wilson. *Complete Cross-Country Skiing and Ski Touring.* New York: W.W. Norton, 1972.

McMartin, Barbara. *Discover the South Central Adirondacks.* Woodstock, Vermont: Backcountry Publications, 1986.

McMartin, Barbara. *Discover the Eastern Adirondacks.* Woodstock, Vermont: Backcountry Publications, 1987.

McMartin, Barbara. *Hides, Hemlocks and Adirondack History.* Utica, New York: North Country Books, 1992.

Murie, Olaus J. *A Field Guide to Animal Tracks.* Boston: Houghton Mifflin Company, 1974.

Petrides, George A. *A Field Guide to Trees and Shrubs.* Boston: Houghton Mifflin Company, 1972.

Schaefer, Vincent J. and John A. Day. *A Field Guide to the Atmosphere.* Boston: Houghton Mifflin Company, 1981.

Shuttleworth, Floyd S. and Herbert S. Zim. *Non-Flowering Plants.* New York: Golden Press, 1967.

Stokes, Donald W. *A Guide to Nature in Winter.* Boston: Little, Brown and Company, 1976.

Wadsworth, Bruce. *Guide to Adirondack Trails: Northville-Placid Trail.* Lake George, New York: Adirondack Mountain Club, 1986.

Williams, Wendy. *Cross-Country Ski Waxing and Maintenance.* Chicago: Contemporary Books, 1977.

Wilson, Leile Fosburgh. *The North Woods Club 1886–1986.* Privately printed, 1986.

Woods, Craig and Gordon Hardy. *Cross Country Skier's Trailside Guide.* Brattleboro, Vermont: Stephen Greene Press, 1983.

Index

Books from Countryman Press

Written for people of all ages and experience, these popular and carefully prepared books feature detailed trail and tour directions, notes on points of interest and natural highlights, maps and photographs.

Discover series
Guides to the Adirondacks
Discover the Southwestern Adirondacks, 2nd Ed., $13.00
Discover the Adirondack High Peaks, $13.00
Discover the Eastern Adirondacks, $16.00
Discover the Central Adirondacks, 2nd Ed., $12.95
Discover the Northeastern Adirondacks, $13.00
Discover the Northern Adirondacks, $13.00
Discover the Northwestern Adirondacks, $13.00
Discover the South Central Adirondacks, 2nd Ed., $12.00
Discover the Southeastern Adirondacks, $11.00
Discover the Southern Adirondacks, $13.00
Discover the West Central Adirondacks, $15.00

Other books about New York
Best Festivals Mid-Atlantic, $13.00
Canoeing Central New York, $12.00
Family Resorts of the Northeast, $12.95
Fifty Hikes in the Adirondacks, 2nd Ed., $13.00
Fifty Hikes in Central New York, $12.00
Fifty Hikes in the Hudson Valley, 2nd Ed., $14.00
Fifty Hikes in Western New York, $13.00
Good Fishing in the Adirondacks, $15.00
Good Fishing in the Catskills, 2nd Ed., $15.00
Good Fishing in Western New York, $15.00
New England's Special Places, Rev. Ed., $13.00
20 Bicycle Tours in the Finger Lakes, 2nd Ed., $10.00
20 Bicycle Tours in the Five Boroughs, $8.95
20 Bicycle Tours in and around New York City, Rev. Ed., $11.00

Our outdoor recreation guides are available through bookstores and specialty shops. For a free catalog of these and other books, please write: The Countryman Press, Inc., Dept. ADK, PO Box 175, Woodstock, VT 05091.